To Aminah ~ (

I pray the[r]

and experience __

of God in ever increasing

FAITH

measure

Pete

Published in the UK in 2021 by Pete Carter
Copyright © Pete Carter 2022

Pete Carter has asserted the right to be identified
as the author of this work in accordance with the
Copyright, Designs and Patents Act 1988

Bible quotes are from:
THE HOLY BIBLE, NEW INTERNATIONAL VERSION®, NIV®
Copyright © 1973, 1978, 1984, 2011 by Biblica, Inc.®
Used by permission. All rights reserved worldwide.

Paperback ISBN 978-1-7397222-0-3
eBook ISBN 978-1-7397222-1-0

Cover design and typeset by SpiffingCovers

FAITH

Discovering and using the resources of Heaven

PETE CARTER

Foreword by Lord Jonathan Evans

Arriving at university as a new undergraduate one of my main priorities was, of course, to find new friends, and specifically to find friends who shared my Christian beliefs. On my first evening I joined the dinner queue and fell into conversation with the person standing behind me. To my amazement and delight he turned out not only to be another new arrival but also, like me, he was from Kent. Further conversation revealed he lived only a few miles from me and most importantly he was also a Christian, and a like-minded Christian at that.

You will have guessed that my new friend in the dinner queue was Pete Carter, and we have been close friends ever since. Though our lives have taken radically different paths we have stayed in touch and Pete has been a source of wise advice to me on several occasions over the years. You might imagine that a Christian leader with such a radical vision of God's work in the world might be a little detached from the everyday challenges of life. That could never be said of Pete. He combines a deep faith with a sharp intellect and a very strong dose of down to earth practicality.

It is part of the human condition that we have to put our faith in something or someone – whether that is in an ideology, in friends or family, in science, in colleagues or in God. However independent and self-reliant we might imagine ourselves to be, we are in reality interconnected and dependent on others. And if we rely on others then we have to trust them, place our faith in them. So one of the biggest questions facing us all is who or what do we trust. Where do we place our faith?

Pete Carter's book explores faith in God, not just as an exercise in theology or biblical exposition but in stories from Pete's own experience and those of other Christians. But it is more than a series of anecdotes. From the Old Testament onwards, the truth of God's engagement in the world has been best shown not by abstract statements or tomes on systematic theology but by stories of how people encounter God in their everyday lives. Stories embody the elusive truth in a much richer and more vibrant way than theory can ever do. They stay in our memory and continue to challenge us. I am sure that the stories you will find here will do the same.

Lord Jonathan Evans - former Director General of MI5 and Crossbench member of the House of Lords, UK.

About the Author

Pete Carter is a medical doctor and a church leader combining both skills to demonstrate that Christianity provides resources applicable to everyday life on earth.

He is one of the senior leaders at Eastgate Church in Kent, England, where his heart to see the full potential of Christianity realised through daily lives is evidently being fruitful in the people and places that he influences. The resulting wonderful stories of God's manifest activity through ordinary people, who believe God can do extraordinary things through them as their faith in God grows, give testimony to this. You will find such stories filling the pages of this book.

Pete also has a particular passion to see the world of medicine affected by the power and love of God, and for Christian healing to sit alongside good medicine for the sake of any who choose to benefit from it. Along with others, he founded the Healing Centre at Eastgate in 2011 and since then thousands of people have experienced the presence and peace of God in a joyful environment; and many miraculous healings have occurred. Towards the end of 2018 the Healing Centre was acknowledged by local doctors as a Complementary Service which could be recommended to patients.

In recent years together with a great team he has been developing *"Heaven in Healthcare"* which provides support and resources to help Christians involved in all aspects of healthcare to access and manifest the fullness of heaven in their environments. www.heaveninhealthcare.com

Pete is also the author of Unwrapping Lazarus, an

inspirational book subtitled *"Free to live as God intended"* which has reached the shores of nearly every continent in the world (not Antarctica that we know about!).

He spends his time developing the people of Eastgate, teaching about healing and miracles in many nations, and helping churches and christian ministries to grow structures that reflect a heavenly model. He is on the teaching staff of the Eastgate School of Spiritual Life and has helped to form the Living Fire community of churches, open to all churches who wish to pursue all the fullness that Jesus offers to us.

He loves life with his family; wife Kim, his children and grandchildren. He also loves sport and aims to keep active and competitive for many years to come.

You can follow Pete on Instagram - petecarter1958 and on Facebook - Pete Carter, for other information you can visit the following websites.

- Eastgate www.eastgate.org.uk
- Heaven in Healthcare www.heaveninhealthcare.com
- Living Fire www.livingfire.church

Endorsements

Pete Carter has a passion that shines through every page of his book, *Faith: Discovering and Using the Resources of Heaven*. He wants to help people successfully navigate "the greatest adventure that exists" — the journey of faith for a child of God.

Pete reminds me of a seasoned mountain guide, who teaches his students both to master mountain-climbing techniques and to recognize and avoid possible pitfalls that could abort the success of the expedition. If you were one of that guide's students, you'd want to learn both sets of skills to make sure you got safely to the top of the mountain!

In this book, Pete is working to help you navigate every type of "terrain" or tight situation you might face on the way to your ultimate destination as you follow Christ. Pete uses a unique blend of tools to accomplish that task, mixing in key scriptural principles with stories of his own and others' faith experiences that open a window to help you see more clearly.

It's very evident that Pete is doing everything he can to help you recognise faith, as well as the potential destroyers of faith, when you see them. He also wants to help you know how to develop your faith muscles by using them to conquer obstacles you find along the way.

What's the point of it all? *That your part in God's great plan will not be aborted on your way to your final destination.* I believe Pete has done well to help ensure that one day you'll be able to stand on your personal mountaintop with a broad view of a life lived fully for God and say with confidence, "Through faith in Jesus, I have finished my course for Him!"

Dr. Roberts Liardon
Author of God's Generals series

I have known Dr Pete Carter for over 20 years now. As a doctor and a pastor, I have seen Pete marry both his sharp intellect and robust faith seamlessly, and this has produced many moments of breakthrough in physical healing, emotional health, and financial miracles. The stories in this book, combined with practical theological insights into faith, are lived out of his experience. Beyond Pete's ability to live a life of risky faith is his gift to bring others into the same understanding of faith for themselves. *Faith: Discovering and Using the Resources of Heaven* is not a theoretical book to fill your head with an idea called faith but an invitation to experience the joy of living in faith. This book will produce in you a robust faith that will see the supernatural life of Jesus at work in you and through you. Reading this book has stirred in me fresh faith for miracles and the impossible to invade the earth today. Please read it. Mediate on it and then live it.

Julian Adams,
Director of Frequentsee, author of "Terra Nova: Fulfilling your call to redeem the earth and make all things new."
Founder of Vox Dei School : Training Prophets and Pastor at The Table Boston.
www.frequentsee.org
www.VoxDeischool.com
www.thetableboston.com

In his book *Faith, Discovering and Using the Resources of Heaven,* Pete Carter breaks down the foundational element of our lives as believers in Jesus Christ, faith. He masterfully sets the stage of not only the imperative importance of faith but also teaches practical wisdom on how to understand and grow our faith. He extends an invitation to every believer to enter into a new realm of faith, one that requires us to trust and obey the voice of God in our lives. Pete has a beautiful way of making complex concepts and revelations, become simple truths that every believer no matter their place in the journey can easily apply to their lives, to live a fruitful and joy-filled life of abundant faith.

Renee Evans
Co-Senior Leader Bethel Austin

It is so appropriate that Pete Carter has written a book on faith, because Pete is himself a man of extraordinary faith who raises faith in others. In all the years that I have known Pete, he has never failed to stir in me a greater revelation of Gods goodness and an increased expectation of God's power. I am so grateful that Pete has penned a book that will be a legacy of faith for the many who will read its pages and be changed by the words they read.

Phil Wilthew is the author of Developing Prophetic Culture, and also an elder of Kings Arms Church, Bedford, UK.

This book is your practical guide to moving in the supernatural things of God and seeing the impossible happen in your daily life. Dr. Pete Carter is a trusted friend, physician and church leader. We have partnered together many times over the years in seeing God do extraordinary things in the realm of faith and miracles. I find Pete to be an anointed teacher in the things of faith and appreciate his unique ability to partner his faith with his analytical medical training. As a result, you will find this book to not only be inspiring but also an easily understood guide in helping you grow your personal faith. I encourage you to read on as you will find both education and impartation among these pages.

Joaquin Evans,
Co-Senior Leader, Bethel Austin

Pete Carter is a fine leader, and practices what he preaches in the realm of faith. His book is biblical and practical, inspiring, understanding of our struggles in faith, but offering clear and reliable ways to grow in faith. This book will be such a help to church leaders wanting to see their churches grow in faith, and to all of us on the journey of what faith looks like for us. Highly recommended!

Reverend John Valentine,
'Theologian and Church Plant Trainer at the Gregory Centre for Church Multiplication'.

Dedication.

This book is dedicated to my children and my wife - "the Carters"! Thank you for helping to build a family life that I have found so rich, such fun, so adventurous, and so loving. My life story has unfolded as we have pursued life and God together, and would be so incomplete without you.

My beautiful daughter Kerry I delight in you: you are probably the most courageous person I know and I draw inspiration from you as do so many other people. Your passion for life and compassion for the world is a constant stimulation to me and I have learnt much from you. Your determination to move forward continually and overcome challenges is an extraordinary example to many. Your faith in God and the fruit of the Holy Spirit in your life will move the hearts of many people as you continue to step forward in life.

My son David - you are so full of integrity, compassion and wisdom that I believe heaven looks on and applauds you. I personally take great delight in you; your passion for God, delight in Him and love of the Bible are an ongoing inspiration to me. Your sense of humour and fun help you to engage with people from all backgrounds and is a valuable component of your excellent communication skills; the humour that we share has also been a wonderful feature of "Carter family life." Your life is a demonstration of the fruit of the Holy Spirit and power of his gifts and is a shining example that many choose to follow.

I look back on every season of life that we have had together recalling the fun, laughter, adventures, challenges, hardships, the affection and love that flows between us, and I can truly say that I am so proud of you both, and you bring great delight to me. Your own personal faith in God combined with compassion for the world truly make you world changers. I hope that my life and that of your mum, Kim, serve as a platform for you both to live extraordinary lives.

It goes without saying and yet I want to acknowledge the fact clearly: my beautiful wife Kim's input into the lives of David and Kerry and her relationship with both has played an integral part in their development.

Kim it has been and continues to be a great delight to walk alongside you and build life together. Your pursuit of God and passion for sharing his love and power with others has helped create an extraordinary journey of faith that we have travelled together.

My love for all three of you is a foundational reality in my life, and I dedicate this book to you.

Pete/Dad.

With Gratitude to many:

This book encapsulates my own journey of discovering the nature of God in ever increasing measure and learning how to trust him in every circumstance of life. Many people have inspired, instructed, corrected and encouraged me along the way, far too many to mention them all personally, but I want to thank all who have played a part in helping me to keep moving forward in my pursuit of God. Particular thanks to members of Eastgate church, students at the Eastgate School of Spiritual Life, those involved in Heaven in Healthcare and also those who are part of the Living Fire community of churches.

Particular thanks also to two of my spiritual mentors, Ray Lowe and Mike Frisby, who helped to lay a firm foundation in my spiritual life and set an example to me of an abundant overflowing life that could enrich the world around me.

Thanks to Sasha Caridia, Janice Pleasants, Dave Foggon and Karen Wellspring whose real life stories not only contribute to this book but are also lived out in front of my eyes as a constant encouragement and inspiration.

Thanks to my "big sister" Christine Watkins (known as Floss to many) for introducing me to Jesus and encouraging me continually. And thanks to my parents Derek and Kathleen Carter - you courageously chose and created a family life of unconditional love, free of religious restrictions, and full of hope and dreams. You gave me a foundation to enjoy the love of God without limits once I had discovered Jesus, and you also entered into this yourselves when you discovered it.

Contents

Introduction

As relational beings, we choose who to trust in all areas of life and the question of trust is fundamental to us. It pervades almost everything we do and think about. Life is an experiment in trust: Who can you trust? Who do you trust? What do you trust? Relationships are formed on the basis of trust and often damaged by suspicion, mistrust and betrayal of trust. A new born baby soon learns where to place its trust in terms of basic needs such as food, comfort and safety. The inquisitive toddler discovers the opportunities of friendship. When a child starts school, parents trust teachers with aspects of their children's education and safety. In turn, children face the challenge of being part of a bigger social context. Teenagers learn the more complex issues of freedom and responsibility on their journey towards adulthood and start to make choices about their lives in general. Adults negotiate the complexities of life - choosing life partners, which bank to trust, a preferred supermarket to shop at, where to live, what job to pursue and who to trust to help with health issues. So many questions, and decisions to make, and all of them require trust.

Put simply, faith is trust. Who do I put my faith in? This is something we discover as we walk through life. Finding faithful people who you know you can trust is a very precious thing, something money cannot buy. The Bible says that Faith is worth more than gold. (1 Peter 1:7) How far would you travel to find such wealth? It is a journey worth pursuing. Here are some further remarkable statements made in the Bible about faith:

Anything is possible for he/she who believes. (Mark 9:23)

When the Son of Man comes, will he find faith on the earth? (Luke 18:8)

Faith is the assurance of things hoped for. (Hebrews 11:1)

These are statements that lead to many questions. Questions that if pursued honestly can take us on an amazing adventure of discovery, the journey of discovery regarding trust in an eternal, infinite, faithful, loving God. Sometimes I refer to this as 'Faith - the journey from hope to assurance'

This book is designed to help you develop your faith in God with increasing confidence as you journey through life. Between each chapter is a true story, each one from friends of mine or myself, to encourage and inspire you further on your journey of faith.

I invite you to join me on this adventure, to my mind the greatest adventure that exists. Let's go.

SECTION 1. WHAT IS FAITH?

Faith is not a mystery. It is an everyday reality lived out by every human being. Let's discover what I mean.

Chapter 1 The River

A puzzle that I have spent many years trying to solve is understanding what faith (or belief) is, why it seems to work in some situations but not in others, and whether the Bible has answers for us in regard to these things. I have studied and taught on this subject in many different contexts and as I have studied the Bible I have found numerous answers addressing this question. However, as I tried to share these answers with other people I found that I was struggling to put the answers together to make a complete picture. Something was missing.

The Bible teaches that nothing is impossible for those who believe, it also teaches about the reasons why we do not always see the reality of this. This seems to provide quite a significant tension within Christianity and this is certainly true at Eastgate Church where I am one of the leaders. For instance, when people are prayed for in regard to healing, some people get healed but others do not; this is probably one of the biggest challenges facing Christians who are pursuing the supernatural lifestyle that Jesus modelled for us and asked us to follow. In order to address this whole issue, I decided to do a sermon series at Eastgate on Biblical reasons for why we do not see the fullness of Biblical promises in our current experience and why sometimes our prayers are not answered as we would hope. During this process I was not convinced that I was managing to communicate my thoughts clearly enough, and I was a little frustrated with myself. So one Sunday I asked God to help me by showing me some specific way to approach the problem. Immediately I heard his voice in my head making a suggestion, Study the River

Thames. This was an encounter with the Spirit of wisdom and revelation, as the part of God that is the Holy Spirit is referred to in the Bible. God revealed something to me that opened up a way to greater wisdom. He gave me a key to open the door to further understanding on the particular subject of faith. I now had the missing piece of the puzzle that would enable me to finish writing this book. My heart and my spirit were stirred with expectation as I began my study of the River Thames.

Did you know that once you are 'born again', as the bible puts it, and become a Christian you have a river inside you? Here is what Jesus says about this in the book of John chapter 7:

> *John 7: 37 On the last and greatest day of the festival, Jesus stood and said in a loud voice, "Let anyone who is thirsty come to me and drink. 38 Whoever believes in me, as Scripture has said, rivers of living water will flow from within them. 39 By this he meant the Spirit, whom those who believed in him were later to receive. Up to that time the Spirit had not been given, since Jesus had not yet been glorified.*

This is a powerful image - rivers of living water flowing within us. It builds on other images of rivers throughout the Bible narrative, for instance the four rivers in the creation story in Genesis; in Ezekiel 47 we read about a river flowing from the Temple and carrying life wherever it flows, and at the end of the Bible narrative in Revelation 21 we read of the river of the water of life'.

During my research, I came across this article published in 2010 in one of the UK daily newspapers, The Daily Telegraph.

"Standing statue still on the shoreline, the heron is almost impossible to spot against the reeds behind it. Only once our boat draws near does the bird stir, flapping its broad, grey wings to lift itself into the air.

Other smaller birds dart across the skyline before settling in the water while there is the occasional plop as a fish breaks the surface. It is an idyllic riverside scene that is found in many places throughout the English countryside. The difference on this occasion is this stretch of river sits in the midst of the country's biggest city. We are on the lower reaches of the River Thames, in the middle of a large industrial estate at Creekmouth, in Barking, London.

It was near this spot in 1878 that more than 600 passengers on the steamship Princess Alice died when the pleasure boat sank in a collision. As they swam towards the safety of the shore, the passengers were overcome by the noxious cocktail of pollution in the water. In 1957, the pollution levels became so bad that the River Thames was declared biologically dead. The amount of oxygen in the water fell so low that no life could survive and the mud reeked of rotten eggs.

Fifty years later, the Thames has become a very different place. It teems with life: 125 species of fish swim beneath its surface while more than 400 species of invertebrates live in the mud, water and river banks. Waterfowl, waders and sea birds feed off the rich pickings in the water while seals, dolphins and even otters are regularly spotted between the river banks where it meanders through London.

Environmental officials now say the Thames is the cleanest it has been in more than 150 years and nearly 400 habitats have now been created to allow wildlife back into the river.

Back in Barking, the evidence of this recolonisation of the Thames is all around. The water itself still looks murky - due to the large quantities of silt and mud the water carries downstream - but it now supports a huge diversity of fish. Juvenile Sea bass, until recently never seen before in the Thames, now fill the creeks that feed into the Thames while flounder, a flat fish, have returned in ever growing numbers. Adult salmon have even been reported migrating up the river.

Above the water too, there are signs of how life has taken hold again.

Crouched among the reeds beneath Barking Barrier is Dennis Ellisdon, a 72-year-old retired marine surveyor and avid birdwatcher. He has been coming to the area, a short drive from his home in Bredbury Station, for 11 years and has spent the morning searching for a pair of peregrine falcons that have been reported nesting in the area.

"You often get kingfishers and a lot of wader birds when the tide is out," he said. "There are also a lot of migrating birds that stop here now like red starts - that was a big surprise."

"I seldom go out without getting a bit of a surprise. You can hear the clank of metal from the scrap yards nearby and the planes at City Airport, so it is not necessarily a haven of peace and quiet, but it is definitely a wildlife haven."

Rare species of wildlife are also making surprise appearances. Water voles are critically endangered across much of the country, but at Thamesmead, just a mile upstream from Barking, the tiny aquatic creatures are thriving. Regular flashes of blue and green can also be seen on many stretches of the river, such as by Dartford Creek, revealing the presence of kingfishers in surprising numbers.

Otters have also set up home in several areas along the river while seals, more normally seen on the coastline than in rivers, are regularly spotted hauled out onto the banks after a good meal. Dolphins also often swim up the river.

Even one of the most fragile and rare sea creatures, the seahorse, have been found in the saline waters of the Thames Estuary.

David Curnick, marine and freshwater programme co-ordinator for the Zoological Society of London, said: "We have had reports of 4 short snouted seahorses over 4.5 years. The Thames has obviously undergone a tremendous transformation since the 1950's. It is feasible that there are significantly greater populations than our results suggest."

Much of the return of wildlife to the Thames has been due to improvements in water quality. Strict legislation now prevents industry from dumping polluted effluent into the river and its tributaries. Sewage from London and the surrounding area is now treated and then exported.

"Improving the water quality is only half of the battle though," explains Antonia Scarr, a senior marine advisor with the Environment Agency. "We have had to create habitats to allow the plants, fish and wildlife to move into.

"If you look along a lot of the River Thames as it passes through London, it is lined with concrete and pilings. Water can't get into these and so there is no way plants can get a foothold."

The Environment Agency, along with local authorities along the Thames, have now set about removing many of these old concrete barriers that contained the rivers. Instead they have been building up mud banks and allowing reed beds to take hold. Piles of rubble at the side help to capture sediment that provides a rich habitat for invertebrates and molluscs that are food for many other species. In areas where they have been unable to remove the barriers completely, they have tried putting sediment behind wooden panels along the walls.

"This essentially turns what would have been a horizontal mud bank on the river floor into a vertical one," said Mrs Scarr. "When we have sampled them, we have found they are full of invertebrates.

"The fact that we have species like otters on the Thames shows we are getting rid of the pollution and creating the right kind of habitats for them."

Even on the smaller rivers and streams that feed into the Thames there is a transformation underway. In Greenwich and Lewisham, extensive work is underway to re-naturalise rivers that for decades have passed unnoticed beneath residents feet. During the 1960s and 1970s extensive work was undertaken to help prevent rivers from flooding into the surrounding neighbourhoods and many were simply diverted into underground tunnels.

The river Quaggy in Greenwich is one such example. In an area called Sutcliffe Park, the river passed through a culvert hidden beneath a large flat area that was used for football pitches. But in an attempt to restore the wildlife and rich biodiversity that once lived on the river, the Environment Agency opened up the culvert and allowed the river to meander through the park. It is now lined with bull rushes and reeds while dragonflies and damselflies dart between the huge number of plants that have established themselves there. Frogs, geese, grebes and other waterfowl also flourish on the site. The park also provides space for the water to spread into when it does flood, so it doesn't flood the houses downstream.

Dave Webb, biodiversity team leader at the Environment Agency who helped lead the project, said: *"The idea in the past was to get water as fast as possible from A to B so these smooth concrete channels were created. Sadly, they are completely barren when it comes to life as nothing can get a grip there.*

"In Sutcliffe park we now have huge diversity of life and it is providing a corridor to allow species to move up and down stream to places they couldn't get to because of the old culvert that was here before."

But for people like Dennis Ellisdon, the simple pleasure of having a river that supports the kind of wildlife he loves to watch is enough.

"The sheer variety of birds you can see here now is what amazes me. You would never have seen a heron here before as there wasn't the fish to support them. Now the river seems to be doing well."

What a transformation! It is startling to think that the River Thames was declared biologically dead in 1957 and 53 years later it teemed with life.

A further 10 years on I wonder how much more life has been nourished in this river? Within the last few months a Beluga whale was spotted in the River Thames not far from where I live, the seal population has doubled in the last five years indicating an ecosystem rich enough to now support even large predators. How did this happen?

First of all, the problem had to be realised for what it was. Secondly, hope had to arise that a solution could be found. Thirdly, a concerted and coordinated effort to overcome the problem had to be vigorously pursued.

Fourthly, signs of encouragement had to be acknowledged and celebrated, leading to hope of further progress. In the case of the River Thames the problem of pollution had to be acknowledged. Pollution was so bad that life had been extinguished. So what had contributed to this problem? The answer was complicated and manifold. There were so many contributions to the overall problem and each one needed to be addressed. Imagine for instance that there were 100 sources of pollution into the River Thames and only 20 of them were tackled and eradicated, there would still be a very polluted river. Also think of the many tributaries that flow into the river each one capable of causing pollution.

I was born in 1958 and grew up not far from the River Thames as it flowed through London and out towards the English Channel. I was made aware of the danger of the river and I certainly didn't want to swim in it. I also knew that there were no fish in it. My expectations of the river were very limited. However, hope was arising in the hearts and minds of some people that change could happen and that the river could be restored to life. Campaigns began; government took notice; a concerted effort started to take place across many fronts. I have to admit I was unaware of any of this and my expectations remained low (not that I gave it much thought). Until one day, I can't remember exactly when, but I was probably in my lower teens: on the television news was a report saying that fish had been found in the River Thames near London. I was very surprised: fish in the Thames! Who would have thought of that? Certainly not me. I don't think there were many fish seen, probably only a couple, but it was a sign of life, and it was much celebrated especially by the pioneers who had started the clean-up process. Like many others I suddenly became aware of the potential of life in the river. Suddenly the river mattered to me in a way it hadn't before, and I became aware of the problem of pollution and also the fact that I could either play a role in being a part of the pollution or a part of the solution. Now many years on, attitudes have changed beyond measure, pollution has been much reduced and people in general care about the whole issue. They also get to enjoy the life that the river brings. A different expectation and reality has arisen.

This illustration of the River Thames got my mind going in overdrive. The source of the River Thames is roughly 100 miles west of London and the water comes from an underground spring - this water is unpolluted. However, on its journey eastward until it empties into the English Channel it risks becoming polluted, and this is especially true as it flows through London although pollution is possible anywhere along its route. Christians have a spiritual river inside of them with a pure source, the Holy Spirit inside them interacting with their own spirit and creating life. The full potential of this life is beyond measure, indeed it is infinite and eternal. However, it is possible for this spiritual river to become so polluted that the life it should produce becomes restricted or even damaged (for example think of the damage that 'The Inquisition' in the Middle Ages produced, all done in the name of Christianity). Let's look at a couple of Bible passages to help us understand this:

> *Matthew 17: 14 When they came to the crowd, a man approached Jesus and knelt before him. 15 "Lord, have mercy on my son," he said. "He has seizures and is suffering greatly. He often falls into the fire or into the water. 16 I brought him to your disciples, but they could not heal him."*
>
> *17 "You unbelieving and perverse generation," Jesus replied, "how long shall I stay with you? How long shall I put up with you? Bring the boy here to me." 18 Jesus rebuked the demon, and it came out of the boy, and he was healed at that moment.*
>
> *19 Then the disciples came to Jesus in private and asked, "Why couldn't we drive it out?"*
>
> *20 He replied, "Because you have so little faith. Truly I tell you, if you have faith as small as a mustard seed, you can say to this mountain, 'Move from here to there,' and it will move. Nothing will be impossible for you."*

Here we have a story of someone not getting healed by Jesus' disciples, unfortunately a situation not unfamiliar to our common Christian experience. Jesus steps into the story and the boy gets healed. The disciples then ask the very relevant question "Why couldn't we drive it out?" This is an honest question and to be commended. Jesus gives an honest answer and then finishes this story by reaffirming the potential of Christian faith - Nothing will be impossible for you. What is the condition for this truth to become our reality? 'If you have faith.' So Jesus diagnosed the problem in this way: 'because you have so little faith.' What is the implied solution to this diagnosis? The need to grow in faith. The implication is not a condemnation but an invitation. Jesus also indicates what is standing in the way of faith and whose problem this is: 'You unbelieving and perverse generation.'

The problem is unbelief. Unbelief is the overarching term that describes spiritual pollution. To whom did the problem belong? The whole generation. The Greek word, Genea, used here implies a cultural reality, a race of people living in an area at the same time with shared belief systems. Jesus describes them as a 'perverse generation' meaning that their belief systems had become corrupted. Jesus was pointing towards a communal problem of polluted beliefs that stood in the way of true faith in Jesus and its resultant possibilities (any mountain can be moved).

Mark chapter 6 tells the story of Jesus returning to his hometown of Nazareth:

> *6 Jesus left there and went to his hometown, accompanied by his disciples. 2 When the Sabbath came, he began to teach in the synagogue, and many who heard him were amazed.*
>
> *"Where did this man get these things?" they asked. "What's this wisdom that has been given him? What are these remarkable miracles he is performing? 3 Isn't this the carpenter? Isn't this Mary's son and the brother of James, Joseph, Judas and Simon? Aren't his sisters here with us?" And they took offense at him.*
>
> *4 Jesus said to them, "A prophet is not without honour except in his own town, among his relatives and in his own home." 5 He*

could not do any miracles there, except lay his hands on a few sick people and heal them. 6 He was amazed at their lack of faith.

The people of Nazareth acknowledged the wisdom and miracles of Jesus but they rejected Him nonetheless. He was amazed at their lack of faith which meant that 'He could not do any miracles there, except lay his hands on a few sick people and heal them.' Unbelief or lack of faith is such a powerful pollutant that it can affect our ability to receive the fullness Jesus offers to us.

How about the story in Numbers 13 and 14 where the 12 spies were sent to spy out the promised land. The land had been promised to them by God and victory had been assured to them as well. However, 10 spies were overwhelmed by the size of the challenge facing them which silenced the voice of faith in Joshua and Caleb. God gives His assessment in chapter 14 verse 11: *'The Lord said to Moses, "How long will these people treat me with contempt? How long will they refuse to believe in me, in spite of all the signs I have performed among them?"* Here, refusal to believe is highlighted. The outcome of such unbelief was that a whole generation of Israelites did not enter the promised land. Unbelief is not neutral. It is pollution.

Whose problem is it? I like the answer given by the father of the boy that the disciples could not heal, it comes in Mark's gospel chapter 9 which also tells the story. 21 Jesus asked the boy's father, "How long has he been like this?"
"From childhood," he answered. 22 "It has often thrown him into fire or water to kill him. But if you can do anything, take pity on us and help us."

23 "'If you can'?" said Jesus. "Everything is possible for one who believes."

24 Immediately the boy's father exclaimed, "I do believe; help me overcome my unbelief!"

All Christians are a mixture of faith and unbelief. In some areas our faith is strong, in other areas unbelief has polluted our river. My invitation to you is to confront the problem of unbelief and push on in the adventure of growing in faith. Let's go on an adventure of faith as we travel through this book.

Invite Duncan to family prayer

Story by Janice Pleasants:

The bravest thing I did was at a London railway station. I was just coming into the forecourt when I noticed a man on a mobile phone who was looking very agitated, and the Holy Spirit said to me, "Tell him, 'I'm here to help you' and offer to buy his fare." The difficulty was he looked like the kind of person who would threaten to punch your lights out if you just said, "Excuse me." A little reluctantly I went up to him and said, "I'm here to help you, how much is your fare?" He said, "What kind of special lady are you?" I replied that I was a Christian, practising hearing from God and I felt that God wanted me to say this to him. He gasped, "Wow, no way!" I asked, "What do you mean?" He explained that just before I came over to him in desperation he had said, "God if you are real, please help me!" I said, "He is real and He's helping you." It turned out that the transmission on his car had gone, he hadn't got his wallet with him, he had just phoned the last person he knew who could possibly help and yet no one was available to help him. He didn't know how he could get home, his wife had tried to buy a ticket for him online but they wouldn't accept it at the ticket machine without the credit card. He'd been there an hour and no one would help. I gave him the cash for his fare then I offered to pray for him. I prayed peace over him and he said, "What was that? I felt something go right through me." He was wiping away tears from his eyes and said he hadn't cried since he was a little boy. I asked if I could give him a hug, he held on and said that his Nan was a Christian and he was going to talk to her about this tonight. He then went over to the ticket office to buy his ticket home.

It showed me the importance of saying the phrases you hear from the Holy Spirit, not adding to or embellishing them; it was the exact wording of the phrase that spoke so powerfully to him, as he had just used the exact same words in his emergency prayer to God.

Chapter 2. Faith is Worth More than Gold

I want you to try and imagine experiencing the world without sound in any form. No music, no baby's cry, no laughter, no wind blowing through the trees, no sound of running water. No sound at all. Complete Silence. Life, but not in all its fullness. Take a few moments to imagine that.

Now let me tell you a story of an experience I had in 2009. I was participating in a meeting where God was doing what he loves to do - restoring people to wholeness. People were thrilled to see what was happening around the room as people experienced the love and power of Jesus in different ways the anticipation grew as we prayed for a woman who was about 40 years old and had been profoundly deaf since birth, no sound had ever impinged upon her brain, she had lived in a world without sound. But then...

We asked God to touch her and do what he alone can do and then stepped back to watch. All of a sudden her face changed to one of absolute amazement. She started to look around the room, a quizzical look on her face, stopping to stare for some moments before moving on to something else of interest. A man playing the guitar grabbed her attention and she pointed at him. I realised that this woman could hear sound for the first time in her life. Visually, she knew about someone playing a guitar, but the accompanying sound had never found its way into her experience. I watched as she swivelled her head from side to side, learning to locate sound and to identify its source. A beautiful smile broke out on her face as the visual image of a guitar being played was now joined by the melodic sounds coming from it. She started to experience the world through the wonder of hearing alongside her other senses. Her smile just grew and grew. I was so excited to be alongside her and witness this miracle brought about by faith in Jesus. I started to talk to her, in English of course, expecting a joyful conversation; instead she looked at me with kind puzzlement on her face and suddenly I realised that the noises coming from my mouth were just that - noises that we interpret as language. However, she had never heard, let alone learnt this language - her language was sign language. Fortunately, a sign language interpreter was with her and we were able to converse in this manner.

This lady had a whole new world to discover, a world full of sound. No money could have bought her that. On that same day I met two women who had previously suffered severely from Multiple Sclerosis but both of whom had been restored to full health. They both told me their stories and I got to marvel at the love and power of Jesus. The potential of 'faith in Jesus' had been revealed to me in a greater way, providing memories that no money can buy and no difficulty I face could ever erase from my mind. I recall previous experiences such as that of Debbie, who had become deaf in adulthood, awaking to hear for the first time the sound of her baby crying and the sound of bird song for the first time in many years. I remember a large youth camp where a 16-year-old girl with dyslexia, who had struggled through school with a reading age of about 5 years old, suddenly found that she could read a passage of the Bible previously inaccessible to her. Her friends and herself crying as she read the passage aloud to me is indelibly printed in my mind. Then with great bravery she agreed to go up on stage and read the passage out loud to 5,000 young people and tell her story so that they also could marvel at this wonderful Jesus who can do the impossible.

Faith in Jesus worth more than gold

Hope restored

Such memories are not only priceless but also provide momentum for faith to grow. The Bible tells us that genuine faith in Jesus is worth more than gold and can produce things that money cannot buy. Such things as joy, peace of mind, assurance of eternal salvation, and miracles, can all result from such faith. In the first chapter of my previous book, Unwrapping Lazarus, I tell the story of two amazing miracles I experienced in 1995 whilst visiting a remote indigenous tribe in Mexico, the Pame. These experiences had an enormous impact upon me and also that whole region. The stories are of Otilio who had been paralysed in all four limbs for ten years following a vicious assault, and of how he instantly regained the use of his arms and legs in response to our prayers. The second story is of a little girl whose life came to an end because of amoebic dysentery but then she was restored to life. Both miracles happened on the same day - the day HOPE arrived amongst the Pame people.

The Pame people were extremely isolated from the rest of Mexico and poor almost beyond measure. They had no hope for the future, just a day to day existence accepting the harsh realities of life even to the extent that one quarter of their children died from amoebic dysentery despite advice that this could be avoided simply by boiling their water before drinking. However, the miracles experienced there began a remarkable change for the whole people group, such that the whole atmosphere and social infrastructure was transformed and continues to develop positively to this day. At the end of our time there, it took us a ten-hour drive to return to the city of Leon and back into communication with the outside world. I was looking forward to communicating with home about the things we had experienced and also to hearing news from there. At that time using a Fax machine was the optimal way of communicating, so that evening I excitedly wrote a letter to my wife, Kim, with the plan of sending it via Fax the next day from the office of the church we were working with. The next morning, I set off with a spring in my step, hoping for a Fax to have arrived from home with love and good news. And indeed, there it was! I diligently sent my Fax via the machine before reading the news from home. Not the news I was expecting or hoping for. A friend called Phil who lived close to us had fallen gravely ill and had been admitted to our local hospital. Instead of improving, he continued to get worse and was transferred to a specialist hospital in London, where he was placed on the Intensive Care Unit. But even there the doctors were struggling to make a diagnosis. Every organ system in his body started to fail and he was placed on a life support machine. He was not expected to live. I wished I could be there to help everyone, including Kim, who was very involved, but more especially Phil's wife, Anne, and their children. I wanted to pray and see him recover just as I had done with the Pame. However, I still had another week in front of me in Mexico. I tried to keep in touch and be supportive as best I could, holding the miracles I had just experienced in tension with the challenge being faced at home.

It was a long journey back to the UK (about 21 hours in total) and I was very tired and jet lagged when I got home, very happy to see Kim and my children, but also wanting an update on Phil's condition. The news was not good, he had septicaemia and pretty much every part of his body was failing. His life was slipping away.

That first night home I was early to bed, exhausted from a long and busy trip alongside the jet lag I was experiencing. I was hoping for a full night's sleep to replenish me. However, around midnight we received a phone call at home with the news that Phil was not expected to 'make it through the night.'

Wearily I rose from my bed and got dressed and waited for our friend Jim to arrive with Anne, to take us to visit Phil at the Hospital in London. We prayed en route and asked God once again for a miracle.

At his bedside I took stock of the situation, my medical brain taking in the familiar sights and sounds and assessing Phil's condition. Then we talked with the nurse caring for Phil - every system in his body was failing - kidneys, liver, lungs, heart, even his skin was breaking down and brain scans showed evidence of significant damage to that most vital of organs with at least three different parts of his brain now effectively dead. His test results indicated a serious deterioration which meant that death was imminent. Medical hope was almost at an end and I understood this fully as did Anne who is a nurse. But hope in God is never at an end, and we placed our hope in Him with great confidence, knowing that our faith in Him could somehow release the answer from heaven. So we joined together and prayed. Nothing happened immediately but our trust in Jesus was alive. After a relatively short visit we returned home and I gratefully found my bed once again.

The next morning I awoke somewhat groggy and disoriented. As I came to, I remembered Phil and eagerly sought the latest news - he had 'made it through the night' and 'somehow' his vital signs had improved. We had a chink of light to focus on in this most dark situation. However, his condition did not improve further, he remained on a ventilator and the doctors could give no real hope of recovery. The days went by and no change happened and we continued to visit and pray. Eventually a potential cause of the septicaemia was identified within the gallbladder, surgery was necessary to remove it, but with Phil's overall condition surgical intervention and anaesthesia carried very serious risks to his life. However, the surgery was successfully performed and he was returned to

ITU and we hoped for a turnaround in his condition. One day shortly after, Anne and I went once again to the hospital to visit Phil in the ITU, the ventilator still enabling each breath and other mechanisms keeping his body functioning but only just. The staff informed us that his ventilator tube needed changing and asked us to wait in the waiting room whilst this procedure was carried out, so we took our leave and took a break from the intensity of Phil's immediate surroundings. After about 10 minutes a senior nurse came to see us and gave us the news that Phil had suffered a cardiac arrest and attempts were being made to resuscitate him but things were not looking good. She left us alone with our thoughts and our prayers - in our distress we cried out to God, the giver of life. After some minutes the nurse returned to say that it looked very unlikely that Phil would come back to life but the team were still trying their best. After another few minutes she came back with the news that things were not going well and gave us some technical details - the most significant one being that Phil's blood potassium level was now extremely high. The team were about to call time on their efforts to bring Phil back. The shock hit us and emotion swept over us, obviously Anne more than I, and once again in our distress we called out to God - and we waited. Eventually the door to our waiting room opened once more, and the nurse returned, but this time with a smile on her face. She said that to everyone's surprise Phil had suddenly returned to life and that his heart was beating once again. Anne and I sat and took this news in - unbelievably happy and grateful to God and also the medical staff. Phil had returned to life.

I lost track of time but eventually we were allowed back to see Phil, still on the ventilator, but with his heart beating on its own accord. Sometime later a doctor asked to speak to Ann to try to explain things further and stated that the outlook for

Phil was still extremely poor - even if Phil could come off the ventilator, he would probably never regain full consciousness and would likely remain in a vegetative state. He would never interact with his wife and children again and the doctor wondered whether such a fate was worse than death. This news was obviously shattering and bewildering; our emotions swung backwards and forwards, but in the middle of all this we allowed our faith and hope to rise above human realities and look to a supernatural Jesus and the possibilities that exist within Him. It was the end of November and Christmas was approaching, the time when we especially remember that Jesus was born into this world in order to enable the realities of heaven to be expressed here.

Day by day Phil's condition improved, his kidney and liver function returned towards normal, he came off the ventilator and his heart grew stronger, even his skin seemed to improve. But Phil remained in a coma and the medical staff informed us (correctly in terms of human possibilities) that in their opinion Phil would remain in a vegetative state with very little brain function and that return to normal life was impossible. Not long before Christmas Phil no longer needed to be on the ITU and was transferred to a general ward where more general ongoing care could be provided. Anne continued to visit and pray but Phil remained unconscious; she and her two children were facing a difficult Christmas and a very difficult future. On Christmas Eve, Anne was sitting by Phil's bedside when suddenly and unexpectedly he opened his eyes, looked at Anne and mouthed "I love you." The future had just changed. The children came to visit their dad, now back to life and starting to interact with them - surely one of the best Christmas presents ever. Over the next few weeks Phil got stronger and stronger, and towards the end of February he was released from hospital back to his home where his recovery continued and by the end of June he returned to his work as a school teacher confounding all predictions which had understandably stated that he would never return to a normal life. No amount of money could purchase what I have just written about; the potential of faith is worth more than gold.

How do these sort of things happen? The simplicity of the answer is that 'Nothing is impossible with God.' The complexity of the answer is, how do we connect with this potential that God makes available? That too is the purpose of this book - to explore the simplicity and complexity of faith in Jesus.

Story by Sasha Caridia:
Whilst out at a local pub a while back we got talking to a man and his family. The man had been using a crutch for some time to help him walk due to chronic knee pain associated with arthritis. His daughter was getting married the next day and he was due to walk his daughter down the aisle.

He was happy for us to pray for his knee, but some of those with him were not so sure! However, this changed when the love and power of God was released and all the pain left. He was able to move the knee freely, standing and walking without pain or restriction. The last we saw of the man and his family was him leaving the pub, walking normally and carrying the 'now not needed' crutch.

Walking his daughter down the aisle the following day must have been such a wonderful moment. Made more special by the fact that Jesus, who loves a good wedding, had made it even more beautiful for all of them.

Chapter 3 Faith in the Invisible

Over the course of my life many people have asked me how I manage to live a life of faith in God and at the same time follow a career in medicine which is based upon scientific facts. People perceive these two things to be in conflict and believe that I must somehow separate these two components of my life and build them on different foundations of thought and experience. In some ways I can understand the question, however, it has never truly been a question in my own mind. I simply don't perceive or experience conflict in that regard. So let me try and answer the question by helping you to understand my way of thinking.

First of all, let me ask a question:

Do you put your trust in unseen things that you don't fully understand? Think about that for a moment.

Here are some examples of unseen things in which I believe we commonly place our trust with greater or lesser degrees of confidence and understanding:

- Air
- Gravity
- Electricity
- Radio
- Television
- WiFi
- Mobile telephone signals

- X-rays
- Magnetism

I wake up each day with no concern about the truth that air surrounds me and that it will provide me with the oxygen I need for life itself. Indeed, that confidence is true 24 hours per day - I don't go to sleep at night wondering whether I will run out of oxygen before I wake up. In fact, air has been affecting me since before I was born, it simply exists and I rarely have to think about it. However, I have done some walking at altitude, the highest that I have experienced being about 11,000 feet on Mount Kenya; at that height I found exertion much more difficult and the experience had more to do with lack of air available than to its presence. When I turn on my bedside light I fully expect that electricity will produce the light I am seeking. I may turn on my television, radio or mobile phone fully expecting that they will work as long as they are connected to the appropriate invisible source. The unseen realities that make such things possible are very important in the delivery of a modern way of life. In my work as a doctor I have put great faith in the results of X-rays even though I have never actually seen an X-ray itself, only the image resulting from them. I simply know they exist and benefit from the application of that knowledge. Appropriate understanding of X-rays makes for effective usage and the same can be said of magnetism in Magnetic Resonance Imaging (MRI).

How about electricity? The understanding of an unseen circuit of electrons that has been utilised to help create the world around us.

What about Radio, Mobile Phone connections and WiFi? All unseen things upon which we place so much trust, and that trust is helping to create the world in which we live.

So much of our modern world is based on our trust/faith in unseen things, and there is great frustration when we cannot access the potential they offer. If we cannot get a mobile phone signal when we want to, we generally move to a place where we can find it. If we experience a power cut meaning normal electricity supply is not available, life is affected in a very significant way.

I can remember the days before mobile phones and the internet (I'm showing my age!). When the internet first arrived it intrigued me and I explored it with a degree of enthusiasm, on the other hand when mobile phones first appeared I was not convinced I would ever want one (I enjoyed not being 'contactable') and I was a slow adopter. Even with the internet I was slow to trust it, purchasing something on it seemed extremely risky! I can date precisely when Kim and I decided to trust the internet more significantly and see how that turned out. It was 2005 and we chose to go abroad on holiday, opting for a more exotic than usual destination, we were going to Cuba. Up to this point in time we had trusted travel agents to help us with booking our holidays, but we decided to enter into the brave new world of internet commerce. We searched for a 'good deal' and discovered what we were looking for. We tried to do a bit of research but in those early days internet reviews were not common. So armed with some information we made a choice and decided to trust the internet. We inserted our credit card details into our computer (I think this was also a first experience for us) and a little nervously pressed the button to enable the transaction. A confirmation email arrived that gave us more assurance and we started to look forward to the holiday with increasing confidence and expectation. The flight that was part of this holiday package was to be provided by Cubana Airlines - previously unknown to us (or to any of our friends that we asked) and some degree

of uncertainty remained in our minds. The day finally came
for us to fly off to Cuba and with our bags packed a friend
kindly dropped us off at London Gatwick Airport.

We made our way into the terminal and started to study the
information screens for details of our flight - where to check
in, any delays etc. To our dismay there was no mention of
our flight or of Cubana Airlines on the screens. A degree of
panic started to rise within Kim and I - had we been foolish to
trust the internet? Did the holiday company we had booked
with even exist? Had we lost all our money and our planned
holiday? We wandered further into the terminal searching
other screens for information that could help us - there was
nothing. We felt very foolish. Our trust in the internet was
under question. We then had another thought - to go to
the Information Desk for help - we should be able to trust
them. So we went and asked if they knew anything about
Cubana Airlines? Their reply immediately lifted our hearts,
"Certainly" they replied, explaining that the check-in process
for Cubana, was handled by a different airline and we needed
to go to their check-in desks. Relief from panic arrived, our
trust in the internet had not betrayed us, and we enjoyed an
excellent holiday.

Now our trust in the internet is so much stronger,
purchasing so many things by that route is now commonplace
and well established in our lives with great confidence. This
is an example of trust in something growing stronger and
stronger. The trust gained by the experience of one generation
provides a platform for future generations to build upon; I
recently spoke to the youth group at our church, none of them
had any experience of life without the existence of the internet
or mobile phone. Trust in these things was taken for granted.

And mobile phones? I have to admit that initially I had
not seen their potential to enhance my life and their general

usefulness; but now my mobile phone is something upon which I depend quite heavily and it would be sorely missed if I no longer had access to it.

How about another 'unseen' part of life? Let us now consider the world of emotions and the way they affect our lives. Emotions are another complex part of life that we have to learn about through life experience, but are they visible of themselves?

Can you see joy?
Can you see peace?
Can you see pain?
Can you see love?

I would like to suggest that of themselves these things are invisible, but their impact upon our lives is visible. We can often tell when someone else is experiencing joy or pain, we certainly know when we personally experience such things. They are an invisible reality with very direct effects upon our lives. To my mind they can be thought of as similar to wind. Wind is the movement of air. We cannot see the air and neither can we see it moving, but we can see its effect on things around us. Watching clouds move across the sky gives us an understanding of how strong the wind is; looking at a calm sea we understand that there is less wind affecting it than when the waves are large. How about the branches of trees moving, leaves being blown through the air, or even during hurricanes trees themselves being uprooted. All because of the movement of invisible air.

How do we discern the movement of an invisible thing such as love? I would suggest that we do so by observing the effects it has upon us and other people. It is a very powerful force that governs many of our actions and yet of itself it is difficult to define its substance. Does it exist? Certainly.

Does it consist of a physical substance? No.

Does it affect the way we trust? Definitely. True love enhances trust, but betrayal of love is one of the most damaging things in human experience.

Our journey through life involves learning how to trust, who to trust, what to trust. How much weight can we place on those things we trust and how does that change with experience? Many of the things we trust are invisible but we are confident that they exist.

Both my parents were brought up in families with strong traditional religious expressions of Christianity which had a lot of guilt, shame and fear attached. They learned through these experiences and when they reached adulthood both decided that the effect of religion upon themselves had been negative and they did not trust the institution of the church and so they turned their backs on religion. Their understanding of the nature of God was fashioned through their religious experiences and as a result they effectively decided that they didn't trust God either - a very understandable thought shared by many others. When they decided to get married they also made another decision - that they would raise their children in a non-religious way. So my sister and I had no church or religious experience, and God was not a feature in our household. We were aware of Christmas and Easter and that Jesus was an important figure in those stories, and that he was in some way connected to 'church', but we understood very little. However, Christmas presents and Easter chocolate led me to some positive expectation of Jesus! Then my sister joined a 'Brownie Guides' group for fun and activity; this group was attached to a church and attendance at some church services was expected. A new experience was entering our lives. When I was about five years old for some reason my mum took me to one of these church meetings. My sister dressed in her Brownie uniform, and the three of us set off 'to church' (Dad decided not to come). So for the first time in my memory I entered this huge (to a five year old) church building and sat down with my mum, somewhere near the back on uncomfortable wooden benches. I didn't realise that I was meant to be still and quiet - I wanted to explore! I stood up and gazed around, uncertain but expectant, and foremost in my mind was that Jesus was here somewhere. All of sudden some music started and some people began to walk down the centre of the building carrying various things - I was intrigued and began to ask my mum some questions. Then all went quiet - all except for one small voice asking a very important question - "Where is Jesus?" My mum, somewhat embarrassed, tried to quieten me down, but I was insistent, after all I had never seen Jesus and my experiences of Christmas and Easter were very positive so I wanted more. I continued with my question, "Where is Jesus?" Heads turned in my direction and mum's efforts to quieten me down increased. No answer was coming, apparently Jesus wasn't there or he was invisible!

This was an intriguing thought for a 5 year old - an invisible God. Indeed, it is an intriguing thought for many people, and is probably the main reason behind the question at the beginning of this chapter - how can you believe in someone who is invisible? But as I have pointed out we believe and trust in so many invisible things.

What does the Bible have to say on this subject?

1 Timothy 1:17
Now to the King eternal, immortal, invisible, the only God, be honour and glory for ever and ever. Amen.
God is invisible.

Romans 1:20

*For since the creation of the world God's invisible qualities—
his eternal power and divine nature—have been clearly seen, being
understood from what has been made, so that people are without
excuse.*

*The invisible qualities of God can be clearly seen as we
look at the world around us. For example, creative design, beauty,
majesty, power.*

Hebrews 11:27

*By faith he left Egypt, not fearing the king's anger; he
persevered because he saw him who is invisible.*

This passage says that Moses saw God who is invisible. If you
study the timeline of this passage of the Bible, this verse sits
at a time before the Passover which led to the exodus of the
Israelites from Egypt. So what had Moses seen by that time?

In Exodus chapter 3 verses 1 to 6 we read

*"Now Moses was tending the flock of Jethro, his father-in-law,
the priest of Midian, and he led the flock to the far side of the
wilderness and came to Horeb, the mountain of God. There the
angel of the Lord appeared to him in flames of fire from within a
bush. Moses saw that though the bush was on fire it did not burn
up. So Moses thought, "I will go over and see this strange sight—
why the bush does not burn up."*

*When the Lord saw that he had gone over to look, God called
to him from within the bush, "Moses! Moses!"*

And Moses said, "Here I am."

*"Do not come any closer," God said. "Take off your sandals,
for the place where you are standing is holy ground." Then he said,
"I am the God of your father,[a] the God of Abraham, the God of*

Isaac and the God of Jacob." At this, Moses hid his face, because he was afraid to look at God."
Moses saw a bush on fire but not burning up.
Moses heard a voice. He experienced evidence of God's presence and activity and responded to God himself.

Colossians 1:15
The Son is the image of the invisible God, the firstborn over all creation.

Jesus is the image of the invisible God, in other words if we want to know what God looks like we need to consider Jesus.

Hebrews chapter 1 verse 3 says *"The Son is the radiance of God's glory and the exact representation of his being."*

The invisible God can be known by what he has made visible, namely His creation, also through His direct actions into our world such as miracles, and most importantly through Jesus Christ himself. Learning to place your faith in the invisible God is a wonderful adventure of discovery, much like a discovery of the possibilities of the internet, the wonders of science or the majesty of our planet.

This is the purpose of this book, to help you go on this adventure of discovery that is Faith in God.

Story by Dave Foggon:
One day I was rushing across a busy bridge in London, desperate to make an important meeting after my train was delayed. Through the crowd of people, I spotted a homeless man begging, but I pressed on, worried about the meeting. Halfway across the bridge, I felt my heart pulled toward the man. I ran back, and quickly gave him all the money I had in my pocket, before once again pacing towards the office. This time, I was almost at the end of the bridge when I felt the Holy Spirit nudge my heart to stop. Although still concerned about my meeting, I knew I couldn't ignore Him.

I then heard God's voice clearly speak to me: "His name is Mark. Go back and tell him that I know his name is Mark, and I sent you back, even though you're rushing to work, to tell him that so he knows that I love him." I ran back to the man and asked, "Is your name Mark?" His jaw dropped. "How did you know that?" I explained exactly what had happened, and as I did, he began to weep. I told him, "God loves you. He is pursuing you, to the extent that even as I was rushing off with another agenda, He interrupted my journey to get me to come back here and tell you."

I asked him if he knew what it meant to have a real relationship with God, and he replied he didn't. I explained how he could have a loving relationship with God the Father, Son and Holy Spirit. Right there, he responded to Jesus receiving the eternal life that he offers to all.
God also told me he had been abused as a child, and he broke down into tears as I prayed. Later he revealed more details showing me how important this moment truly was.

Realising I'd surely missed my meeting now, I told him that since he was now royalty, I'd buy him breakfast fit for a king. We celebrated together like old friends, and then I left. I saw him again a week later, and he was a new man. No longer depressed, he was full of joy and hope! Oh, and that meeting I was worried about missing? It was cancelled.

Chapter 4 Who Do You Trust?

Learning to trust other people and things around us is essential to life. Learning to trust ourselves is also important. We all have to place our faith outside ourselves as well as in ourselves. As we journey through life we make choices about where to place our trust and these things can change as life moves on. Let's take the example of learning to swim. I remember having swimming lessons as a child. My parents placed their trust in a swimming instructor to enable me to learn this life skill but they also came to watch my lessons to see my progress. We started in the shallow end of the pool where I could safely put my feet on the bottom and the first lesson was to walk across the pool - not much like swimming, but wisely increasing my confidence of being in the water and feeling safe. Imagine instead if the instructor had thrown me in the deep end out of my depth and told me to swim - I think my parents would have been out of their seats in a shot to rescue me and that would have been the end of those lessons, their trust obviously misplaced. Thankfully my instructor was wise and kind, gradually helping me to become confident, try new things and learn new skills until I was swimming across the width of the shallow end. My confidence in my instructor grew and grew, I happily obeyed his instructions knowing that he was leading me forward through his superior understanding. He used buoyancy aids to help me at first but eventually these became unnecessary. When he was confident enough in my ability, we ventured into deeper water where my feet could not reach the bottom. This took more courage, but my faith was producing appropriate (but not reckless) courage because it was placed in someone who was competently guiding me.

As time moved on I became confident in my own ability to swim and the need for lessons stopped. My instructor had succeeded in making a confident swimmer out of me, this was what both I and my parents had hoped for and now assurance had been developed. Success for my instructor meant that I no longer needed his help, but I still respected him and was very grateful. From then on I have loved swimming. At the age of eleven I went to a senior school which had its own indoor heated swimming pool and I got to swim a lot. I trained hard under the instruction of my coaches, learnt more skills, increased in confidence and began to swim in competitions and became quite successful. Through this whole process one thing was essential to my progress - obedience to my instructors, taking note of their instructions and putting them into practice, understanding that they knew more than me and were helping me move forward. Sometimes it was hard work and took courage and perseverance but it was more than worthwhile. Some of my favourite times in life have resulted from my willingness to learn from my swimming instructors - I have snorkelled in the seas around Britain, in the Mediterranean Sea, the Indian Ocean, the Caribbean, the Pacific Ocean and the Red Sea seeing some of the amazing wonders of life within the sea. I have shared these experiences with my wife, Kim, and our children, David and Kerry. So many shared memories. Kerry has pursued this even further, training in Scuba diving which has become one of her favourite pursuits. And it all began in the shallow end obeying the first instruction.

Not everyone in the world will have the opportunities that I have just outlined but there is one area of life that is universal to all mankind.

Finding, preparing and eating food is essential to all human life. Our ability to do this safely and enjoyably is dependent on learning from others. One of the first things a newborn baby does is search for food, it has a need for nourishment and it has a way of making this need known - crying. It also has an inbuilt reflex called the rooting reflex, whereby gentle stimulation of the area close to the infant's mouth will cause the infant to turn its head towards that stimulation, then try to put its mouth around the object of stimulation and start sucking. Obviously the desired object is the mother's nipple (or a feeding bottle) from which milk will flow to nourish the child, however, you can stimulate with other things such as a finger and the rooting reflex will still work causing the baby to suck for a short while before rejecting this counterfeit and search once again for the genuine article. As the child grows its need for food develops and changes, solid food is introduced and different flavours are experienced. Individual preferences become more obvious and experimentation can continue. The child is learning about the world of food. In fact, this is one area of life that continues to engage the minds of Kim and myself, often amusing us in the process. When we were in Kenya working at a mission hospital we came across the vegetable Cassava which seemed to be a staple part of the diet for the local people. However, if eaten raw Cassava can be very dangerous because it contains Cyanide. It has to go through a thorough preparation for many hours before it is safe to consume. We wondered to ourselves - how did people acquire the knowledge of how to use Cassava safely? However it happened, you can be sure that the safest way to consume it is to obey the instructions of those who have more experience. We chose not to prepare it for ourselves but happily ate it in meals prepared by the local people, placing our faith in them.

Also in Kenya, I was placed in situations way beyond my level of experience in Medicine, as was Howard, a young doctor with about 3 years more experience than myself. On one occasion a young lady came into hospital with abdominal pain, which was such that she needed surgical intervention. We thought she had appendicitis, but in those conditions with little to help us in our diagnosis we had to move forward with open minds. She was taken to the Operating theatre where I applied the anaesthetic. Howard was surgically qualified and so undertook the actual surgery. It was a Sunday evening and Kim came to check how long we were likely to be before we would be finished and ready for supper. Howard was just ready to make the first cut with the scalpel and as he did so blood started to gush from the incision. Our minds started to race as to the possibilities and Howard very effectively started to deal with this unsuspected situation. He soon discovered that the lady had a ruptured ectopic pregnancy which was bleeding profusely.

The next problem we faced was that Howard had never performed this operation before! Fortunately many other surgeons had, and one of them had written a brilliant book on surgical technique which included the necessary operation. This book happened to be on a shelf in the operating theatre - but neither Howard nor I could leave the patient easily. Kim came to the rescue - she found the book and under our instruction found the correct page, she then read out the instructions which Howard followed. The surgery was successful and the patient recovered well. In this instance, trust and obedience to someone else's instructions saved someone's life.

How about making a cake? That seems a little more trivial but the same principle applies. Say you like cakes but had never made one yourself and decided you wanted to start baking your own cakes. Where would you start? I would start with a recipe book, carefully following the instructions to the letter, placing my faith in Mary Berry or some other established cook. This is simple wisdom, and it is simple obedience that comes from trust and free choice not external obligation. And neither is the recipe book a straight-jacket that limits creativity but rather it can stimulate confidence that will lead to creative exploration and innovation.

Sometimes obedience stems from orders given by a chain of command, and it is not really a matter of free choice. This is not wrong, indeed it is necessary in places such as the army, police force and many lines of work. At other times obedience may be rooted in fear; fear of punishment, fear of failure, fear of shame, fear of rejection (so many fears). However, in the New Testament of the Bible we are told what sort of obedience Christians are called to in their relationship with God.

Romans 1:5 Through him we received grace and apostleship to call all the Gentiles to the obedience that comes from faith for his name's sake.

Obedience that comes from faith. This is the New Testament principle. It is important also to contrast this with the Old Testament when the Jewish nation lived by the principle of obedience to the law of God's commandments and the consequences of disobedience. This distinction sometimes causes confusion but a passage in Jeremiah helps us to understand:

Jeremiah 31: 31 "Behold, the days are coming, declares the Lord, when I will make a new covenant with the house of Israel and the house of Judah, 32 not like the covenant that I made with their fathers on the day when I took them by the hand to bring them out of the land of Egypt, my covenant that they broke, though I was their husband, declares the Lord. 33 For this is the covenant that I will make with the house of Israel after those days, declares the Lord: I will put my law within them, and I will write it on their hearts. And I will be their God, and they shall be my people.

In the Old Testament the nation of Israel was ruled by external commandments, it was an issue of compliance to rules and regulations not necessarily of internal trust in God and his nature. There were examples such as King David who went outside the external regulations but was still commended by God and referred to as 'a man after God's own heart.' The Bible tells us the Law of the Old Testament (The Old Covenant) was a steward to take us forward to the New Covenant where God's ways would be written on the hearts of those who choose to put their faith in Him; such people would not be led forward by adherence to external rules and regulations, but instead through relationship with God himself and the trust that grew through relationship.

Just as I learned to trust my swimming instructor, and people when seeking to produce good food turn to recipe books or people more knowledgeable in cooking, God wants us to know and trust Him as we journey forward on the adventure of life. We start in the shallow end of the pool following simple instructions and gaining confidence, but can end up in vast oceans exploring the wonders of creation.

The word 'obedience' is often viewed from a perspective of obligation, a lack of choice and freedom and this is very understandable. I remember when our son, David, first went to school; we took him to his classroom and left him with his teacher for the school day. About 3.30pm we collected him and he seemed reasonably happy and we talked with him about what he had experienced. He chatted along recounting his activities and seemed happy that he had 'done school' and would now be happy to resume "normal life" at home playing with his toys and friends. He certainly didn't consider another day at school as a good option. We had to explain to him that school was not an option but that he would have to go every day. So on the second day David went to school somewhat reluctantly. At the end of the day he came out and, with definite determination in his voice, announced to us that he 'definitely' didn't want to go to school again. We had to explain that the government required us to make sure that he received 'schooling' and that we had no choice in the matter. After the third day at school David proclaimed, "It is no good you will have to write to Mrs Thatcher (the prime minister) and tell her that I don't want to go to school!"

Obedience to God is not rooted in obligation, fear or lack of freedom. It is rooted in love, faith and freedom. In the story of creation, we read of God's instructions with clear indications of consequences that follow actions; we also see the freedom of choice that He gave to Adam and Eve. Love without choice is not love. God did not create us as robots with no free will, simply obliged to obey him, but rather as human beings who can make free choices. The choice of whether or not to obey God is an extraordinary aspect of His relationship with us. He loves us and love requires choice. All of us get to choose in whom we put our trust.

Who and what do you trust? This is a fundamental question in life.

A Story from my Family

It was our first day on holiday and we were very excited for a great week ahead of us. We were settling into our self-catering accommodation on the holiday park we had chosen, looking forward to using the various sport and leisure facilities on offer. David, Kerry and I were doing some unpacking and Kim was preparing our evening meal after which we would be going to play ten pin bowling together.

The cooking hob was different to our one at home in that it showed no difference when it was on or off, no change in colour to indicate it was hot. Kim got the meal ready and called us to eat, David wandered into the kitchen area to see what he could do to help and put his hand down on one of the cooking rings not knowing that it was very hot. Immediately he screamed in pain – he had a serious burn to his hand.

My doctor's brain leapt into action and we got his hand under cold running water from the tap. Despite this we watched in horror as the skin on David's hand went red raw and bubbled up into huge blisters, a sure sign of severe injury. David was in very considerable pain.

The meal was put to one side and all four of us started to pray and release the healing power of God and then our eyes watched a remarkable miracle unfold in front of us. The blisters on David's hand started to disappear, the redness receded and all his pain went away.

Twenty minutes later we sat down to our meal with David completely healed, then we went and played ten pin bowling. We went on to have a great week full of fun and activity, David was completely unhindered, it was like his hand had never been burned.

Chapter 5 Everyone Places Their Faith Somewhere.

Everyone places their trust in things and people in different ways at different times, and experience from those circumstances teaches us where to place our trust and where not to place it. Life is an experiment in trust. Babies are born needing to trust that people will meet their needs and they cry to bring attention to that need. They soon learn where to place their trust when they need feeding.

Parents trust school teachers with their children's welfare and education. As children mature gradually into adults their parents have to appropriately increase the levels of trust in the relationship in order to prepare them for life.

Let's return briefly to the subject of electricity. Every day we put our trust in many people and many things. I live in the UK, where the electricity supply is very good and I confidently expect power to be delivered to my house, so that I can use it in various ways. Behind that confident expectation is a whole industry involving many people and much infrastructure to supply electricity. I trust these organisations to supply my needs and it is a surprise if I cannot access electricity. However, I have been in other places in the world where electricity is not available in such a manner, other mechanisms are necessary in the normal walk of life and in that context I learn to put my trust in different things such as batteries or generators. I remember being in a remote part of Mexico with the Pame people where there was no central electricity supply and I slept on a bench in the small chapel there. It was pitch black in the room when I woke up in the mornings and the most important thing to do was turn on my torch hoping the batteries were still working so that I could check for scorpions and black widow spiders before putting my feet to the floor. This confidence in batteries definitely helped my peace of mind!

I like to be adventurous and one time I went abseiling with my wife, Kim, and my daughter, Kerry. It was the first time for each of us. We were going to descend 50 metres down a cliff face using climbing ropes to help us and keep us safe. We had, as best we could, carefully chosen our instructors on the recommendation of other people. They explained the procedure to us, explained how safe it was and then one by one attached the ropes around our bodies with the other end of the rope firmly attached to some rocks. As I backed towards the edge of the cliff and looked over at the 50 metre drop it occurred to me the level of trust I was exercising - literally my life was at stake. I was trusting the instructors, the ropes, and the rocks! And yet it was a well informed decision and I not only lived to tell the tale I chose to do it a second time and have subsequently done it in other places. My confidence is fairly high in that particular activity and yet I can fully understand why fear might stop other people from attempting it.

Fear and faith generally oppose each other. Taking a taxi for a journey in London is a very safe choice and involves little risk; however, when I visited Lima the capital of Peru in 2006, the local people instructed me very firmly not to trust in taxis, or more precisely taxi drivers, because of the risk of abduction and theft. People put their faith in different things and different people at different times.

Faith requires context. Both my grandfathers were great men. Despite difficult circumstances which assailed them throughout life they maintained their dignity, generosity and kindness towards those around them. It was a privilege to

know them and be part of their family. I trusted them and
their love for me.

I was closer to my maternal grandfather because I saw
him more often. He would call me "Pete-boy" and we enjoyed
being together; I particularly enjoyed hearing his stories from
life. Born in 1905, his family suffered some of the ravages
of the First World War. His name was Martin Ryan and
he came from an Irish Catholic background, his ancestors
on both sides having fled Ireland during the potato famine
seeking a better life in England and finding a place to settle
in London. He was one of thirteen children and poverty was
close at hand. In the 1920's he married Elizabeth Stone, also
an Irish Catholic, so my mother, born in 1931, was fully Irish
in her blood line, which makes me at least one half Irish,
a strange thought for someone who has lived all his life in
England and feels thoroughly English. My dad was born in
1928, also lived in London and similarly to my mum endured
the dangers and difficulties of the Second World War up
close; both of them coming extremely close to death with
their lives and education disrupted by the battle for freedom
against the Nazis. They met around 1950 in the post war
era, fell in love and got married in 1953, the year of Queen
Elizabeth's coronation and the year that rationing finally
ceased after the war. My parents deliberately chose to form a
stable family in which love was unconditional. As previously
stated my parents decided that religion would play no part
in the upbringing of their children, thus my sister and I were
raised without any religious obligations or tendencies.

The story in chapter 2 of this book left me with a
question:

Where is Jesus? This was a question I soon forgot once
I had left the church building (where I supposed that Jesus
lived and remained) and I carried on very happily with my

life untroubled by religious thoughts. Years passed by and my life developed in an agreeable way, stable family, nice home, success at school, success at sport and thoughts of a career in medicine. So it came as a complete shock when around the age of 16 my thoughts returned to the question of Jesus, or rather the questions about Jesus:

> Who is He?
> What is he like?
> Where is He?
> What does it matter to me?

These questions started to grip my mind and as I pursued them I made a great discovery. To the surprise of everyone including myself, I discovered that Jesus really is alive, and He is amazing, and my life took on a whole new meaning and purpose. I didn't find religion (as I was quick to point out to my friends) I found another person in whom I put my trust. I say 'another person' because I already had many people I could trust, one of whom was my Grandad Ryan. He was intrigued by this new found faith of mine and asked helpful questions. Over several years he and I interacted on this subject of faith, and he observed my life as I embarked on my medical career, got engaged then married to Kim and started a family. He was intrigued and eventually he said to me, "I wish I could have your faith."

"You can" I replied, certain that it is available to everyone who seeks it. However, he wasn't quite so sure because his religious upbringing had led him into a different sort of relationship with God, one based more on fear than confident trust. Our conversations continued and I believe my confidence in God started to change his perception of God.

Let me once again make a statement that might surprise you, Everyone has faith.

"Not me!" I hear some people replying, keen to avoid any connection with religion, which I understand entirely because the word faith is closely associated with thoughts of religion. However, it has a much broader meaning than that - it carries the meaning of trust. We place our faith in things and people all of the time. Faithfulness is a cherished thing. There is a geyser in Yellowstone National Park in the USA called Old Faithful because it reliably gushes steam and boiling water from the bowels of the earth in such a consistent way that you can be assured of a spectacular viewing any time you may choose to visit. When I visited my grandparents it was a sure fire certainty that I would be offered food, my nanny made sure "her boy" never went hungry, probably because she knew what hunger was when she was growing up, and after all she was sure that I was still growing (even at the age of 25!) When I introduced Kim into this setting, she learnt how to navigate through the mountains of food on offer!

Certain things are a sure fire certainty:

The sun will rise and set each day.
Gravity works.
There are stars in the universe.
Water runs downhill.

We trust these things and incorporate their reality into our everyday lives with assurance that is often buried in our subconscious thought and sometimes pulled forward into our conscious minds - for example when you choose to experience a glorious sunset, or a starry night sky. When constructing a building, drainage of water has to be considered, but it doesn't even cross our minds that water won't run downhill, we are assured of this. Such things are so stable and constant that trusting in them is easy and normal, rather than a struggle. However, each one is learnt through experience after birth and is not an inbuilt quality. Trusting in people, however, has different considerations: who can I trust with different aspects of my life? Appropriate trust is learnt through experience and knowledge. For example, I am a family doctor and generally my patients trust me and trust my opinions, but I am not a gynaecologist nor a dentist, for such issues another doctor is the appropriate choice of trust. Neither am I a car mechanic so trusting me in that area of life would be inappropriate and, almost without doubt, unhelpful to you.

Learning who you can put your faith in is part of the substance of life and without it life is very difficult and diminished.

What about trusting God?

Is he trustworthy?
Is he a constant reality or does he change?
What is He like?
Where is He?
How far can I trust Him?
What does it matter to me?
What does faith in God look like?

This is a beautiful lifelong adventure that is available to everyone. Just as I said to my grandad 'my faith' is not centred around me, but rather the certainty of the very being of God himself. The God who loves all mankind and who meets and rewards all who genuinely seek him.

Story by Janice Pleasants:
I was due to go away for 4 days to a Healing Rooms conference, when my elderly mother went into her garage for something, and whilst in there she tripped over her walking stick and fell, first onto the arm of a wooden bench and then on to the concrete floor. She just managed to get herself back into the house. When I came to see her she looked like she'd been in the wars; she had such pain in two fingers of her left hand that she couldn't move them, a sharp pain in her ribs which hurt as she moved or took a deep breath, a huge fist sized blood red bruise just below her left rib, bruised and swollen knees and other bruises. My initial thoughts were, I have to get her to A&E to get her checked out, and I wonder if I'm going to have to cancel going away, but before anything I'm going to pray. She sat in a chair and I felt the Holy Spirit say, just wait on Me. So I laid hands on her knees, invited the Holy Spirit to come and simply waited on Him. About 30 seconds later she started to giggle, then laugh, then she let rip with full blown Holy Spirit, joy-filled laughter for a good 10 minutes, rocking back and forth in her chair and gasping for breath between laughing. At the end of the 10 minutes, as the laughter subsided, I asked her how she was feeling. She could immediately move her two fingers and clench them into a fist, the pain in her ribs had gone, her bruise was fainter just a purplish colour and the swelling and pain in her knees had gone. By the next morning the blood red bruise was just a faint yellow outline. The joy of the Lord was truly her strength!

Chapter 6 Faith is Assurance

"Faith is the assurance of things hoped for." Hebrews 11:1
If you ask me, "Can you swim?" I will tell you with great confidence and assurance that "I can."

As I recounted in a previous chapter, this confidence and assurance was gained through placing my trust and obedience in someone with greater experience than myself.
Stating that "I can swim," is not arrogant or proud, simply a matter of truth.

Many things in life follow the same pattern:

- learning to drive a car
- training as a doctor
- starting to use computers and other technology
- parenting
- marriage
- bereavement

Learning from other people with more experience is wise and helps us grow in confidence. If you ask me, "Can you swim" and I reply "I hope so" you would have every reason to lack confidence in my ability.

There is a big difference between Hope and Assurance.
Compare these three statements:

We are hoping to fall pregnant vs We are pregnant.
We hope to have a holiday this year vs We are going on holiday.

I hope to get married one day vs I am getting married tomorrow.

Hope is a great starting place but not the final destination.

Our children were brought up in a secure environment and we did not lack money, so imagine if one day when they were 8 and 6 years old I had said to them, "I hope we will have enough food this week." Do you think they would feel confident and at peace? I suspect not, more likely a sense of unease and anxiety would be the result, after all this was an area of life in which they experienced assurance, they had never had to consider lack of food as an issue. The same statement given by parents to children the same age in a country overwhelmed by famine for a long period of time would probably elicit a different emotional response of joy and peace. In such a situation the ability to keep hope alive is essential, but the overall aim of such hope is an assured future. Hope is essential to progress in life, but assurance is essential for stability and confidence. Understanding the difference between hope and assurance is extremely important, and understanding their place in our journey through life helps us to continue to make progress.

Generally speaking, something that I am assured about requires much less thought and attention than something that I am hoping for.

In various conversations with Christians I have found that many have a distorted view about their level of faith, regarding themselves as low in faith and struggling to somehow grow in this area. They tend not to take into consideration some of the areas of their Christianity where they already experience full assurance of faith, for example:

- God so loved the world that He sent Jesus
- The gospel of Jesus Christ has the power to save
- Assurance of eternal salvation
- Confidence in some of the spiritual gifts
- The Bible is inspired by God and instructs us about Him.

I remember vividly the moment that God baptised me in the Holy Spirit, it came out of the blue and was not something I was aware of previously. I had been born again for only a few months and was not particularly confident in my Christian faith especially when it came to an assurance of eternal salvation and a desire to tell other people about Jesus. Then all of a sudden during a 'time of worship' I experienced what I could only describe as pure joy and power: it felt like a fountain started inside me drenching my internal reality with warm water, it felt refreshing and peaceful, then joy started to develop, firstly deep inside me then overflowing into my mind and my thoughts. It was such an exhilaration that I felt that I had to express it out loud and as I did so I was hit by a wave of power that almost knocked me off my feet. I was overwhelmed and felt unable to contain what was being poured into my life, I simply couldn't stop myself overflowing with joy and then came an intense desire to tell other people about God's love.

Almost simultaneously a strange sound escaped from my lips, it sounded like some Asian language that was incomprehensible to me.

Unknowingly I had received the gift of 'speaking in tongues' - but for a 17-year-old boy with no frame of reference for such a thing (my Bible knowledge was still very poor) it was somewhat alarming! I was already concerned about my friends thinking I was crazy, what would they make of this? This unearthly gift and ability to speak a language of heaven that is largely unintelligible in human terms seemed a bit 'freakish' to me. The Bible actually refers to it as "the language of angels" - could I now converse with angels?!

Also I was concerned that my Christianity would be genuine and not false in any way. My concern was so great that it overcame my hope that this gift was genuinely from God and the result was that I decided not to use this beautiful gift from God and it lay dormant in my life and therefore of no benefit. Fear had extinguished it, I had believed the lies that the devil had whispered in my ear although I didn't realise it, instead I was rather proud of myself for being so genuine. I had been robbed.

What I had experienced was a spiritual battle concerning my hope and fear had prevailed. About 9 months later I was having a conversation about this with a more mature and experienced Christian who had taken me under his wing. He used the Bible to help me understand about God being a good father who wants to give gifts to his children and for these gifts to grow in effectiveness as we develop them through faith. He pointed out that, "For the Spirit God gave us does not make us fearful, but gives us power, love and a sound mind" *(2 Timothy 1v7)*

He asked me a very helpful question. What factor had influenced my thinking the most - fear of getting it wrong, or hope and confidence in a good God? I realised that the answer was that fear had guided my thoughts rather than hope in God; the result was not to my benefit and also reduced my fruitfulness and positive impact on the world around me. With this realisation, I determinedly threw off fearful thoughts, allowed hope to rise within and studied the Bible for myself trying to find out as much as I could about this 'gift of tongues.' Alongside this I dared to try speaking in tongues again, starting rather hesitantly and awkwardly but allowing the journey from hope to assurance to commence. My internal conversations went something like this: "I hope I can speak in tongues, God gives good gifts and he loves me. Fear is not my friend and the devil is a thief, I will not allow myself to be robbed therefore I reject fear and lies." I started to thank God for giving me good gifts, confidence started to rise, I practiced speaking in tongues some more, and then more still. Within a month or so, I no longer hoped that I could speak in tongues, I knew with full assurance that I could. The soil of hope had allowed the assurance of faith to grow in me and doubts and fear had receded. For the last 44 years I have had full assurance about this gift, and have followed the Bible directive to pursue more spiritual gifts using a similar pattern. This has established more of the fullness of Christianity as an assured and normal part of my life and my relationship with God and my effectiveness in the world has been enhanced as a result.

Hope makes great soil and it needs to be nurtured carefully in our lives but it is not sufficient on its own, it needs to lead to confident faith and that is the fruit that we should expect to grow there. As an illustration, imagine you are sharing the good news of Jesus with someone who does not have a personal relationship with him by saying "I hope Jesus loves you"; this is not a powerful statement, neither is "I hope I am going to heaven when I die." Both are unconvincing. Assurance of faith is vital in confidently communicating the goodness of God with other people.

This truth came home to me when I first went to university. I had a room in a university residence and I was on the lookout for fellow Christians, and much to my surprise there were a lot of them - about 100 in our hall of residence alone. So I was having a lot of stimulating conversations and developing friendships. Many of these people had been brought up in Christian households and had a lot more experience than myself in spiritual matters and I was keen to learn. During one conversation I mentioned to one of my new found friends that I spoke in tongues; a look of concern came over his face and he told me, "You can't do that!"

Somewhat confused, I answered, "Why?"

"You just can't," came back the reply.

"But I do."

"You can't."

"Why?"

"It stopped a long time ago."

I was now very confused and puzzled. I went back to my room, got out my Bible and started to study the subject of speaking in tongues once again. I had done this before and come to a conclusion, but this was now being challenged by a more experienced Christian. The conclusion of my study was that I could find a lot of evidence about speaking in tongues being a normal Christian experience, for example, Mark 16 v 14-18: *Later Jesus appeared to the Eleven as they were eating; he rebuked them for their lack of faith and their stubborn refusal to believe those who had seen him after he had risen.15 He said to them, 'Go into all the world and preach the gospel to all creation. 16 Whoever believes and is baptised will be saved, but whoever does not believe will be condemned. 17 And these signs will accompany those who believe: in my name they will drive out demons; they will speak in new tongues; 18 they will pick up snakes with their hands; and when they drink deadly poison, it will not hurt the at all; they will place their hands on people who are ill, and they will get well.'*

However, I could not find any evidence that it had stopped. A few days later I came across my friend and I recommenced our conversation; with my Bible in hand I showed him passages that to me gave clear expectation of the gift of tongues continuing as part of Christian life. Then

I invited my friend to show me passages that talked about the gift stopping. He looked at me in surprised fashion and said, "I have no idea where that might be in the Bible."

I replied, "So why did you tell me that?"

"I was just passing on what I have been taught," he answered.

"Is it possible that you have been taught incorrectly?" I asked gently, and then I asked him if he would like to be baptised in the Spirit and speak in tongues.

"Yes" he said eagerly, so we went back to my room and I laid hands on him and prayed. Immediately he felt the power of God touch Him and started to speak in tongues.

My previous internal battle to establish the gift of tongues in my life as an assured reality had led to a place of confidence that opened up the same spiritual opportunity for other people. Following on from that a steady stream of people asked me to pray for them in this regard as hope arose within them of the availability of spiritual gifts. I am not sure that would have happened if I had not overcome fear, regained my hope and turned that into confident faith. It was a big lesson that has played an important part in my life.

Story by Janice Pleasants:

I was waiting in the reception area of a hairdresser's salon when I noticed a lady hobble in and walk up to the reception desk, obviously wincing with pain. I overheard her say that this would be her last visit as she was about to lose her job as her ankle was so messed up she couldn't work. I immediately heard the Holy Spirit say to me, "I want you to pray for her." I wondered how that could possibly work out as it is a big salon and she was taken straight through to have her hair washed whilst I waited. However, I ended up sitting next to her in the hairdresser's chairs. I got into conversation and ended up telling her a story about my shoulder being miraculously healed 6 months after a disabling injury in a car crash when a friend simply prayed for me. She said, "Where can I go to get prayed for by this man?" I said, "You don't need to, I'm a Christian and it's Jesus who heals, so I could pray for you." My hairdresser said it would be okay and he went to the reception desk and said in a loud voice, "Turn off the music, Janice is about to pray for someone!" He then led the woman to a more comfortable chair in the middle of the salon, so I ended up praying for the woman with the ankle problem, in my gown and sopping wet hair, with all the other clients and hairdressers turning round to watch what was going on. She felt some warmth but that was it. So I was disappointed for her that not more had apparently happened. I was passing the hairdressers sometime later, and he popped out of the salon to say, "Janice, we had your patient in here the other day." I explained that he'd got me confused with someone else as I wasn't a doctor. He said, "It was the lady you prayed for with the bad ankle. She came into the hairdressers the other day to let us know that over the next 24-36 hours her ankle was completely restored and totally pain free and that her GP had confirmed this and she had been able to return to work without any difficulty."

Chapter 7 Faith is a Journey.

My wife, Kim, and I were on holiday on the Spanish island of Majorca enjoying the sunshine, riding bikes, swimming and sampling the local food. Usually on holiday we isolate ourselves from the world news to give our minds a break from such things and concentrate on quality time together. Thus we were blissfully unaware of events in Iceland in the North Atlantic.

It was April 2010, and on the island of Iceland the volcano called Eyjafjallajökull, which had been active for a while, entered its next phase of eruption.

Beginning on 14 April 2010, the eruption created an ash cloud that led to the closure of most of the European airspace between 15th and 20th April as approximately 250 million cubic metres of ash shot into the air above Iceland and started to drift south towards the rest of Europe. Flights needing to use major parts of the European airspace began to be cancelled. About 20 countries closed their airspace to commercial jet traffic and it affected about 10 million travellers.

Our friends, David and Carol Webster were also away from home having a holiday on the Caribbean island of Antigua and visiting one of their sons who was working there, unaffected so they thought by anything 'happening at home,' and joyfully enjoying for a few days the sunshine and relaxed lifestyle offered in the Caribbean. Our holiday was drawing to a close on Sunday 18th April and that evening we started to move our thoughts to returning home the next day and back to work. We started to organise ourselves with a little bit of packing before we went down for our evening meal in the hotel. As we entered the reception area we noticed a number of people gathered around the television set with some animated conversation ensuing. Curious, we walked over to see what was going on; the TV screen was showing pictures of a volcano erupting and a cloud of ash rising into the sky. The commentary and subtitles were in Spanish and we didn't immediately understand the situation, so we started to ask some people what was happening and they explained to us what they had ascertained to that point. Nearly every flight into or out of the United Kingdom was cancelled until further notice because the ash cloud was a danger to planes due to the possible effect on their engines. We would not be returning home the following day.

Fortunately, we had booked our holiday through a tour company and their representative was in the hotel to help us. He confirmed that it was very unlikely that we would fly home the next day, but the situation was evolving, so to go and enjoy our meal and the rest of the evening and await more news the next morning. We awoke on the Monday morning, got dressed quickly and went to the hotel reception area for an update. Many people were in the same position as us, uncertain as to what might be in store.

The tour company representative was there to greet us with the news that flights were not leaving from Majorca for the UK. He said that it was not certain when circumstances would change and not to go far from the hotel in case things changed suddenly. Also as there were no new guests arriving we could keep our hotel room and all meals would be provided. So we set about enjoying another day in the sun, but with our minds preoccupied with uncertainties.

Monday passed and Tuesday came. The news that morning was that there was "no chance of flights today so go ahead and enjoy yourselves and ask again tomorrow." We tried to make the most of the situation but our minds were a bit preoccupied, especially as Kim and I were due to be working in France from the following Friday to Sunday. I had been in touch with David Webster by text messaging; he and Carol were stuck in the Caribbean with no hope of a flight for about a week. They had been transferred into a luxury hotel with all expenses paid. David said he was enjoying swimming in the pool and drinking cocktails whilst talking with other stranded tourists. Wednesday arrived - still no flights. However, we were asked not to go far and to stay in touch with the hotel. There were no further details. Intriguing! Kim and I decided to make the most of the day and set out to enjoy ourselves. Early in the afternoon our mobile phone rang and we were asked to return quickly to the hotel and prepare to leave at 3.00pm. We hurried back, grabbed our already packed bags from our room and with expectation gathered with the others waiting to return home. Here was the news; we were going by coach back to England! The small matter of crossing part of the Mediterranean Sea came quickly to mind! It was explained to us that a coach would take us to the port at Palma on the other side of Majorca, from where we would be taken by sea to Barcelona, and from there back to England by coach - all the way!

"How long will that take?" we thought. We were to find out!

The coach arrived about 5.00pm (but what was two hours in the grand scheme of things?). People got on board and with somewhat mixed emotions set off on the journey home. Relieved to be on the move, uncertain of the details and length of journey. We waved goodbye to the few hotel guests remaining. I texted David Webster to tell him our news; still enjoying the sun, swimming and cocktails for a few more days came back the reply. I chose to rejoice with him!

One hour into our journey we reached Palma port where a boat was waiting for us. Our tour company had arranged for one of its cruise liners to be brought out of a refit to act as a ferry for us, which was an impressive solution. This particular company had about 1500 British customers stranded on Majorca and the boat could accommodate 750 at a time. We were in the first group.

Everyone was assigned to a cabin and informed that an evening meal and breakfast would be provided, this was a great relief as hunger and sleeplessness were not attractive options. We boarded the boat around 8.00pm, had a meal and went to bed with the information that we would set sail around midnight and arrive in Barcelona around 8.00am. We slept reasonably well, got up, had breakfast and readied ourselves for the day ahead. As we were docking in Barcelona we looked out across the scene of the port in front of us and observed many coaches arriving in convoy. As we disembarked we were told to get on any coach because they were all headed in the same direction - towards Calais in Northern France, our next destination. It was 9.00am - 16 hours so far! (Normally it is a two hour flight back to England from Majorca.)

Dragging our cases behind us we found our way to a coach and got on board. Looking around we realised that this was not a coach designed for long distances but rather for shuttle runs to hotels and airports. No toilet on board! We were joined by families with young children, an elderly couple in their eighties and others. As soon as the coach was full, we set off with a driver and tour company representative who gave us some more details about our journey. We would stop every three hours for a refreshment and relief break!

We left the port and joined the motorway along with throngs of other similar coaches. Our tour company alone was trying to get 10,000 people home from mainland Spain in addition to those from the Spanish Islands. It started to feel like Dunkirk, the great evacuation of World War Two trying to return people to the UK, but obviously less dangerous. People were helping one another and looking out for each other. I texted David Webster to update him on our progress. Still enjoying the Caribbean came the reply. I rejoiced again! Time passed slowly! After three hours we pulled into a service area to find food, drink and toilets. At the same time, seemingly dozens of other coaches did the same. "You have thirty minutes," said our guide. Kim joined the queue for 'the ladies,' I navigated the shorter queue for 'the men's' and then set off in search of supplies. Kim made it back to the coach just in time and we set off again for the next three hours. We ate our provisions and drank enough to keep ourselves hydrated (but not too much because of other considerations!). The elderly couple on our coach were amazing in their good humour and well supported by everyone else. The children behaved brilliantly. We were all in this together and the atmosphere amongst us was extremely positive.

Time passed. Breaks at service stations were negotiated; humour kept up. As we drove through France it occurred to us that we could ask to get off here as we would be due back the next day, but we soon realised that was not practical.

Seventeen hours after leaving Barcelona we approached Calais and the ferry port where we could start to feel like we were nearing home. We drove into the port and a sense of relief engulfed us. We could see the ferries, we would be able to get off the coach and stretch our tired bodies. We drove around the port and to our dismay drove away from it. What was happening? Our guide spoke over the intercom to give us an explanation. We needed to transfer to other coaches and suddenly it made sense. On our coach were people from all over the UK: us from the South East of England, some from further north or west in England, and some from Scotland. We all needed to transfer to a coach specific to our final destination and these coaches had come from the UK to collect us. Only there was no room to park them all in the port of Calais.

So began our search of Calais, looking for the car park where our coaches awaited. Tiredness suddenly swept over us both, like a tsunami wave, would this journey never end? One hour later after many twists and turns we found our target. We disembarked from our coach and said farewell to our companions who somehow had become friends in such a short space of time. We collected our bags and were directed to another coach whose final destination would be Gatwick Airport where we had flown from at the start of our holiday and where our car was parked. Luxury! A toilet! As we settled into our seats, we were informed that we would leave as soon as everyone had arrived! At that stage there were about six of us. Over the next couple of hours more coaches found the elusive parking area and names were ticked off on a list. Everyone expected had arrived! It dawned on me what a massive logistical exercise we were benefiting from, thousands and thousands of people from many different places being cared for in an effort to get them home. Gratitude began to grow above my tiredness, and any frustration started to fade away. Shortly after 5.00am we arrived back at Calais port and our coach joined the queue for a place on a ferry. We were allowed to get off and try to find some refreshments. 36 hours journey time so far.

There were thousands of people, each one with a story to tell. We met a couple who had managed to find their way from South America via Spain, it had taken them 5 days! Another couple had been on holiday in Northern Africa, with very little help on offer as they had booked their travel independently of any travel company. They had taken small boats, a ferry, buses, and cars to get them as far as the border between Spain and France; in all there had been 12 different components of their journey to that point, but their money was running out and they still needed to get back to England. They had a relative who lived in Germany who decided to help; he chose to drive from Germany to Southern France to collect them, he then drove them all the way through France to Calais, not only that but he was going to drive them back to Gatwick airport to collect their car, before he would drive back home to Germany. What generosity of heart and mind. We heard story after story and the overall picture grew. Each story told with a sense of triumph over adversity and a mutual respect for fellow travellers. There is something powerful in finding fellow travellers with a common goal, to overcome obstacles in their paths in order to reach their destination. People were helping one another, there were tales of generosity and sacrifice. We started to feel a sense of privilege to be participating in this unfolding story. Tiredness seemed less relevant. Eventually we re-boarded our coach and drove onto the ferry and settled down for the crossing of the English Channel. Strong emotions rose in us as the White Cliffs of Dover came into view, somehow a potent symbol of our identity and our homecoming. Pride swelled in my heart, a strange feeling towards the end of such a journey; but I realised that I had been part of something that would be recorded in people's hearts and minds for a long time to come. Even now as I retell the story positive feelings flood my mind. The coach deposited us at Gatwick airport, and we noted that airplanes were landing and taking off, service being resumed. Kim and I made our way to the car park office. I went inside to sort out any details about our delayed return whilst Kim waited outside with our bags. The staff

were very friendly, helpful and understanding towards us,
asking how long our journey had taken - "42 hours from
hotel to airport," was the answer, sympathy the appropriate
response. A man came and stood next to me obviously for the
same reason as myself. I asked where he had travelled from,
and he replied "Majorca".

Thoughts formed in my mind, "a fellow traveller",
"respect", "instant camaraderie". Certain of another
encouraging story I asked him how long his journey had
taken. (Somewhere in the region of 42 hours I was guessing,
possibly more, possibly less).

He looked at me with a slightly puzzled expression, and
matter of factly replied "Two hours. Our plane took off this
morning as flights restarted."

Two hours!?

Instantly other thoughts invaded my mind, this time of a less
positive nature. Why? Respect was challenged. After all this
man had 'had it easy', he wasn't part of the 'true journey.'

A new thought came up: 'unfair' - a sense of inequality
rising. But then reason started to show its face; no one was at
fault, the man had simply had his expected journey, we had
an unexpected journey and many people had helped us; we
had been blessed in an unusual way.

I took my car keys, went to Kim outside and we found
our car and started the very last stage of our journey home.
En route I recounted the story to Kim of my encounter with
the 'other man from Majorca' and we both laughed and
groaned at the irony. We walked through our front door and
a sense of relief enveloped us. Our own beds that night had
never felt so welcome. We made it to France for the weekend
and on the Tuesday following went into our office for our
staff meeting. David Webster was there, having returned from
Antigua the day before, feeling refreshed after his prolonged

"luxury holiday". In contrast we felt somewhat tired but we had realised something over the previous few days; we had an amazing story to tell, an out of the ordinary story of ordinary people thrown together on a common mission.

Every part of life gives us opportunities and stories to tell, many parts may seem ordinary, some parts give more intriguing or amusing stories, others give stories of courage, perseverance and overcoming difficulties, still others give stories of blessing and abundance.

Such is the tapestry of life. And as with a tapestry, life looks different from different aspects. One thing I have learnt is that God can use every part of my life to weave a unique tapestry, and from his perspective it all makes sense. However, sometimes from my perspective life looks like a tangle of loose threads; at such times I choose to trust in His craftsmanship in my life rather than my limited understanding and I realise that the tapestry of my life is still under construction. I am on a journey into the fullness of life and I have the privilege of being on this journey with many other people; with countless life stories being formed. Life is a journey that includes other people.

Who are you journeying with? Who are you trusting? Is friendship with God part of your story?

Story by Karen Wellspring:
Our 19-year-old son, without warning, decided to leave home, writing a letter saying he didn't want to have any more to do with us, his friends, or siblings.

"Oh, and don't come looking for me either". He went off to university with his girlfriend. We thought we knew where he was heading but even that turned out to be a lie.

To say we were devastated was an understatement. We cried, got angry, tried to find him, Google searched for him, cried out to God for help. At one point we did find an address for him and wrote, only to be pushed away again. Years of heartache and years of shame. For me the hardest thing, apart from not having contact with him, was the shame. I didn't even tell my work colleagues what was going on, I didn't want it to affect my work. Just a few friends and our church family knew.

It was such a difficult time, it was like living with a bereavement that never ended. I did not talk about it and pushed it further away in my mind. If I thought about it, I cried and I didn't want to be out of control. But we still believed God would somehow bring him back.

Three years later I met Pete, Kim, and a team from ESSL (Eastgate School of Spiritual Life). They were like no other Christians I had met before. Full of the Holy Spirit and living life to the full. Living with joy, abundance, power, and the authority of the living God. They arrived in our house like a whirlwind, and we really didn't know what had happened. They came to the church for the weekend and then returned the following year for another weekend. It was at that point I decided I needed to do ESSL.

The week before I started the course, we received, out of the blue, a letter from our son. He had got married and had a baby daughter. He asked if it was possible to come back into our family and lives.

On my first day of ESSL I thought I could just sneak in and be unnoticed. God had other ideas. Somebody had a prophetic word about reconciliation coming, I just burst into tears, sobbing uncontrollably (not my style at all). I knew God was bringing reconciliation to our family again. Within a week we had met up with our son, new daughter-in-law and grand-daughter, and welcomed them back into our family. What a journey! God taught me so much about myself, about forgiveness, and about how crippling shame is. What the enemy planned for harm; God has used for good.

We now have complete reconciliation with our son. Our story of reconciliation has also helped other people to hope and trust in God in what seems like impossible situations. "And we know that in all things God works for the good for those who love Him."

Chapter 8 Faith Comes in Different Shapes and Sizes.

I have many relationships. All of them are different.

I have two children, David and Kerry, I love them both equally and am fortunate to have very close relationships with them. But my love and relationship with David is expressed differently to that with Kerry.

This is true of all people because every human being is a unique creation, even identical twins have different personalities and life paths. God is a Father to human beings, that is how Jesus introduced Him in the Lord's prayer, "Our Father in Heaven ..."

Therefore, it is fair to conclude that each one of us will have a unique relationship with God the Father, Son and Holy Spirit - the three aspects of the personhood of God. This means that our faith in Him, which is essentially our connection with Him, will have unique expressions, but like in any family there will be a lot of common ground. In this regard I find Hebrews chapter 11 in the Bible fascinating. Let's take a look at some of it and I will make some comments en route.

1 Now faith is confidence in what we hope for and assurance about what we do not see.

Faith is confidence growing in the soil of hope. It has confidence in the unseen realm, the invisible things.

2 This is what the ancients were commended for.

Throughout the ages, God has been looking for people who will trust Him with great confidence in His ability and character.

3 By faith we understand that the universe was formed at God's command, so that what is seen was not made out of what was visible.

God is the creator of the universe, He created what is seen out of what was invisible. Understanding the issue of creation is a matter of trust in a creator God. Any other theory of how the universe came into being also requires a faith system, but not necessarily faith in God.

4 By faith Abel brought God a better offering than Cain did. By faith he was commended as righteous, when God spoke well of his offerings. And by faith Abel still speaks, even though he is dead.

The story of Cain and Abel in the book of Genesis can look confusing at first glance:

Genesis 4; Now Abel kept flocks, and Cain worked the soil. In the course of time Cain brought some of the fruits of the soil as an offering to the Lord. And Abel also brought an offering—fat portions from some of the firstborn of his flock. The Lord looked with favour on Abel and his offering, but on Cain and his offering he did not look with favour. So Cain was very angry, and his face was downcast. Then the Lord said to Cain, "Why are you angry? Why is your face downcast? If you do what is right, will you not be accepted? But if you do not do what is right, sin is crouching at your door; it desires to have you, but you must rule over it."

Now Cain said to his brother Abel, "Let's go out to the field." While they were in the field, Cain attacked his brother Abel and killed him. Then the Lord said to Cain, "Where is your brother Abel?" "I don't know," he replied. "Am I my brother's keeper?"

The Lord said, "What have you done? Listen! Your brother's blood cries out to me from the ground. Now you are under a curse and driven from the ground, which opened its mouth to receive your brother's blood from your hand. When you work the ground, it will no longer yield its crops for you. You will be a restless wanderer on the earth."

Cain said to the Lord, "My punishment is more than I can bear. Today you are driving me from the land, and I will be hidden from your presence; I will be a restless wanderer on the earth, and whoever finds me will kill me." But the Lord said to him, "Not so; anyone who kills Cain will suffer vengeance seven times over." Then the Lord put a mark on Cain so that no one who found him would kill him. So Cain went out from the Lord's presence and lived in the land of Nod, east of Eden.

Why did God not look favourably on Cain's offering?

I have heard many thoughts and theories on this over the years, in particular about the substance of the offerings, one being a blood offering and the other not, but I am not convinced by these explanations.

In Hebrews 11 an explanation is given: *"by faith Abel …"* It is possible to do things for God that can look good externally and resemble what other people are doing, but God is looking for the internal faith/trust in Himself that is the motivation for the action. We will explore this a whole lot more in this chapter and throughout this book. Cain did a similar external action to Abel but it was not motivated by faith.

"Anything that is not from faith is sin" Romans 14 v 23

Very often "sin" is seen as something done wrong, not in line with the commandments of God and therefore displeasing to him. However, this verse reveals a deeper root that we need to understand. If faith is defined by our connection to God, then "anything that is not done in faith" is defined as doing something without connecting to God. When God created human beings he designed them to live in constant connection to him; sin results from disconnection and the consequences of sin are very damaging causing humanity to fall short of its glorious destiny (Romans 3 verse 23 all have sinned and fallen short of the glory of God). Jesus came to restore the connection so that we could live by faith in constant connection with God.

Back to Hebrews chapter 11:

5 By faith Enoch was taken from this life, so that he did not experience death: "He could not be found, because God had taken him away." For before he was taken, he was commended as one who pleased God.

Wow! I don't know how you react to Enoch's story, but I am overwhelmed by it. According to the Bible he is one of only two me–n (the other being Elijah) who did not experience death and were taken up into heaven by God. Surely his life story would be worth telling so that we could learn from him. Certainly he is worth a few chapters in the Bible (the story of Elijah spreads across eight chapters).

But no - Enoch gets seven verses in Genesis chapter 5:18-24

When Jared had lived 162 years, he became the father of Enoch. After he became the father of Enoch, Jared lived 800 years and had other sons and daughters. 20 Altogether, Jared lived a total of 962 years, and then he died.

When Enoch had lived 65 years, he became the father of Methuselah. After he became the father of Methuselah, Enoch walked faithfully with God for 300 years and had other sons and daughters. Altogether, Enoch lived a total of 365 years. Enoch walked faithfully with God; then he was no more, because God took him away.

And only one verse of explanation about what he did with the 365 years of his life. In actual fact just five words; *"Enoch walked faithfully with God."* In my opinion if you want to know what the Christian faith looks like it is summed up in those five words.

Who are you walking faithfully with?

6 And without faith it is impossible to please God, because anyone who comes to him must believe that he exists and that he rewards those who earnestly seek him.

This is quite a statement - without faith it is impossible to please God. It is the explanation for Cain and Abel. On the other side of the equation, it is also the explanation for Enoch - God finds faith so attractive that he draws people who walk faithfully in relationship with Him closer and closer to himself. It appears that Cain offered something to God out of duty rather than relationship and God tried to correct him and point him back into relationship, acceptance and favour. God also warned Cain that sin was a malicious force trying to overwhelm him and rule over him and if he let that happen the consequences would not be good. God was offering repentance and the good fruit that follows, Cain chose sin and had to accept the consequences that brought, the prime one being separation from the presence of God. However, even in that condition God still loved and protected him.

7 By faith Noah, when warned about things not yet seen, in holy fear built an ark to save his family. By his faith he condemned the world and became heir of the righteousness that is in keeping with faith.

For me this is another 'wow' moment. Imagine trying to build an ark of that size from scratch. God gave Noah instructions to build an ark in order to escape from something not yet seen or experienced on earth. So much rain that it would produce a flood.

So what did Noah do each day 'by faith?'

Pretty much the same thing: cutting down trees, making planks of wood, getting them into shape and putting them together. Day after day, year after year, for very many years. No power tools, no large number of helpers, not much encouragement from other people, more likely he suffered mockery. Just himself and his family obeying God, doing the same thing over and over, following God's instructions, getting ready for what God said was going to happen. That is faithfulness, that is everyday life walking in faith.

It is important to note that faith is not primarily about the more extravagant aspects of Christianity such as miracles and healing, but about our everyday lives dedicated to God and walking alongside Him.

8 By faith Abraham, when called to go to a place he would later receive as his inheritance, obeyed and went, even though he did not know where he was going. 9 By faith he made his home in the promised land like a stranger in a foreign country; he lived in tents, as did Isaac and Jacob, who were heirs with him of the same promise. 10 For he was looking forward to the city with foundations, whose architect and builder is God. 11 And by faith even Sarah, who was past childbearing age, was enabled to bear children because she considered him faithful who had made the promise. 12 And so from this one man, and he as good as dead, came descendants as numerous as the stars in the sky and as countless as the sand on the seashore.

The story of Abraham has had a great impact upon my life. It is a great story of relationship with God, endurance, keeping hope alive, and growing in faith. In Romans chapter 4 Abraham is called the father of us all and we will look at that chapter in detail later in this book. Hebrews 11 goes on to tell us more about Abraham:

17 By faith Abraham, when God tested him, offered Isaac as a sacrifice. He who had embraced the promises was about to sacrifice his one and only son, 18 even though God had said to him, "It is through Isaac that your offspring will be reckoned." 19 Abraham reasoned that God could even raise the dead, and so in a manner of speaking he did receive Isaac back from death.

Our faith is tested by God, not in order to produce a sense of failure or shame, but always to offer the opportunity to grow in faith. Hebrews 11 lists people from the Old Testament, names such as Isaac, Jacob, Moses, Rahab, Samson, and David, amongst others - all examples of people walking by faith in God.

We will be picking up more details about all this as we travel through this book together. Hebrews chapter 11 ends with some amazing thoughts -

"These were all commended for their faith, yet none of them received what had been promised, since God had planned something better for us so that only together with us would they be made perfect."

All of these people were commended for their faith and yet those of us who live in the reality of the New Testament have a greater reality of faith available to enter into.

Story by Janice Pleasants:

I was in London and went into a large department store to do some window-shopping during a very wet lunch break between meetings. As I walked towards two women assistants in a very posh part of the store, I got a severe pain in my abdomen like someone had punched me in the stomach. The older woman left, and I walked up to the younger woman and engaged her in conversation about the cashmere jumpers she was selling. Then I said, "This may seem like a strange question, but do you have pain in your abdomen?" I then described the pain. She said, "Yes, how did you know?" I explained that I was a Christian practising hearing from God and that sometimes I get sympathetic pains which indicate that God wanted to heal that condition. I asked if she would like me to pray for the pain to go away. She was a Catholic and said that would be lovely but we would be seen on the shop floor. I said as there was a changing room behind her, I could try something on and she could come with me. She agreed that would work. On the way she asked me who my favourite saint was. I explained we wouldn't be praying to a saint but asking Jesus to heal her pain. There was a little changing room of three cubicles, with no one else there. I released peace and prayed for her. I then asked how the pain was, and she said it was smothered in a blanket of peace. I went into one of the cubicles and tried on a £300 jumper – very carefully – I then came back to her and asked how she was getting on, she said that all of the pain had left. I explained that the jumper wasn't 'quite' me and left.

Chapter 9 Faith and Authority

The Bible teaches a clear link between faith and authority and I believe this needs to play an important part in our understanding. In Matthew 10 verse 1 Jesus called his twelve disciples to him and gave them authority to drive out impure spirits and to heal every disease and sickness. And yet they did not always succeed in the use of their delegated authority.

In the first chapter of this book we looked at a story in Matthew chapter 17 where Jesus' disciples were unable to bring healing to someone despite the fact that Jesus had given them authority over demons and every disease and sickness. When they did not succeed in setting people free from such affliction and they asked them why, he answered them, "because you have so little faith." Spiritual authority operates through faith. Lack of faith means that spiritual authority is not put into operation.

Imagine someone gives you a brand new television, one that you have been thinking about acquiring. It is a generous gift and you are excited to get it out of the box, you put it in the place you want it to be and you sit down to watch it, but nothing happens. You get the instruction manual out and read the instructions: you need to plug the television into an electricity source! Electrical devices operate through electricity and without that they do not work. Faith is like the power cord that plugs authority into its power source.

Let's look at another story in Matthew's gospel, it is found in chapter 8 starting at verse 5.

5 When Jesus had entered Capernaum, a centurion came to him, asking for help. 6 "Lord," he said, "my servant lies at home paralyzed, suffering terribly."

7 Jesus said to him, "Shall I come and heal him?"

8 The centurion replied, "Lord, I do not deserve to have you come under my roof. But just say the word, and my servant will be healed. 9 For I myself am a man under authority, with soldiers under me. I tell this one, 'Go,' and he goes; and that one, 'Come,' and he comes. I say to my servant, 'Do this,' and he does it."

10 When Jesus heard this, he was amazed and said to those following him, "Truly I tell you, I have not found anyone in Israel with such great faith. 11 I say to you that many will come from the east and the west, and will take their places at the feast with Abraham, Isaac and Jacob in the kingdom of heaven. 12 But the subjects of the kingdom will be thrown outside, into the darkness, where there will be weeping and gnashing of teeth."

13 Then Jesus said to the centurion, "Go! Let it be done just as you believed it would." And his servant was healed at that moment.

Jesus gives an amazing accolade to this centurion - "such great faith." What had Jesus seen that made him say such a thing? He saw that the centurion understood how spiritual authority operated and he put his faith in Jesus to use that authority to heal his servant. The word "Go" would carry sufficient authority to cast out darkness from the servant's body. The centurion likened it to his own military authority delegated to him by Rome. He knew the power that Jesus' authority carried. It had been given to him from heaven.

Jesus saw his faith and responded, "Go! Let it be done just as you believed it would." The centurion's belief produced his desired outcome.

When I qualified as a doctor I was instantly given authority to access the resources of the British National Health Service and increasing experience gave me increasing confidence and competence in the use of that authority. This has helped my understanding of spiritual authority in a similar way to how the centurion gained understanding from his work. However, it is very important to state that such authority was only given to me for the benefit of other people and not so that in some way I could rule over their health. Medicine not only tries to destroy sickness it also aims to help people live life fully and healthily. For that benefit to be realised it needs to operate through trust. I can give people medical advice but it is their choice whether or not to follow that advice. I can access medical resources in a way that others cannot but I cannot impose them upon people. I depend upon trust from my patients in order to be an effective doctor. Similarly, Jesus has given his followers authority to destroy darkness and to give life so that people can be fully healthy. Jesus states about himself in John 17 v 2 For you granted him authority over all people that he might give eternal life to all those you have given him.

The purpose of authority delegated from heaven is to release the resources of heaven so that life can be lived in all its fullness. The way that is activated is by faith in Jesus. Also when authority is delegated to someone they have a responsibility to use that authority. Authority and responsibility work vitally together.

Let's look at a Biblical example in the life of Moses. In Exodus 3 God says to Moses, "8 So I have come down to rescue them from the hand of the Egyptians and to bring them up out of that land into a good and spacious land, a land flowing with milk and honey—the home of the Canaanites, Hittites, Amorites, Perizzites, Hivites and

Jebusites. 9 And now the cry of the Israelites has reached me, and I have seen the way the Egyptians are oppressing them.

God is responding to the cry of his people and He has come down to earth to rescue them. How does he choose to do this, bearing in mind he doesn't need human help?

10 So now, go. I am sending you to Pharaoh to bring my people the Israelites out of Egypt."

He finds someone to send, giving them authority and power to command the power and resources of heaven. Although God is sovereign and all powerful he chooses to work through human beings to do his work on earth.

11 But Moses said to God, "Who am I that I should go to Pharaoh and bring the Israelites out of Egypt?"

This is a good question - why me? When God calls us to a specific task it is not uncommon to feel not properly qualified nor equipped to do the amazing works of God. God gives an interesting answer!

12 And God said, "I will be with you.

That is all you need to know. The answer to every question and challenge is found in these five words. "God with us" is a sufficient answer to any circumstance.

Moving on further in the story of Moses we get to Exodus 14, the Israelites have been released from Egypt and God has led them to the edge of the Red Sea. Pharaoh has changed his mind and wants his slave workforce back, so he gathers his army, pursues the Israelites and catches up with them at the Red Sea effectively holding them captive. Nothing is separating them from the Egyptian Army; the cloud of God's presence which turns into a pillar of fire at night is in front of them. God has led them to this impossible and dangerous situation.

> *13 But Moses told the people, "Don't be afraid. Just stand still and watch the Lord rescue you today. The Egyptians you see today will never be seen again. 14 The Lord himself will fight for you. Just stay calm."*

This is a suitably reassuring bit of communication by Moses and with the history of the ten plagues suffered by the Egyptians in their recent memory I can imagine the Israelites waiting for God to act.

> *15 Then the Lord said to Moses, "Why are you crying out to me? Tell the people to get moving.*

This answer is astonishing. God is effectively saying, "Get on with it! I have delegated leadership authority to you, so use it."

So often we think God is not doing anything, when he has already done everything we need. Moses expected God to part the Red Sea and was waiting for him to do so but God's expectation was different. His expectation was that Moses would use his delegated authority.

> *16 Pick up your staff and raise your hand over the sea. Divide the water so the Israelites can walk through the middle of the sea on dry ground.*

The staff is a symbol of authority and it needed to be used.

Moses is instructed to divide the water and lead the Israelites
to freedom and safety.

> *19 Then the angel of God, who had been leading the people of
> Israel, moved to the rear of the camp. The pillar of cloud also
> moved from the front and stood behind them. 20 The cloud settled
> between the Egyptian and Israelite camps. As darkness fell, the
> cloud turned to fire, lighting up the night. But the Egyptians and
> Israelites did not approach each other all night.*

God changes his position from leading to protecting. He
expects Moses to lead the people.

> *21 Then Moses raised his hand over the sea, and the Lord opened
> up a path through the water with a strong east wind. The wind
> blew all that night, turning the seabed into dry land.*

Moses takes the initiative, steps out in faith and uses his
authority. As He did this, God responded in power. This is
the way that spiritual authority usually works, we choose to
step out in faith and God blows upon our effort doing what
only He can do. Authority and faith release the resources of
heaven upon earth. That is how healing occurs. That is how
deliverance occurs.

> *22 So the people of Israel walked through the middle of the sea on
> dry ground, with walls of water on each side.*

The people were led to freedom and in addition their enemies
were swallowed up by the Sea. God expects us to use our
spiritual authority with faith, trusting that as we step out in
faith he will respond with the resources only he can release.
An example of this would be healing: Jesus instructed his

disciples to heal the sick, not to pray to God to do it, however, as we step out in faith he releases healing power. This interaction between authority and faith is very important to understand. Jesus is the best model to follow in learning how to use spiritual authority and studying the gospels to ascertain this is a wise thing to do. I talk about how Jesus used authority in my book Unwrapping Lazarus - broadly speaking Jesus used his authority over anything linked to the kingdom of darkness in order to destroy it, however, with regard to people he used his authority to give them life and freedom.

Story by Dave Foggon:

Recently I was on a packed commuter train into London to meet a client. On the seat opposite me sat a man in overalls, wincing in pain. Every so often, he would struggle to stand up, and try to move his back around with great difficulty, wincing and groaning loudly as the pain was so great. He'd then hobble back to his seat again.

I asked him what the problem was and he told me that he was playing football at the weekend, and had been challenged by another player whilst going up for a header. This had caused him to be flipped up, higher into the air, and then land on the hard ground, directly onto his back. He'd been carried off the pitch and then taken to hospital, where he was told he'd damaged his coccyx (tailbone). The problem was, he was a roofer and it was going to make doing his job that day almost impossible as he wouldn't be able to climb ladders and carry out his work.

I asked him if he'd like to be completely healed right there and then. He looked at me strangely, and then asked, 'Why are you some kind of doctor?' I told him I wasn't, but that if I prayed for him, he could be healed. Thinking I might well be mad, he seemed to decide it was worth the risk and said yes.

I walked over and placed my hand on his shoulder. I thanked God, then released grace into his back. Then I walked back to my seat and told him to stand up and check it out.

He stood up and moved, and immediately started swearing loudly on the train carriage for all to hear. 'WHAT DID YOU DO TO ME?!!' With amazement, and more expletives, he moved freely in any direction he pleased without any pain. He was totally pain free.

Other people in the carriage began asking what was

happening. A man told a lady, 'That man has just been prayed for, and God healed him. Amazing.' Pretty much the entire carriage heard what happened that morning.

Before the roofer got off for his stop, he thanked me, and I reminded him it was Jesus that had done this for him because he loves him - and to never forget that.

Chapter 10 Faith Can Calm Any Storm.

Faith is very powerful.

It was July 1985, Kim and I knew that the next few weeks would present opportunities both for great joy and great challenges. Kim was pregnant with our second child, her due date was 30th July, and our son David was two and a half years old and full of life. David enjoyed playing with his friends, in particular two boys around his age who lived in the houses immediately next to ours in the very pleasant surroundings of Biggin Hill in the South East of England

I was working as a hospital doctor in 'Internal Medicine' but was planning to work towards becoming a General Practitioner, and in order to do this and work effectively as a family doctor I felt the need to gain paediatric experience so that I could be confident when treating children as well as adults. I needed to find a paediatric job in a hospital for six months and despite trying hard I could not secure one in a hospital near to where we lived. However, in April 1985 I was offered just such a job in Liverpool in the North West of England, which is a long way from Biggin Hill; Kim's sister and family lived not far from there, as did Kim's mum and this played a big part in our decision. I accepted the job in Liverpool, which would start on 1st August, and resigned from my existing employment with effect from 12th July. On the 15th of July a removal van came to collect the furniture and belongings that we were taking with us to the house near Liverpool that we would rent for the next six months. We would meet them there the following day; our house in Biggin Hill would be rented out to two friends for the same amount of time. Once the removal van had left we looked around our nearly empty house, locked it up and after we had said our goodbyes to our neighbours including David's two close friends, we started the drive north towards the next part in our adventure of life. Kim was 38 weeks pregnant - not an ideal time to move house! Fortunately, Kim did not go into labour en route and we safely arrived at Kim's sister's house for an overnight stay. We were given a very warm welcome in our new location.

The next day Kim had an appointment at the Maternity Hospital in Liverpool to transfer her antenatal care to them and after that we would also move into our new home - quite a full day.

The removal van arrived and our new home welcomed its new furniture and its new occupants. Kim's family helped us to settle in, and we started to unpack lots of boxes.

David was somewhat bewildered by his new surroundings, there was no back garden, just a small patch of bare concrete, and there was no front garden. In fact, there was virtually no green at all. And no friends! We had chosen to live in an area where I could get to work by public transport, meaning that Kim would have use of our car, as this was a priority to us. However, that limited our options of where to live and we found ourselves living in a deprived inner city area with 60% unemployment. It was a very big contrast to Biggin Hill. We were hoping that Kim would give birth not too long after we had moved house so that we could have time together as a family before my job started on 1st August (I was not allowed to take any leave for the first six weeks of the job). However, that did not happen and eventually Kim went into labour late on 29th July and our daughter Kerry was born on 30th July, thankfully uneventfully. David was excited to visit his sister. Mother and baby were well and allowed home on Wednesday

31st July. Less than twenty-four hours later I left the house, took a bus into the centre of Liverpool and walked into my new job, thankfully I was not on duty that night, nor over that weekend, but that was the calm before the storm. Not that there was much calm to be enjoyed!

It was a very high pressure job, with an enormous workload; my contract was to work on average 84 hours per week, this consisted of two weeks working 56 hours per week and then every third week working 136 hours which included an 80 hour shift over a weekend with little or no sleep. The Hospital was called The Royal Liverpool Children's Hospital and it was partnered with the world renowned Alder Hey Children's Hospital; my major work was the care of children with severe heart problems before and after they had surgery. Much of the work was groundbreaking, trying to save children from untreatable conditions and unfortunately it was not uncommon to see children die despite the heroic endeavours of the staff. I found it extremely demanding on my emotions. In addition, I had to cover the Accident and Emergency department and other areas of the entire hospital when I was on duty overnight and at weekends. I lived with the spectre and prospect of the '136 hour week' constantly over me. When I came home from work it was difficult to work out which one of Kim and I was more tired, both of us working so hard in the different aspects of our life together. David was settling in but very much missing his friends and his green surroundings. Kerry was a delight, smiling and laughing, healthy and bouncy, but it was still a lot of work for Kim with a newborn and a toddler. In addition, as I looked at my own two healthy children I found it difficult not to bring to my mind the sick children under my care who faced very different futures. It was a tough time emotionally for all of us, except Kerry who kept on smiling.

After six weeks we were able to take a weeklong holiday and we booked accommodation on a holiday resort in Devon in the south west of England, a part of the country that held fond memories for us. Our holiday home had large picture windows looking out over a beautiful valley, green with grass and trees and as we entered it for the first time David toddled over to the windows, looked out and said, "I like this garden". Never before had four simple words expressed his emotions so profoundly. We had a great week, relaxing, swimming, going to the beach, and being together just the four of us. During the week Kim was taking notice of the freckles on my back (little brown spots) of which I have many. They are harmless and never caused me any concern. However, Kim was concerned about one particular spot and so I agreed that once I was back working in the hospital I would get a Dermatologist to check it out. I did this for the sake of Kim's peace of mind, not because I shared any concern. I put it out of my mind and enjoyed our time together.

The hospital I worked in had a dermatology department so as soon as I got back I arranged to pop in to one of their scheduled clinics. I went in to see a doctor with whom I was familiar and explained the situation. He agreed to look at my back there and then, both of us thinking it would only take a very short time. We chatted a bit as I took my shirt off and then he walked behind me to look at my back. He started to touch various spots on my skin and things became studiously quiet, in particular as he found the area on my back causing Kim's concern. His fingers prodded with a bit more intent and after what seemed an age a small sigh exited from his lips and he said to me, "I think it would be best if I remove that for you."

I was surprised but agreed without hesitation, "Best to be rid of it" was my thinking, still not particularly concerned. But

that all changed with his next three words: "It is pigmented."
My medical brain was suddenly racing at extreme speed as
I realised what his concern was and what he was expressing
to me. He was effectively saying, "I think that could be a
Malignant Melanoma" and that was very bad news. I was
suddenly facing the possibility of having a form of skin cancer
that could be very aggressive and spread to other parts of my
body very readily. In 1985 such a diagnosis would mean that
my life expectancy was likely to be less than five years.
We moved into a side room, where I laid on a small surgical
bench. He injected local anaesthetic to the area to make it
numb so that he could remove the suspected cancer. It was all
over in about ten minutes but it seemed like a lifetime ("What
was my lifetime?" I thought to myself).

    He explained that he would send the section of skin off
to the Pathology Laboratory for analysis and that I should
come back the same day next week for the result and then
he left me in order to continue with his clinic. I got up off
the bench, and started to put my shirt back on, my mind not
concentrating on the buttons. I knew that I needed to get
back to my patients, that I was part of a team endeavouring
to save lives, and yet was my own life now in peril? I talked to
God about it all, and set my requests in front of him and then
I put my mind into 'doctor mode' and allowed my optimism
to come to the fore, trying to push back any foreboding
thoughts. Fortunately, it was not a 136 hour week, I would be
sleeping in my own bed tonight alongside my lovely wife, the
night probably disturbed by my own healthy children rather
than ones battling for life: welcome disturbances awaited me
I thought. When I arrived home that evening, after David
was in bed and Kerry was settled, I told Kim that my skin
lesion had been removed. She was relieved.

    I also told her that I would be reviewed in a week, but

I did not tell her the details possibly indicating a malignant melanoma as I saw no point in troubling her with something as yet unknown as she did not need extra emotional pressure. I kept talking to God, pulled on the reality of praying in tongues and worshipping in the spirit in order for the River of God's Peace to flow into my heart and my mind. At the end of the evening with both Kerry and David asleep we went to bed together. I cuddled Kim for quite a while, my mind registering that there was a possibility that I had limited opportunity to do this. We read our books and then turned out our lights.

I closed my eyes but sleep would not come, my mind turning over and over with the words 'malignant melanoma' and all the potential consequences. My mind was in turmoil and the peace of God seemed beyond my grasp. Once I was certain that Kim was asleep I got out of bed and looked at her for a period of time and then left our bedroom. I went to look at Kerry, still asleep, so peaceful and beautiful, just seven weeks old; and then into David's room enjoying the sight of my young son so full of life. I didn't want to die. I alternated between the three bedrooms all night, looking at Kim, Kerry and David, occasionally getting into bed and searching for elusive sleep that never arrived. I talked to God telling him that I wanted to grow old with Kim, to see David and Kerry grow up into their adulthood, to make cherished memories and enjoy my family. I was sad beyond measure. Would my life be snatched away from me at such a young age? I don't know how I got through the next day except I know I did and that my work was okay (after all I was used to working without sleep!). I don't remember much about that evening either, but I remember the night very well. It was the same as the previous night, alternating between three bedrooms, no sleep acquired, sadness increasing, and peace disappearing beyond the horizon. I had a longing in my heart to be with my wife and my children. The size of the mountain facing me was all consuming in my mind and I could not find anything else to focus my thoughts upon. I had no idea how to access the "peace that passes understanding", how to come to Jesus and find "rest for my soul", the spiritual battle raging inside was very intense and I did not seem to be winning. The next day passed in a similar fashion, somehow I got through. This was the longest week of my life with the longest nights ever and I dreaded going to bed. It was another night I would never forget. We went to bed and I cuddled Kim for a length of time, then I waited for her to drop off to sleep and got out of bed once again. I spent some time downstairs as well as in the bedrooms looking at Kim, Kerry and David. I was battling with thoughts of my mortality and who would look after my family if I died. I was talking to God about it all but nothing seemed to be coming back the other way. Perhaps I wasn't listening correctly. What was God saying? I started to ask myself some questions about trusting God as I had never faced such an extreme test of my faith. Did I trust him? Could I trust him in this circumstance? I was sitting downstairs with all these thoughts circling through my mind. I decided to go and look at David, Kerry and Kim all asleep in bed, peaceful and at rest, it was about 3.00am. I prayed for each one of them to enjoy the abundance of life God offers even if I wouldn't be there to share it with them. Then with tears running down my cheeks, I stood on the landing outside the three bedrooms and I said to God, "I choose to trust you that if I die, somehow you will look after my family in a way that will surpass what I can do. I choose to entrust you with my family." Instantly peace flooded my being, it was like a tidal wave hitting me from the inside out. It did not start in my mind but in my spirit from where it flowed into my mind. It was the "peace that goes beyond all understanding" as promised in the Bible. I had never experienced it in such depth and intensity before, and maybe I had never needed to. I was overwhelmed in the presence of the Prince of Peace and I knelt on the floor in wonder and adoration. It was strange in many ways that the peace I was experiencing was not due to a change in my circumstances as I still did not know about my future and God was not reassuring me about my health and future life on earth with my family. My circumstances hadn't changed but God had entered into my internal reality and changed me. As I reached out in faith to him, expressing my trust in him, He had connected with me in the most extraordinary way. I felt peaceful, my mind no longer raging with uncertainty and anxiety, but I also felt tired so I climbed into bed and instantly fell asleep. The next morning I woke up alongside Kim and explained to her what I had experienced and indeed was still experiencing - utter peace. I spent some time with David and Kerry as well and then set off to work. The next few days I remember enjoying the presence of God and his peace as a constant reality. It was an extraordinary transformation.

The following week I returned to the Dermatology clinic for the results regarding my skin lesion. I was feeling fine, optimistic and peaceful as I registered myself with the receptionist for the clinic. She said, "Hello Dr Carter, I have been asked to put you in one of our side rooms." That was a small surprise. She then explained that the senior Dermatology doctor would come and see me and explain the results to me rather than the doctor I had seen previously. My medical brain went into action again: this did not sound good, this was usually a sign of bad news to be conveyed to a fellow doctor by a senior doctor. My peace was challenged as I anticipated the news that I had a malignant melanoma, all sorts of emotions rose up within me.

I sat alone in the small side room and quite quickly I made the decision to reaffirm my trust in God no matter what the circumstances. My peace returned.

After about five minutes the senior doctor, whose name I cannot remember, entered the room and sat down. Here came the results.

"I am pleased to tell you that you don't have a malignant melanoma" - relief enveloped me. "However, the lesion we removed was a skin cancer, a basal cell carcinoma (or rodent ulcer), all of it has been removed and you will have no further problem with it because this form of cancer does not spread to other parts of the body. Moving forward I suggest that you undertake a regular review of your skin and seek help again if there is anything suspicious."

We chatted briefly over a few details and I thanked him for his help. I left the clinic and returned to work with a spring in my step.

When I got home that evening I embraced Kim and told her the result. I gave both Kerry and David hugs and as I looked at them I thanked God for the gift of life that I could enjoy with them and for our future together. That life and future were enhanced through the greater understanding I had acquired about an eternal perspective sitting alongside the reality of our time limited earthly existence. My faith had been tested not so that I would fail, but so that I could grow and acquire something that money cannot buy - Peace of Mind.

It was a very difficult experience but my whole life following was enriched by it as I had learned a very important lesson about being able to live in the peace of God that can guard my heart and mind in any circumstance. Trials and tests still come but the lesson learned back in 1985 has served me well. The river of God flows within me and peace is contained within its waters. On that dark night in July 1985 I found that faith can calm any storm.

A story by Sasha Caridia

I work in an Urgent Treatment Centre in a hospital and one day I was discussing with a patient the suggested management plan for her problem: who had debilitating foot pain and needed to use crutches. She explained that she was a former Chaplain and it turns out that she led the ministry team at a church attended by one of my work colleagues. All of a sudden the management plan now included prayer and I went and found my colleague to include her. We all shared stories of what we have seen the love and power of Jesus do and as we did the presence of God filled the room. My colleague and I prayed - the woman and her daughter who was accompanying her were physically overcome by the Holy Spirit, which was fun to watch given how unexpected it was for them. The woman was now able to walk unaided, feeling heat in her foot as the pain was leaving. And her daughter felt as though a heavy weight had lifted from her, she looked visibly different. My colleague and I were enthusiastically hugged and then we watched as the woman pushed the wheelchair she had used whilst in the department down the corridor. I love the Holy Spirit surprises; the love of God is so wonderful.

Workplace revival, on earth as it is in Heaven.

Chapter 11 Faith Needs to be Tested.

A lot of Christians think that they don't have much faith and I would like to challenge that thought. If you are a Christian, you probably already experience assurance about various aspects of your faith but other parts are a work in progress.

"Your faith is worth more than gold"

The Christian life is like a gold mine and I would encourage you to imagine that you have access to this mine at all times.

God is the gold mine.
How much gold is available?
How many seams of gold are in this mine?
Is there still more to discover?

Let's explore some of the treasure:

Assurance of eternal salvation
For all who are born again there is the assurance of eternal salvation. Believing this requires extraordinary faith. Being certain that God has prepared a place in heaven for you gives extraordinary (dare I say supernatural) security in your inner being. Ultimately we are trusting God with our eternal destiny.

The book of Ephesians is very clear about the gift of eternal salvation by grace through faith. However, for centuries this Biblical truth was in question and assurance of salvation was absent, instead the fear of hell and purgatory held people captive to religion and religious structures. Then God raised up Martin Luther and the Reformation came into being - based on the assurance of salvation through faith alone and not by works. Gold was rediscovered and that aspect of Christianity is readily accessible nowadays compared to previous centuries.

> *Ephesians 1; 11 In him we were also chosen, having been predestined according to the plan of him who works out everything in conformity with the purpose of his will, 12 in order that we, who were the first to put our hope in Christ, might be for the praise of his glory. 13 And you also were included in Christ when you heard the message of truth, the gospel of your salvation. When you believed, you were marked in him with a seal, the promised Holy Spirit, 14 who is a deposit guaranteeing our inheritance until the redemption of those who are God's possession – to the praise of his glory.*
>
> *Ephesians 2: 8 For it is by grace you have been saved, through faith – and this is not from yourselves, it is the gift of God – 9 not by works, so that no one can boast.*

Assurance of the love of God
I know that God loves me because He is love. His love is not dependent on my works or my performance, it is simply his nature to love and I am certain about that.

Assurance of the power of God
He demonstrates his power and I know He is all powerful.

Assurance of the gifts of God
A number of spiritual gifts are now an assured part of many Christians lives. For instance, speaking in tongues was a seam of gold that was rediscovered in the early part of the 20th

century during the Pentecostal awakening which spread across the world. It is now experienced as a normal part of Christianity by millions of Christians and (I believe) openly available to all.

Prophesy is another gift having a wider and wider impact. The Bible instructs us in Romans 12:6 to *"Prophecy in accordance with our faith."*

Many more things come to mind where generally speaking we don't experience much doubt, the existence of angels and the second coming as examples. However, there are areas where doubt is a bigger feature, the areas of healing and other miracles, for instance, even though they stand alongside the other gifts mentioned in the Bible. To my mind these are seams of gold that are not as easily accessible at this moment in time to large parts of the Christian experience. We are less assured about them but as long as we hope that they are potentially accessible we can pursue them. Once hope is extinguished then endeavour to discover more will cease.

If you believe that there is no more gold to discover in a gold mine, you will cease exploration. However, if you believe that there are seams of gold as yet undiscovered or not fully accessed you will continue. 'Hope for more' inspires endeavour.

Some people say that too much hope will only lead to disappointment, that we must be real about our Christianity and not lead people into false hope. My reply to this is simply that in reality God is infinite and eternal, therefore there can be no limits placed on our potential to discover more about him. Therefore, our faith always has potential to grow. There will always be more seams of gold to discover and use.

However, if we do not believe we have been granted access to these seams we will not have the hope for our faith to grow in. We need to resist any notion of limits to our Christian experience remembering that it is an eternal journey through infinite possibilities. This journey will continue past the death of my human body, but even before that I do not believe I will exhaust the possibilities of my Christian life.

Once I have mined one seam of gold, I am confident there will always be more seams to seek out, explore and appropriate into my life.

The Bible teaches us about the possibility of spiritual deception and we need to be aware of this without becoming fearful or shrinking back from endeavour.

Imagine you were part of a gold rush and you staked your claim to a plot of land that you could mine. As you work in the mine day by day you will be looking carefully for any sign of gold and then one day there it is in front of you. Amongst the rock is something gold coloured and your excitement rises. You start to chip out the rock and discover there is more to uncover.

At this point in the process something very important needs to happen. Your rock needs to be inspected and tested to see if you have found genuine gold because there are other rock types that can look similar but are not gold. As an example, Iron Pyrites is commonly called 'Fools Gold'. Without that testing you could spend years accumulating something that is almost worthless and certainly disappointing.

A positive test would help to fuel your future endeavour, a negative test will redirect you and help to avoid unnecessary disappointment and heartache.

Similarly, our faith needs to be tested.

1 Peter 1: 3 Praise be to the God and Father of our Lord Jesus Christ! In his great mercy he has given us new birth into a living hope through the resurrection of Jesus Christ from the dead, 4 and into an inheritance that can never perish, spoil or fade. This inheritance is kept in heaven for you, 5 who through faith are shielded by God's power until the coming of the salvation that is ready to be revealed in the last time. 6 In all this you greatly rejoice, though now for a little while you may have had to suffer grief in all kinds of trials. 7 These have come so that the proven genuineness of your faith— of greater worth than gold, which perishes even though refined by fire—may result in praise, glory and honor when Jesus Christ is revealed. 8 Though you have not seen him, you love him; and even though you do not see him now, you believe in him and are filled with an inexpressible and glorious joy, 9 for you are receiving the end result of your faith, the salvation of your souls.

God allows our faith to be tested so that it will be found to be genuine or not. Trials passed give greater confidence and energy for endeavour. Trials failed can inform and redirect us so that genuine faith will grow.

It is important to say that trials of our faith are also an assessment of our spiritual capacity. What degree of spiritual responsibility can we carry, how many of heaven's resources have we gained access to? The Bible says that we have received "every spiritual blessing in Christ" but how many are we experiencing? If we understand that our mission on planet earth is to bless every nation on earth then we will also understand the need for increasing our spiritual capacity, or to put it biblically, to enlarge our storehouses, or stretch out our tent pegs.

God promises that if he finds us faithful with small things that he will entrust us with greater responsibilities. How does he find us faithful? He tests our faith - not for failure, but to ensure future growth.

Kim and I are not really 'into cars' in that we happily use cars as a form of transport but it is a very functional reality for us. We don't derive much pleasure from driving or owning cars and all our cars that we had purchased were second hand. A few years ago we needed to find another car as one of ours (we have two) was definitely heading towards the end of its useful life. We had a type of car that served our services particularly well and we decided we would get another one, so we started to search the internet for what we wanted and we had a price bracket in mind. Much to our surprise we found the type of car we wanted within our price bracket quite quickly, but it was actually a new car (a demonstration model with just a few miles driven) and it was about half the normal price. We decided that this was a provision from God and for the first time in our lives we had a new car to own and drive.

Interestingly we were far more aware of its quality and newness than we had anticipated and it made us more careful to look after it well. Another thing was that it came with more advanced technology than we had experienced previously. One of these features was an automatic display of the tyre pressures. Very handy, we thought!

A few months after our purchase I was driving along and a warning light came on: at first I did not understand what it was warning me about so I stopped and got out the instruction manual. I discovered that the car was informing me that one of my tyres was at a low pressure of 22psi instead of the regulated 29psi. I was very pleased to discover how helpful this technology was and armed with this information I made my way to a petrol (gas) station to pump up the tyre. Following this, the warning light turned off, the car registered 29psi and we were all happy.

A few days later the same thing happened - 22psi on the same tyre so I promptly went to the petrol station and pumped up the tyre to 29psi and drove on my way. This process was repeated 3 days later.

On the 4th occasion that it happened I decided on a different course of action. I decided on no action! I was intrigued to find out whether the pressure would drop below 22psi - I must add that it was still safe to drive the car for short distances but slightly suboptimal. I kept an eye on the pressure reading for the tyre in question and it stayed firmly at 22psi for the next few days.

The car was giving me information but I was struggling to understand it. The remedy that I had applied three times did not take away some underlying problem. Simply doing the same thing over and over was not a satisfactory solution. I put my scientific brain into gear! Somehow the tyre would tolerate a pressure of 22psi but nothing above that pressure. It was limited in its capacity to hold enough air for it to function correctly. Then a thought occurred to me - there must be something causing a leak of air that stops at 22psi. However, there was nothing obvious to see from my inspection of the tyre, so I took the car to a tyre repair shop for them to inspect. They lifted up the car on a hydraulic jack and sure enough there on the inside of the tyre tucked away from sight we found a screw embedded in the tyre. The screw was removed, the hole was repaired and the tyre returned to full capacity and function.

I found this a very helpful lesson. God wants to continually increase our capacity to receive his blessings and for them to flow from us into the world around us. However, if we have 'screws in our tyres' we will not be able to attain our full potential. God will test our faith by applying pressure in our lives in order to give us information about ourselves as to our current levels of capacity. He will also help us to understand where 'our screws are' by using his much fuller perspective on life so that we know what and where we need to mend.

God tests us so that we can be more successful and fruitful, giving us information that will enable us to drive through life more fruitfully and effectively.

Praise God for trials. He wants us to grow in capacity. Pressure is a friend not an enemy as long as it is handled well. The result can be that we will share the apostle Paul's sentiment of "being hard pressed but not crushed."

The key to a car tyre working properly is its internal pressure - what are we like internally? Our key to travelling through earthly life and withstanding the inevitable pressures this entails, is based on our internal reality of being full of the Holy Spirit - his power, his love and other spiritual fruit.

Another form of testing that most of us find less easy to recognise as a test is identified in the parable of the sower in Matthew 13: 20 The seed falling on rocky ground refers to someone who hears the word and at once receives it with joy. 21 But since they have no root, they last only a short time. When trouble or persecution comes because of the word, they quickly fall away. 22 The seed falling among the thorns refers to someone who hears the word, but the worries of this life and the deceitfulness of wealth choke the word, making it unfruitful.

This passage talks about trouble, persecution and the worries of this world which are not very difficult to recognise as trials. However, it also talks about the deceitfulness of wealth.

Wealth and abundance can be trials and tests for our faith. They strike against our connection with God from a different angle - independence from God. Wealth can satisfy much of our human need and we can develop a trust in our human resources such that we don't feel the need to trust in God so much. Wealth goes beyond that by offering us opportunities of material gain, influence and power - these can be alluring temptations. The Bible says that we can't love God and love money (Matthew 6:24).

God wants to entrust us with sufficient resources to bring his blessings to the whole world and he will test us in order to make us ready.

Luke 16:11 So if you have not been trustworthy in handling worldly wealth, who will trust you with true riches?

God will examine our response to worldly wealth and that will determine how many true riches he will entrust to us. Such testing will not only examine any wealth we may personally have, but also examine our attitudes towards other people - coveting, jealousy, envy and selfish ambition are all corrosive entities that can damage our internal reality and choke spiritual life out of us. The way we use whatever money we have, and our attitudes regarding wealth and prosperity are tests that can either propel us forward or cause us to lose ground.

God's intention for us is that our faith in Him, our internal reality, grows through increasing experience of Him and connection with Him. That is what I will cover in Section 3 of this book. Before that we need to recognise our enemies!

Sasha Caridia:

Whilst at a large Christian event I met a young guy who had been radically saved by Jesus just over two years previously whilst in prison. We spent around 30 minutes chatting with him and in that time he was visibly transformed by the love and power of God.

When he started the conversation he said, "I don't see anything supernatural happening." Knowing how good and kind and loving Father God is, I felt this was an open invitation for this man to see for himself. He had a long standing painful clicking elbow and was very surprised when after praying for him the elbow became pain free and stopped clicking. He told us that his arm felt brand new! For the next 30 minutes as we talked he was constantly checking and rechecking the elbow. The physical healing opened the door for the Holy Spirit to speak directly to his heart. He was being awakened to the fullness of the good news of the Kingdom and all that Jesus has made available to him, to the good news of outrageous grace as the condemnation and lies of the enemy were being replaced by the truth of his true identity as a beloved son of a good, loving Heavenly Father. He kept saying how he was seeing things differently and he left full of hope with a smile on his face. We too had smiles on our faces - Jesus does that to you!

SECTION 2. ENEMIES OF OUR FAITH.

There are spiritual forces who are determined to influence us in order to reduce our faith by diminishing our confidence in God and our expectation of him. They will try to use testing times to discourage us, accuse us, make us fearful and persuade us that our Christianity is limited. They will tell us that we are not worthy of more experience of God, that thoughts about performing miracles somehow demonstrate a lack of humility and reality. They seek to rob us of assurance, sowing fear and doubt into our minds to rob us of joy, peace and confidence. I regard these forces as enemies of Christian faith that we need to be aware of and then overcome.

In Section 2 of this book we will examine this issue of 'Enemies of our Faith" so we can recognise them for what they are.

Chapter 12 The Spies who Robbed
Their Own People

The Bible story in Numbers chapters 13 and 14 is an extremely powerful one and to my mind one of the saddest in the Bible and it carries great instruction for us. The context is that the Israelites had travelled through the wilderness and stood at the edge to the promised land, a land flowing with milk and honey. God had promised them victory over their enemies and given them repeated experiences of his awesome power. Under the instruction of God, one leader from each of the 12 tribes of Israel was sent to explore the promised land and bring back a report of what they discovered:

Numbers Chapter 13 v 17-33

17 When Moses sent them to explore Canaan, he said, "Go up through the Negev and on into the hill country. 18 See what the land is like and whether the people who live there are strong or weak, few or many. 19 What kind of land do they live in? Is it good or bad? What kind of towns do they live in? Are they unwalled or fortified? 20 How is the soil? Is it fertile or poor? Are there trees in it or not? Do your best to bring back some of the fruit of the land." (It was the season for the first ripe grapes.)

Moses gives them clear instructions of what to look for.

21 So they went up and explored the land from the Desert of Zin as far as Rehob, toward Lebo Hamath. 22 They went up through the Negev and came to Hebron, where Ahiman, Sheshai and Talmai, the descendants of Anak, lived. (Hebron had been built seven years before Zoan in Egypt.) 23 When they reached the Valley of Eshkol, they cut off a branch bearing a single cluster of grapes. Two of them carried it on a pole between them, along with some pomegranates and figs.

They discovered amazing fruit.

24 That place was called the Valley of Eshkol because of the cluster of grapes the Israelites cut off there. 25 At the end of forty days they returned from exploring the land.

They returned from their exploration.

26 They came back to Moses and Aaron and the whole Israelite community at Kadesh in the Desert of Paran. There they reported to them and to the whole assembly and showed them the fruit of the land. 27 They gave Moses this account: "We went into the land to which you sent us, and it does flow with milk and honey! Here is its fruit.

The fruit is put on display. The promise is shown to be true - a very fruitful land.

28 But the people who live there are powerful, and the cities are fortified and very large. We even saw descendants of Anak there. 29 The Amalekites live in the Negev; the Hittites, Jebusites and Amorites live in the hill country; and the Canaanites live near the sea and along the Jordan."

There are enemies to overcome. No great surprise.

30 Then Caleb silenced the people before Moses and said, "We should go up and take possession of the land, for we can certainly do it."

Caleb is confident of victory. (Joshua son of Nun was with him in this opinion).

31 But the men who had gone up with him said, "We can't attack those people; they are stronger than we are."
32 And they spread among the Israelites a bad report about the land they had explored.

The other ten leaders had a different opinion and they began to spread their fear amongst the Israelites.

They said, *"The land we explored devours those living in it. All the people we saw there are of great size.*

They started to exaggerate their fears and allowed the problems to get out of proportion - now every problem was of great size.

33 We saw the Nephilim there (the descendants of Anak come from the Nephilim). We seemed like grasshoppers in our own eyes, and we looked the same to them."

Their view of themselves diminished dramatically and with it their confidence drained away. They made the mistake of assessing the enemy's position on the basis of their own fear.

Chapter 14:1 That night all the members of the community raised their voices and wept aloud.

Fear spreads across the whole community.

2 All the Israelites grumbled against Moses and Aaron, and the whole assembly said to them, "If only we had died in Egypt! Or in this wilderness!

Grumbling against their God given leaders starts to take a stronghold in the communal thinking and pessimism grows.

3 Why is the Lord bringing us to this land only to let us fall by the sword? Our wives and children will be taken as plunder.

The grumbling and discontent grows to the place where the purposes of God are viewed negatively (despite all He has done for them up to this point in time!)

Wouldn't it be better for us to go back to Egypt?" 4 And they said to each other, "We should choose a leader and go back to Egypt."

The people want to choose a leader who will give in to their fears rather than one who trusts God.

5 Then Moses and Aaron fell face down in front of the whole Israelite assembly gathered there. 6 Joshua son of Nun and Caleb son of Jephunneh, who were among those who had explored the land, tore their clothes 7 and said to the entire Israelite assembly, "The land we passed through and explored is exceedingly good. 8 If the Lord is pleased with us, he will lead us into that land, a land flowing with milk and honey, and will give it to us. 9 Only do not rebel against the Lord. And do not be afraid of the people of the land, because we will devour them. Their protection is gone, but the Lord is with us. Do not be afraid of them."

Joshua and Caleb appeal to the whole nation, certain of victory because God is with them. They urge the people not to be afraid and not to rebel against God.

10 But the whole assembly talked about stoning them.

The people turn against their leaders.

*Then the glory of the Lord appeared at the tent of meeting to all
the Israelites. 11 The Lord said to Moses, "How long will these
people treat me with contempt? How long will they refuse to believe
in me, in spite of all the signs I have performed among them?*

God appears to all the Israelites, they are without excuse, they
are treating God with contempt.

Refusal to believe in God when he has demonstrated his
power and majesty is an offence to God.

*12 I will strike them down with a plague and destroy them, but I
will make you into a nation greater and stronger than they."*

*13 Moses said to the Lord, "Then the Egyptians will hear
about it! By your power you brought these people up from among
them. 14 And they will tell the inhabitants of this land about it.
They have already heard that you, Lord, are with these people and
that you, Lord, have been seen face to face, that your cloud stays
over them, and that you go before them in a pillar of cloud by day
and a pillar of fire by night. 15 If you put all these people to death,
leaving none alive, the nations who have heard this report about
you will say, 16 'The Lord was not able to bring these people into
the land he promised them on oath, so he slaughtered them in the
wilderness.'*

*17 "Now may the Lord's strength be displayed, just as you
have declared: 18 'The Lord is slow to anger, abounding in love
and forgiving sin and rebellion. Yet he does not leave the guilty
unpunished; he punishes the children for the sin of the parents to*

the third and fourth generation.' 19 In accordance with your great love, forgive the sin of these people, just as you have pardoned them from the time they left Egypt until now."

20 The Lord replied, "I have forgiven them, as you asked.

Moses pleads with God on behalf of the people and He forgives them.

21 Nevertheless, as surely as I live and as surely as the glory of the Lord fills the whole earth, 22 not one of those who saw my glory and the signs I performed in Egypt and in the wilderness but who disobeyed me and tested me ten times— 23 not one of them will ever see the land I promised on oath to their ancestors. No one who has treated me with contempt will ever see it.

Forgiveness does not necessarily remove consequences. This generation of Israelites effectively removed themselves from the Promise of God, they lost their inheritance.

24 But because my servant Caleb has a different spirit and follows me wholeheartedly, I will bring him into the land he went to, and his descendants will inherit it.

Caleb did not lose his inheritance, neither did Joshua; however the unbelief of the nation delayed it for them by 40 years. This is an example of how corporate unbelief can impact people with true belief. One clean tributary will not cleanse an otherwise wholly polluted river.

When we are looking for answers as to why the manifest activity of God is less than we would hope for and expect, we need to look at any areas of corporate unbelief that are polluting our river system.

25 Since the Amalekites and the Canaanites are living in the valleys, turn back tomorrow and set out toward the desert along the route to the Red Sea.

God warns the people about their enemies and directs them towards a different path.

26 The Lord said to Moses and Aaron: 27 "How long will this wicked community grumble against me? I have heard the complaints of these grumbling Israelites. 28 So tell them, 'As surely as I live, declares the Lord, I will do to you the very thing I heard you say: 29 In this wilderness your bodies will fall—every one of you twenty years old or more who was counted in the census and who has grumbled against me.

This shows the level of corporate responsibility.

30 Not one of you will enter the land I swore with uplifted hand to make your home, except Caleb son of Jephunneh and Joshua son of Nun.

Faithful people will prosper, but delays can be caused by corporate lack of faith.

31 As for your children that you said would be taken as plunder, I will bring them in to enjoy the land you have rejected.

God's promise is still true, even if it needs to be delivered to a future generation.

32 But as for you, your bodies will fall in this wilderness. 33 Your children will be shepherds here for forty years, suffering for your unfaithfulness, until the last of your bodies lies in the wilderness.

Pollution can take a long time to eradicate. What we do with our own lives will affect the generations that follow.

> *34 For forty years—one year for each of the forty days you explored the land—you will suffer for your sins and know what it is like to have me against you.' 35 I, the Lord, have spoken, and I will surely do these things to this whole wicked community, which has banded together against me. They will meet their end in this wilderness; here they will die."*
>
> *36 So the men Moses had sent to explore the land, who returned and made the whole community grumble against him by spreading a bad report about it 37 these men who were responsible for spreading the bad report about the land were struck down and died of a plague before the Lord. 38 Of the men who went to explore the land, only Joshua son of Nun and Caleb son of Jephunneh survived.*

The sad story continues.

> *39 When Moses reported this to all the Israelites, they mourned bitterly. 40 Early the next morning they set out for the highest point in the hill country, saying, "Now we are ready to go up to the land the Lord promised. Surely we have sinned!"*
>
> *41 But Moses said, "Why are you disobeying the Lord's command? This will not succeed! 42 Do not go up, because the Lord is not with you.*
>
> *You will be defeated by your enemies, 43 for the Amalekites and the Canaanites will face you there. Because you have turned away from the Lord, he will not be with you and you will fall by the sword."*

The people decide to try to make amends through their own efforts.

44 Nevertheless, in their presumption they went up toward the highest point in the hill country, though neither Moses nor the ark of the Lord's covenant moved from the camp. 45 Then the Amalekites and the Canaanites who lived in that hill country came down and attacked them and beat them down all the way to Hormah.

The Israelites acted in presumption, ignoring the instructions of God, and they suffered the consequences.

This is a very powerful story from which we can learn many things; I have highlighted my thoughts en route through the story and here is a brief summary of the main points.

The land had been promised to them by God and victory had been assured as well.

They could be confident in God, he had demonstrated his power, majesty and glory clearly to them.

However, 10 spies were overwhelmed by the size of the challenge facing them and silenced the voice of faith in Joshua and Caleb.

They regarded themselves as grasshoppers rather than God's warriors accepting a false identity that robbed them of their true purpose.

God gives His assessment in chapter 14 verse 11: "*The Lord said to Moses, "How long will these people treat me with contempt? How long will they refuse to believe in me, in spite of all the signs I have performed among them?*""

Refusal to believe is a very powerful negative spiritual force. The outcome of such unbelief was that a whole generation of Israelites did not enter the promised land.

We will now move further into this section in order to expose "enemies of faith" and see them for what they really are.

Janice Pleasants:

As I approached a homeless man I felt the Holy Spirit highlight him to me. I put some coins in his hat and knelt down to ask about his day. He said he had severe back pain so I offered to pray, and he was glad to accept prayer. I asked how he was doing and he said he felt a little warmth in his back. I then felt the Holy Spirit say, "Ask him this, 'What would you ask Jesus to do for you if he was standing in front of you right now?'" I thought, that's not fair, clearly he's just going to ask again for his back to be healed. But the request came from the Holy Spirit once more, so I posed the question to the man. "That's easy," he replied, "I'd ask Him to hold me." He said he'd been on the streets for 18 months and hadn't had any human touch in all that time. I said that I was a Christian and that meant Jesus was living in me, and that I could give him a hug and that would be like Jesus hugging him. He said that would be lovely. The funniest thing was that as I hugged him, people passing by started to put £1 coins and notes into his hat, it's like we were some kind of street artists! Someone gave a croissant and another a sandwich. He then began to really cry and I asked him what was going on and he explained that he could feel my arms around him but he could also feel a hug of love on the inside of him and suddenly all the pain in his back had gone! He then looked at the money and food that had been left for him and said that he could now go by coach to London to see his family and have food for the journey. He was amazed at God's love and called me his lucky star.

Chapter 13 Enemy Tactics That Can Cause Standstill

A number of years ago I was reading the book of Ezra in the Bible and I was fascinated once again by the story of an amazing God working through people to establish his kingdom on earth. I was caught up in the momentum of the unfolding adventure and then suddenly my attention was grasped by God in a very unexpected way. I was astonished. Let me share with you the things I learned.

The story begins in Chapter 1 (no surprise there!):

> *1 In the first year of Cyrus king of Persia, in order to fulfil the word of the Lord spoken by Jeremiah, the Lord moved the heart of Cyrus king of Persia to make a proclamation throughout his realm and also to put it in writing:*

God in his sovereignty moved the heart of a very powerful pagan king. He was acting in fulfilment of a prophecy spoken by Jeremiah 70 years previously. God will fulfil his plans for the earth and for his people.

> *2 "This is what Cyrus king of Persia says:*
> *"'The Lord, the God of heaven, has given me all the kingdoms of the earth and he has appointed me to build a temple for him at Jerusalem in Judah.*

A temple for the God of Israel is going to be built.

3 Any of his people among you may go up to Jerusalem in Judah and build the temple of the Lord, the God of Israel, the God who is in Jerusalem, and may their God be with them.

At this point the Israelites were exiles from their land living in subservience to King Cyrus - effectively slaves. But they are now about to be set free, to live with a divine purpose and with the divine presence.

4 And in any locality where survivors may now be living, the people are to provide them with silver and gold, with goods and livestock, and with freewill offerings for the temple of God in Jerusalem.'"

All provision was going to be given to them for the purposes of God. Imagine that - going from servitude to abundance.

5 Then the family heads of Judah and Benjamin, and the priests and Levites—everyone whose heart God had moved—prepared to go up and build the house of the Lord in Jerusalem.

Those whose hearts were moved prepared themselves. It is always issues of the heart that move us forward with God.

6 All their neighbours assisted them with articles of silver and gold, with goods and livestock, and with valuable gifts, in addition to all the freewill offerings.
7 Moreover, King Cyrus brought out the articles belonging to the temple of the Lord, which Nebuchadnezzar had carried away from Jerusalem and had placed in the temple of his god. 8 Cyrus king of Persia had them brought by Mithredath the treasurer, who counted them out to Sheshbazzar the prince of Judah.
9 This was the inventory: 30 gold dishes, 1000 silver dishes, 29 silver pans, 30 gold bowls, 410 matching silver bowls, 1000

other articles. In all, there were 5,400 articles of gold and of silver.
Sheshbazzar brought all these along with the exiles when they came
up from Babylon to Jerusalem.

Such amazing provision.

As I read through this chapter I marvelled at the sovereign hand of God transforming a situation in an instant and equipping his people for the works he had prepared for them to do. What a God, and in the words of a well known song, "Who can stop the Lord Almighty." My heart swelled with praise to God and confidence in Him and I couldn't wait for Chapter 2, so I kept on reading:

2:1 Now these are the people of the province who came up from the
captivity of the exiles, whom Nebuchadnezzar king of Babylon had
taken captive to Babylon (they returned to Jerusalem and Judah,
each to their own town, 2 in company with Zerubbabel, Joshua,
Nehemiah, Seraiah, Reelaiah, Mordecai, Bilshan, Mispar, Bigvai,
Rehum and Baanah):
*   The list of the men of the people of Israel:*

And so follows a long list of households; each one important in the purposes of God, called by Him and moved in their hearts to serve Him.

The whole company numbered 42,360, besides their 7,337
male and female slaves; and they also had 200 male and female
singers. They had 736 horses, 245 mules, 67 435 camels and
6,720 donkeys.
*   When they arrived at the house of the Lord in Jerusalem,*
some of the heads of the families gave freewill offerings toward the
rebuilding of the house of God on its site. According to their ability

they gave to the treasury for this work 61,000 darics[b] of gold, 5,000 minas[c] of silver and 100 priestly garments.

The priests, the Levites, the musicians, the gatekeepers and the temple servants settled in their own towns, along with some of the other people, and the rest of the Israelites settled in their towns.

Imagine that: a people in exile for 70 years, now settling again in their towns and getting ready to rebuild the temple of their God. What excitement and expectation there would have been, along with a sense of awe. Imagine the singing, laughter, excited conversation as a long held dream starts to become reality.

My mind was racing, caught up in the excitement of the story. So I kept reading:

3 When the seventh month came and the Israelites had settled in their towns, the people assembled together as one in Jerusalem.

They came together as one, with a common purpose.

2 Then Joshua son of Jozadak and his fellow priests and Zerubbabel son of Shealtiel and his associates began to build the altar of the God of Israel to sacrifice burnt offerings on it, in accordance with what is written in the Law of Moses the man of God. 3 Despite their fear of the peoples around them, they built the altar on its foundation and sacrificed burnt offerings on it to the Lord, both the morning and evening sacrifices.

They overcame their fear. They built the altar in order to have a common place of worship. Worship is our first priority.

4 Then in accordance with what is written, they celebrated the Festival of Tabernacles with the required number of burnt offerings prescribed for each day. 5 After that, they presented the regular burnt offerings, the New Moon sacrifices and the sacrifices for all the appointed sacred festivals of the Lord, as well as those brought as freewill offerings to the Lord. 6 On the first day of the seventh month they began to offer burnt offerings to the Lord, though the foundation of the Lord's temple had not yet been laid.

They reestablished the manifold practices of their faith.

7 Then they gave money to the masons and carpenters, and gave food and drink and olive oil to the people of Sidon and Tyre, so that they would bring cedar logs by sea from Lebanon to Joppa, as authorized by Cyrus king of Persia.

They used their resources to continue the work and the foundation for the temple was laid. As the building work progressed the enemies started to pay more attention as they detected a serious threat arising. We see this in the next chapter.

4 When the enemies of Judah and Benjamin heard that the exiles were building a temple for the Lord, the God of Israel, 2 they came to Zerubbabel and to the heads of the families and said, "Let us help you build because, like you, we seek your God and have been sacrificing to him since the time of Esarhaddon king of Assyria, who brought us here."

3 But Zerubbabel, Joshua and the rest of the heads of the families of Israel answered, "You have no part with us in building a temple to our God. We alone will build it for the Lord, the God of Israel, as King Cyrus, the king of Persia, commanded us."

The Israelites were aware of this enemy tactic: a seemingly friendly collaboration would ultimately lead to compromise.

This subtle attempt at disruption was thwarted and a more direct approach was taken up by their enemies.

4 Then the peoples around them set out to discourage the people of Judah and make them afraid to go on building. [5 They bribed officials to work against them and frustrate their plans during the entire reign of Cyrus king of Persia and down to the reign of Darius king of Persia.

6 At the beginning of the reign of Xerxes, they lodged an accusation against the people of Judah and Jerusalem.

In these three verses we clearly see four schemes of the enemy:

Discouragement
Fear
Frustration
Accusation

But just how effective can such things be against a people called sovereignly by God with a very specific purpose; a people resourced in extraordinary ways by God, and a people united in vision and action? Surely nothing could stand in the way of such a move of God? Such was my thinking as I read on through the chapter. I was totally confident in the sovereign power and purpose of God. Who can stop the Lord Almighty?

I read on eagerly towards the end of the chapter and then gave a gasp of astonishment as I read verse 24:

24 Thus the work on the house of God in Jerusalem came to a standstill until the second year of the reign of Darius king of Persia.

The work of God came to a standstill! How could that be? I
was dumbstruck. My theological thinking was challenged. I
believed in a sovereign, all powerful God, I also understood
that the devil is a powerful enemy, but I also knew that Jesus
has overcome Satan. However, I had not discerned the power
of the enemy's schemes in terms of their potential to interrupt
the sovereign purpose of God. This led to some very serious
thinking on my part, and a serious renewing and changing of
my mindset (literally repentance).

I studied the Bible and Bible history on this subject and
I also looked at church history both modern and old. It is
important to note that "the work on the house of God in
Jerusalem came to a standstill until the second year of the
reign of Darius king of Persia." The standstill was for a
period of time, not forever, similar to the story of the Israelites
entering the promised land which involved a 40-year delay.
So how long was this delay? Bible history shows us that this
standstill was for 14 or 15 years, until the second year of the
reign of king Darius.

> *This is what it says at the beginning of Ezra chapter 5: "Now
> Haggai the prophet and Zechariah the prophet, a descendant of
> Iddo, prophesied to the Jews in Judah and Jerusalem in the name
> of the God of Israel, who was over them. Then Zerubbabel son
> of Shealtiel and Joshua son of Jozadak set to work to rebuild the
> house of God in Jerusalem. And the prophets of God were with
> them, supporting them."*

The people of God were inspired by the prophets and also
their leaders and work recommenced.

I wondered to myself how many times this pattern has
been repeated in church history? In my lifetime I have seen
'moves of God's start and stop, and it seems to me that an

unbiblical theology has built up that explains these matters in terms of the temporary nature of 'visitations of God' or 'Revivals' leading us to accept that such things will stop as if that were the will of God. I believe that what became known as the 'Toronto Blessing' fell into this category for very many churches across the world. The four enemy tactics of Fear, Discouragement, Accusation and Frustration were clearly at work and broadly speaking the Blessing flowing from that move of God was brought to a standstill for many churches and individual Christians. Even now it can be a topic of dispute and accusation.

Other 'moves of God' have continued to be fruitful over decades, having overcome the enemy's tactics to thwart their fruitfulness. For example, the Pentecostal movement that was birthed out of the Azusa Street Revival 1906-1910 still bears fruit to this day and following on from this the Charismatic Renewal overcame much opposition to gain ground in understanding of the gifts of God being freely available to all Christians.

As I have studied this subject it has become clear to me that the devil will always try to oppose God's activity, but his success in doing so is primarily dependent on the people of God being unaware of his tactics and schemes, and also unaware of the power of the spiritual armour at our disposal to overcome all the flaming arrows of the evil one.

Ephesians 6:16 In addition to all this, take up the shield of faith, with which you can extinguish all the flaming arrows of the evil one.

How do you extinguish a flaming arrow?

The most effective way of dealing with it is before it has got past your defences. A fire once started will do damage, so best not to let it get that far. This is what the image of the 'shield of faith' conveys. Stop the arrow before it penetrates your defence.

Let us take a look at the 4 types of arrow we have learned about in Ezra as a starting point.

Fear.

What does fear look like? How do we recognise it? How do we extinguish it?

Anxiety is a form of fear. It flies in our direction on a very regular basis, so often in fact that sometimes we accept it as a normal part of life, and we justify it in our own minds. What does the Bible say about this?

> *Phillippians 4: 6 Do not be anxious about anything, but in every situation, by prayer and petition, with thanksgiving, present your requests to God. 7 And the peace of God, which transcends all understanding, will guard your hearts and your minds in Christ Jesus.*

Peace will guard our hearts and minds from the fiery damage of anxiety and we are given our own tactics in this passage to create a life built on the foundation of peace. Anxiety is more difficult to deal with if it has a hold on our minds, it is best extinguished early on, using the strength of your 'shield of faith.'

What else do Christians possess to extinguish fear?

> *1 John 4:18 There is no fear in love. But perfect love drives out fear, because fear has to do with punishment. The one who fears is not made perfect in love.*

Experiencing the love of God and the love of other people is very powerful; also giving love to God and others is a way of using our shield of faith.

Discouragement.

We have all experienced discouragement. This word literally means to take your courage away. It is probably easier to recognise than fear.

Similarly, it is a bit simpler to extinguish. Encouragement will overcome discouragement and give you your courage back. The ability to encourage yourself, encourage others, and receive encouragement from others is the key to defeating this enemy. More about this later in the book.

Accusation.

The devil is known as "the accuser of the brothers and sisters." Accusation is one of his very common tactics and it can be overcome by confidence in the fundamental truths of Christianity, here are some examples:

Once you are born again all your sin is not only forgiven but removed from you as far as the east is from the west.

We are born again into a new nature, we are not trying to renew our old nature.

- *God calls us to participate in his nature.* 2 Peter 1v4
- We are seated with Christ in Heavenly realms.
- We are clothed in the Righteousness of Christ.
- *We are called to do the works of Jesus and even greater works* John 14v12
- Our eternal salvation is secure.
- God loves us because He is love and His nature is not dependent on our behaviour.
- If we fall in any way Jesus will reach out his hand to restore us.

It is important not only to apply these truths to ourselves internally but also in our attitudes towards other people. Accusation within communication is extremely destructive.

Frustration.

This is not always easy to recognise as an enemy because frustrating things happen in the normal course of life and it is okay to feel frustrated by them. However, when being frustrated is allowed to develop into a state of frustration which negatively impacts upon other people (and ourselves) it becomes a destructive force. Two things in particular can feed into this, impatience and selfishness. Being patient is a good shield against frustration. Patience is a fruit of the spirit and it is important to nurture this fruit and resist impatience.

In terms of selfishness, not insisting upon your own way is a good shield, and this will be strengthened as we actively seek to love other people. As it tells us in 1 Corinthians13 v 5: love is not self-seeking, it is not easily angered, it keeps no record of wrongs.

In most circumstances there is not only one correct way of doing things; respecting the way other people choose to behave is very important (I am referring to positive behaviour not destructive behaviour here).

If you find yourself frustrated I suggest you ask God to reveal the source of that frustration and how he wants you to move forward.

When we are coping with unwelcome delays in life it is not uncommon to experience all four of these flaming arrows. This is an important aspect of our enemy's tactics and so now we will move on and look at the subject of "Dealing with Delay."

Janice Pleasants:

I was in a sandwich bar in London in a break between meetings. I was about to leave when I looked over at the owner who was behind the counter and as I did I felt a sharp pain in my shoulder which I knew wasn't my own pain. So I went up to him and asked if he had any pain in his shoulder. He denied it. There were only two other people there, a lady who was eating who said she was fine and a lady who was just heading to the door, so I asked them both but they both assured me they were fine. At that point the owner said, "You're persistent, aren't you! Okay, it is me!" So I said I was a Christian practicing hearing from God and had a pain in my shoulder that wasn't mine and when that happened it usually meant that God wanted to heal the person with the problem. "Could I pray for you?", I asked. He said, "I guess so, but it's an old sports injury and nothing can be done about it." I leant over the counter, and asked if I could hold his hand, as I did and before I could say anything he jumped back and said, "Jesus Christ!" I said "Absolutely." He said, "But did you feel that?" "What?" I asked. "That surge of energy. All my pain has gone and I can move my shoulder just fine!" He was healed before I could vocalise a prayer.

Chapter 14 Dealing with Delay Part 1

The story of Abraham

Delay can be frustrating, we all know and experience this. Traffic jams, waiting in a queue in a supermarket, delays with planes, trains or other forms of transport, business transactions, legal interactions, internet connection problems, all these have the potential to frustrate us. Similarly, with spiritual life. There are delayed answers to prayer, people not being healed, dreams unfulfilled, 'callings' not materialising, not as many people being impacted by Christianity as we would hope to see, prophecies as yet not working through, other people not meeting our expectations, and so on. How do we handle such things and continue to grow in faith?

This is a very big question, and one that can easily occupy our minds in ways that do not necessarily strengthen us. Let's use some Bible stories to help us learn from some people with amazing faith who endured delays.

Abraham

The story of Abraham is one that I have found very helpful in this regard and I would like to share some of my thoughts with you. So let's have a look at it together. It starts at the end of Genesis chapter 11:

> *27 This is the account of Terah's family line. Terah became the father of Abram, Nahor and Haran. And Haran became the father of Lot. 28 While his father Terah was still alive, Haran died in Ur of the Chaldeans, in the land of his birth. 29 Abram and Nahor both married. The name of Abram's wife was Sarai, and*

the name of Nahor's wife was Milkah; she was the daughter of Haran, the father of both Milkah and Iskah. 30 Now Sarai was childless because she was not able to conceive.

31 Terah took his son Abram, his grandson Lot son of Haran, and his daughter-in-law Sarai, the wife of his son Abram, and together they set out from Ur of the Chaldeans to go to Canaan. But when they came to Harran, they settled there.

32 Terah lived 205 years, and he died in Haran.

At this point in the story Abram is his name and his wife is called Sarai, their names will be changed during the course of the story to Abraham and Sarah. We are informed that they are unable to conceive a child together and this is extremely relevant as we move forward into Genesis chapter 12:

12:1 The Lord had said to Abram, "Go from your country, your people and your father's household to the land I will show you.

2 "I will make you into a great nation,
and I will bless you;

I will make your name great,
and you will be a blessing.

3 I will bless those who bless you,
and whoever curses you I will curse;

and all peoples on earth
will be blessed through you."

This is some promise!
"I will make you into a great nation."

"I will make your name great."

God is describing a great destiny.

"I will bless you and you will be a blessing."

God is describing his method of bringing about this great destiny; Abraham will be blessed so much that he will overflow with blessing.

The outcome of this will be that *"all peoples on earth will be blessed through you."* Sufficient blessing would flow through Abraham that all peoples on earth would be blessed by God.

There is a very important principle at work here; God wants to bless Abraham so much, that blessing will inevitably flow through him and touch the world.

The story continues:

4 So Abram went, as the Lord had told him;

Responding to God's instruction Abraham set out on a journey; chapter 11 of the book of Hebrews in the Bible gives us some more insight telling us "By faith Abraham, when called to go to a place he would later receive as his inheritance, obeyed and went, even though he did not know where he was going."

Abraham chose to trust God without needing to know all the details.

However, the Bible does give us some more details:

Abram was seventy-five years old when he set out from Harran. 5 He took his wife Sarai, his nephew Lot, all the possessions they had accumulated and the people they had acquired in Harran, and they set out for the land of Canaan, and they arrived there.

> *6 Abram traveled through the land as far as the site of the great tree of Moreh at Shechem. At that time the Canaanites were in the land.*

And then God gets very specific:

> *7 The Lord appeared to Abram and said, "To your offspring I will give this land." So he built an altar there to the Lord, who had appeared to him.*

Contained within this promise is the promise of offspring, their own children. This is going to require the intervention of God because as we have already heard Abraham and Sarah are unable to conceive.

Abraham and Sarah need to trust God if their destiny is going to be fulfilled, and their story unfolds through Genesis until chapter 25.

In the New Testament we find references to Abraham and Sarah, and for me in particular Romans chapter 4 provides a very helpful commentary upon the story.

> *Romans Chapter 4 v1 What then shall we say that Abraham, our forefather according to the flesh, discovered in this matter?*

What did Abraham learn? What can we learn?

> *2 If, in fact, Abraham was justified by works, he had something to boast about—but not before God. 3 What does Scripture say? "Abraham believed God, and it was credited to him as righteousness."*

You cannot earn the Righteousness of God, rather it is

given to people who choose to trust in God. Receiving the righteousness of God puts us in right standing with God and releases our spiritual inheritance to us.

> *9 Is this blessedness only for the circumcised, or also for the uncircumcised? We have been saying that Abraham's faith was credited to him as righteousness. 10 Under what circumstances was it credited? Was it after he was circumcised, or before? It was not after, but before!*

God's blessings and righteousness are available to all people on the earth, not to one specific group.

> *13 It was not through the law that Abraham and his offspring received the promise that he would be heir of the world, but through the righteousness that comes by faith.*

Righteousness comes by faith.

> *16 Therefore, the promise comes by faith, so that it may be by grace and may be guaranteed to all Abraham's offspring—not only to those who are of the law but also to those who have the faith of Abraham. He is the father of us all.*

The promise is given by God and received into reality by anyone who chooses to trust in God and His gracious nature. In this way it is not only given by God it is also guaranteed by God. God has guaranteed to fulfil the promise of Genesis 12 in and through the life of anybody who chooses to trust and follow Him.

*17 As it is written: "I have made you a father of many nations."
He is our father in the sight of God, in whom he believed—the God
who gives life to the dead and calls into being things that were not.*

Abraham is called the father of our faith, he is an example for
us to follow and we gain more insight as we carry on through
Romans 4:

*18 Against all hope, Abraham in hope believed and so became the
father of many nations, just as it had been said to him, "So shall
your offspring be."*

I like the way this verse is translated in the New Living
Translation; "Even when there was no reason for hope,
Abraham kept hoping—believing that he would become the
father of many nations. For God had said to him, "That's
how many descendants you will have!"

Abraham did not allow his hope to become a slave to
his circumstances. Even when there was no earthly reason to
hope, he chose to hope in God, trusting that his destiny would
be fulfilled.

*19 Without weakening in his faith, he faced the fact that his body
was as good as dead—since he was about a hundred years old—
and that Sarah's womb was also dead.*

Abraham did not ignore the human circumstances which
confronted him every day, he did not deny that they existed,
instead he faced up to them and kept choosing to trust God.
That is why he didn't weaken in his faith - he chose to keep
trusting that God had the answer. It is very important to state
that faith does not deny human circumstances, rather faith
overcomes such circumstances. For example, Abraham did

not say that "he had a child by faith" when he didn't, he didn't say that Sarah's womb was not barren. Similarly, for us it is not a statement of faith to say that someone has been healed when they clearly haven't, or that I am not in debt when I am. Indeed, such statements attract ridicule to the Christian faith and don't help us to grow in faith.

The next two verses help us to understand this further:

> *20 Yet he did not waver through unbelief regarding the promise of God, but was strengthened in his faith and gave glory to God, 21 being fully persuaded that God had power to do what he had promised.*

Abraham's faith was rooted in the reality of God, in the promises of God and in the power of God. In these things he was unwavering. He made mistakes in life as the Bible story clearly shows. Under pressure from Sarah he took things into his own hands to try and fulfil God's promise (and which one of us hasn't done that under pressure from ourselves or others?!) and in so doing created a more complicated set of circumstances. And yet despite all that Abraham fundamentally trusted in the nature of God and was fully persuaded about the power of God to fulfil those promises.

As he kept trusting God throughout his life Abraham's faith was strengthened and after 25 years of delay Isaac was born, 'the child of promise' rather than "the child of human endeavour".

How did Abraham deal with delay?

- He never lost sight of the promise of God
- He kept hope alive
- He faced the facts of daily life and didn't live in denial
- He kept on trusting God and giving Him glory
- He won the battle against unbelief

Story by Pete Carter:

Like a good dad I was helping one of my children. Kerry was
going to a worship festival called David's Tent which started
on a Friday towards the end of August in a large field in the
south of England. Thousands of people attend this event and
many of them camp in a nearby field, tents everywhere. Kerry
was working in London during the day on the Friday and was
due to arrive on site during the evening. I volunteered to go
down earlier during the day to set up her tent and also enjoy
a short part of the festival with her before driving home late
that evening.

I arrived after about a 90-minute drive from home,
parked the car at the top of the camping field and started the
rather long process of unpacking the car, involving a number
of trips taking the tent, camping equipment and other stuff
quite a distance from the car to the camping site at the bottom
of the field. It seemed to me that the grass was unusually long
in the field for camping. Some people from Kerry's church
were already on site and helped me get the tent ready. They
also kindly supplied me with food and drink.

That done, I went off to enjoy the festival. Kerry arrived
later on, we managed to meet up, I showed her where her
tent was, we set off to worship together and had a great
evening. As I was saying goodbye to Kerry I checked with her
whether there was anything else she needed from the car – I
had brought extra things in case she wanted them. We agreed
that there was one item that would be useful.

I set off to find my car and then her tent in a field that
was pitch black, I hadn't realised just how dark it would be.
I had a small torch with me and eventually found my car
amongst the hundreds of cars at the top of the field. The
next task was to find Kerry's tent amongst hundreds of tents
in the field. I meandered backwards and forwards between

rows of tents with my small torch hoping to see something I might recognise. After about 30 minutes and with great relief I found Kerry's tent and deposited the desired item inside (I can't remember what it was). Next task was to find the car again, thankfully this time it was a bit quicker.

As I arrived at the car I reached into my jacket pocket for the car keys and immediately an alarm hit my mind. No keys! Frantically I searched my jacket but all I found was a hole in the pocket where I had put my keys. Realisation hit me, how on earth was I going to find my keys? I needed help from heaven. I hoped that I had somehow dropped the keys in Kerry's tent but knew that was unlikely so I set off in search. I tried to retrace my steps as closely as I could but really that was futile in the dark and unfamiliar surroundings. I scanned the long grass at each step, my small torch barely illuminating the ground and there were no keys to be seen. I found Kerry's tent and opened it with a glimmer of hope within me and searched the space. No keys. The glimmer of hope was all but extinguished.

I closed up the tent and made my way to the reception area at the top of the field with a hope that someone else might have found them and handed them in. I kept scanning the ground as I slowly walked but still no keys. At the reception desk I asked about my keys: no keys had been handed in and they held out little hope of them being found; maybe in the morning when it was light they suggested, but I had not planned to stay that long.

It was about 10.30 at night and I realised that I needed to phone Kim at home, she might need to come and rescue me in our other car and with the spare car keys. I broke the news to her and said I would do one more quick search near Kerry's tent and then phone her back; we prayed together. I found Kerry's tent, searching en route for my keys. I searched the tent thoroughly but to no avail and I admitted defeat. I would need to ask Kim to come and get me. As I trudged back to the reception area I berated myself for my error and tried to deal with my frustration. In the middle of that God broke into my thinking and spoke to me. "Stop right now!" he said in a rather forthright manner. So I stopped in my tracks in the middle of a dark field in the long grass.

Then in a gentler manner he said, "Look down." Next to my right foot, nestling down in the long grass out of sight, a small glint reflected off the light from my torch. I reached down and picked up my car keys.

144   Faith

Chapter 15 Dealing With Delay Part 2

The stories of King David, Joshua, Caleb and Mary the
mother of Jesus.

King David
Let us take another example from the Old Testament to help
us with this subject, the story of young shepherd boy David
developing into King David.

We find the beginning of the story at the start of 1
Samuel chapter 16 when God talks to the prophet Samuel:
*"The Lord said to Samuel, "How long will you mourn for Saul, since
I have rejected him as king over Israel? Fill your horn with oil and be on
your way; I am sending you to Jesse of Bethlehem. I have chosen one of
his sons to be king."*

God had chosen one of the sons of Jesse to be the future
king of Israel so Samuel goes to Jesse's household. Once
there, God directs him to anoint David with oil; in verse 13
we read, "So Samuel took the horn of oil and anointed him
in the presence of his brothers, and from that day on the
Spirit of the Lord came powerfully upon David."

I think it is interesting to note that the Bible does not
say Samuel anoints David as King; Saul was still the King
of Israel and David respects that as seen in the following
chapters that show him serving Saul wholeheartedly.

The verse tells us that "from that day on the Spirit of
the Lord came powerfully upon David." An anointing of
the Holy Spirit is essential for spiritual destiny to become a
reality. Anointing enables the journey towards fulfilment of
calling and purpose to happen, it also helps the development

of character and maturity to grow, and empowers a person with Heaven's resources and the wisdom to apply such power appropriately. All this is so that at the right time destiny can start to be lived out.

It was a number of years after this first anointing that David was anointed King of Judah, then seven and a half years later he was anointed King over all of Israel at the age of thirty. The delay from first anointing to the fulfilment of the purpose of the anointing was probably in the region of 15 years.

Delay can be a time of learning to move in the power of God. In order to benefit from such time, it is essential that you continue to walk in the anointing of the Holy Spirit, living powerfully and continually trusting God.

Joshua and Caleb

Earlier in this book we looked at the story of the 12 spies sent into the Promised Land, but preceding that moment of opportunity to enter into their promised destiny the people had been on a journey of preparation.

In Exodus chapter 13 the Israelites have just left the captivity of Egypt with the promise of "a land flowing with milk and honey" ahead of them. In the middle of the chapter there is a very interesting insight in verses 17&18

"Now when Pharaoh had let the people go, God did not lead them by the way of the land of the Philistines, even though that was shorter; for God said, "The people might change their minds when they see war, and return to Egypt." Hence God led the people around by the way of the wilderness to the Red Sea; and the sons of Israel went up out of Egypt armed for battle.

If you look at a map of that region, you can clearly see that there was a much shorter and easier route (on dry land) for Israel to take towards the promised land than going via the Red Sea. They weren't chased there by their enemies; they were led there by God with a specific purpose in mind. The people needed to be trained for warfare otherwise they might miss their destiny. It is interesting to note that they had the equipment for warfare but they did not have the mindset for it. They needed training in how to use the resources available to them in order to enter their promised land. This is the same within Christianity; Ephesians chapter 1 says that we have already received every spiritual blessing in Christ, but it is clear from the books of Romans and Galatians that we need to be transformed by the renewing of our minds. The Bible also talks about putting on the Armour of God, not simply regarding it as a spiritual theory.

The rest of the book of Exodus, the book of Leviticus, and the book of Numbers up to Chapter 13 tells a story of a journey of training and preparation, in order to have a people ready to possess the promised land.

The opportunity of development was there for all the Israelites, extraordinary interactions with God and his power, miraculous provision, battles fought and won, discipline, leadership structures, a tabernacle built according to God's design and with anointed people, instructions about health, hygiene, social structure, sacrifices to God, feasts, rest and remembrance - all formed part of this training. This training journey took about a year before they arrived at the edge of the Promised Land - the edge of destiny – where dreams were ready to be realised. All 12 spies had the same opportunities to grow in faith and confidence in God and His promises.

However, 10 spies did not grasp those opportunities, they remained unprepared just as they had been when they left Egypt about one year previously. They were all leaders in their tribes, and they led the whole people of Israel away from their destiny because of their fears and lack of faith. They inflicted a further 40 years' delay on Israel and helped to rob around two million people of their destiny. They did not use their 'delay' to allow themselves to be trained to pursue their destiny. This is a tragedy.

Delay is a time of opportunity for training and preparation. It is an opportunity that needs to be grasped, because it can be missed.

But what about the other two spies, Joshua and Caleb? They were prepared and ready for the Promised Land, they had made the most of the training opportunities. They had grown in faith but the corporate unbelief of others nevertheless impacted them in an enormous way. They faced 40 years of delay not of their own making. Imagine the frustration as they walked away from the edge of the Promised Land which they had already visited. What was different about these two men?

Numbers 32: 10 The Lord's anger was aroused that day and he swore this oath: 11 'Because they have not followed me wholeheartedly, not one of those who were twenty years old or more when they came up out of Egypt will see the land I promised on oath to Abraham, Isaac and Jacob— 12 not one except Caleb son of Jephunneh the Kenizzite and Joshua son of Nun, for they followed the Lord wholeheartedly.'

Wholeheartedness was the difference between defeat and destiny.

What did these two do with themselves for the next 40 years?

Joshua
We learn a lot about him in the following Bible passages:

Numbers 27 18 So the Lord said to Moses, "Take Joshua son of Nun, a man in whom is the spirit of leadership, and lay your hand on him. 19 Have him stand before Eleazar the priest and the entire assembly and commission him in their presence. 20 Give him some of your authority so the whole Israelite community will obey him. 21 He is to stand before Eleazar the priest, who will obtain decisions for him by inquiring of the Urim before the Lord. At his command he and the entire community of the Israelites will go out, and at his command they will come in."

Joshua learned the art of leadership in the power of the Spirit and under prophetic direction. (This is an example of Apostolic and Prophetic foundations.)

Deuteronomy 1:38 But your assistant, Joshua son of Nun, will enter it. Encourage him, because he will lead Israel to inherit the land.

Deuteronomy 3:28 But commission Joshua, and encourage and strengthen him, for he will lead this people across and will cause them to inherit the land that you will see."

Deuteronomy 31:7 Then Moses summoned Joshua and said to him in the presence of all Israel, "Be strong and courageous, for you must go with this people into the land that the Lord swore to their ancestors to give them, and you must divide it among them as their inheritance.

Deuteronomy 34:9 Now Joshua son of Nun was filled with the spirit of wisdom because Moses had laid his hands on him. So the Israelites listened to him and did what the Lord had commanded Moses.

Joshua received encouragement and confirmation of his destiny, alongside wisdom in order to know how to proceed. He continued to follow God wholeheartedly and allowed himself to keep growing and developing throughout the delay rather than living with frustration eating him away.

Caleb

I think the following passage in Numbers 14 sums Caleb up without need for further explanation. What an inspiration this man is. Undefeated by delay.

Now the people of Judah approached Joshua at Gilgal, and Caleb son of Jephunneh the Kenizzite said to him, "You know what the Lord said to Moses the man of God at Kadesh Barnea about you and me. I was forty years old when Moses the servant of the Lord sent me from Kadesh Barnea to explore the land. And I brought him back a report according to my convictions, but my fellow Israelites who went up with me made the hearts of the people melt in fear. I, however, followed the Lord my God wholeheartedly. So on that day Moses swore to me, 'The land on which your feet have walked will be your inheritance and that of your children forever, because you have followed the Lord my God wholeheartedly.' "Now then, just as the Lord promised, he has kept me alive for forty-five years since the time he said this to Moses, while Israel moved about in the wilderness. So here I am today, eighty-five years old! I am still as strong today as the day Moses sent me out; I'm just as vigorous to go out to battle now as I was then. Now give me this hill country that the Lord promised me that day. You yourself heard then that the Anakites were there and their cities were large and fortified, but, the Lord helping me, I will drive them out just as he said."

Then Joshua blessed Caleb son of Jephunneh and gave

him Hebron as his inheritance. So Hebron has belonged to
Caleb son of Jephunneh the Kenizzite ever since, because he
followed the Lord, the God of Israel, wholeheartedly.

Mary

> *Luke 2: 16 So they hurried off and found Mary and Joseph, and
> the baby, who was lying in the manger. 17 When they had seen
> him, they spread the word concerning what had been told them
> about this child, 18 and all who heard it were amazed at what
> the shepherds said to them. 19 But Mary treasured up all these
> things and pondered them in her heart. 20 The shepherds returned,
> glorifying and praising God for all the things they had heard and
> seen, which were just as they had been told.*

What an extraordinary woman of faith Mary was. In the
verses above I have found one of the keys to dealing with
delay which has helped me enormously during my life. The
words and promises of God are to be treasured in my heart,
valued and thought about in advance of them becoming
reality. Indeed, some experiences and promises from God are
best not shared with others immediately. One of the reasons
for this is that God imparts faith and anointing through
experiencing Him and hearing His words, and such faith and
anointing are not always easily transferable to other people.
This can result in awkward interactions as people struggle to
comprehend what God is doing and saying in your life. The
story of Joseph in Genesis is another example of this.

When I was twenty I had an encounter with God in
my university room and he gave me a very specific and very
challenging calling upon my life. I did not want to appear
arrogant to others, and I did not feel mature enough and fully
equipped at that time to be at all public about it, so I kept it

tucked away in my heart and mind allowing it to shape the direction of my life. The only person I shared it with was Kim, my fiancée at the time because we were starting to shape our life together and it helped us to make strategic life decisions.

Daniel

In Daniel Chapter 10 there is a passage that is very enlightening:

> *1 In the third year of Cyrus king of Persia, a revelation was given to Daniel (who was called Belteshazzar). Its message was true and it concerned a great war. The understanding of the message came to him in a vision.*
>
> *2 At that time I, Daniel, mourned for three weeks. 3 I ate no choice food; no meat or wine touched my lips; and I used no lotions at all until the three weeks were over.*
>
> *4 On the twenty-fourth day of the first month, as I was standing on the bank of the great river, the Tigris, 5 I looked up and there before me was a man dressed in linen, with a belt of fine gold from Uphaz around his waist. 6 His body was like topaz, his face like lightning, his eyes like flaming torches, his arms and legs like the gleam of burnished bronze, and his voice like the sound of a multitude.*
>
> *7 I, Daniel, was the only one who saw the vision; those who were with me did not see it, but such terror overwhelmed them that they fled and hid themselves. 8 So I was left alone, gazing at this great vision; I had no strength left, my face turned deathly pale and I was helpless. 9 Then I heard him speaking, and as I listened to him, I fell into a deep sleep, my face to the ground.*
>
> *10 A hand touched me and set me trembling on my hands and knees. 11 He said, "Daniel, you who are highly esteemed, consider carefully the words I am about to speak to you, and stand*

*up, for I have now been sent to you." And when he said this to me,
I stood up trembling.*

*12 Then he continued, "Do not be afraid, Daniel. Since
the first day that you set your mind to gain understanding and to
humble yourself before your God, your words were heard, and I
have come in response to them. 13 But the prince of the Persian
kingdom resisted me twenty-one days. Then Michael, one of the
chief princes, came to help me, because I was detained there with
the king of Persia. 14 Now I have come to explain to you what
will happen to your people in the future, for the vision concerns a
time yet to come."*

Daniel received revelation from God in a vision, in response
to this he spent 21 days in mourning and interacting with
God. Then he has an encounter with an angel who has been
sent in response to Daniel's prayers. The encounter with the
angel is not shared by those around Daniel but they were
affected by it. The angel says that Daniel's prayers were heard
on the first day and ongoing after that, also that the answer to
those prayers was sent immediately in the form of this angel.
And yet the answer didn't arrive on earth for 21 days.

The angel was resisted by a demon called the "Prince
of Persia" for twenty one days and even needed assistance
from the angel Michael in order to fulfil his mission coming
from heaven to earth. This is talking about levels of spiritual
warfare that are not apparent with only an earthly perspective.
Indeed, I have to admit I do not fully understand how angels
and demons interact in that unseen realm, but nonetheless I
realise that it is true.

This spiritual warfare is another reason for experience
of delay from an earthly perspective. However, it is very
important to note that Daniel's prayers were heard on the
first day and the angel was sent in response to those prayers

immediately. There was no delay in the answer to prayer, but there was delay in experiencing the answer. I find it interesting that Daniel continued to seek God during that time. I do not know the full impact of those prayers upon the spiritual battle, but I believe it could only be positive. For this reason, my practice is to continue praying whilst I am waiting for answers. I literally do not know what is happening in those unseen realms but I know that it is relevant to what is happening on earth.

James 5 verse 16 says, *"The prayer of a righteous person is powerful and effective."*

One example of this in my life was regarding our two children whilst Kim was pregnant with them. Asthma has affected many in my family and I suffered with it quite a lot particularly in my early years of life, so much so that I missed a large proportion of my first two years at school. Knowing that asthma is often passed on to one's children I had a very serious desire that my children would not be inflicted with this disease. When Kim fell pregnant for the first time I prayed for our unborn child that he or she would not suffer from asthma. I prayed once and immediately I had a complete assurance that my prayer had been answered, it was an amazing experience and I knew that I did not need to ask God again, my faith had gained me assurance of what I had hoped for. David was born and he has never had any problems with asthma.

When Kim fell pregnant the second time I prayed again in a similar manner fully expecting an instant answer and the assurance that followed it. However, that assurance did not happen, somehow I knew that my prayer was not yet fully answered even though I knew it had been heard. Asthma was still a possibility (or more likely a probability) so I continued to pray. It was in the seventh month of Kim's pregnancy one

day when I was praying and reading my Bible that God led
me to a verse in Isaiah through which he spoke to me and
assured me that my child would not have asthma.

At that point I stopped praying about the issue but
instead turned my attention to thanksgiving. Kerry was born
and has never had a problem with asthma. Do I understand
this fully? No. But I know the difference between hope and
assurance. This matter meant enough to me that I wasn't
willing to leave it in the realms of hope, I entered a battle in
prayer until I was assured of the answer.

Another example was in the process towards construction
of the Eastgate building. It was a very complicated process with
lots of interactions with lawyers and banks, and at one stage
we were at a standstill and we needed to break the deadlock
within two weeks otherwise the whole project was in jeopardy.
We were trying everything we could to help lawyers and
banks meet agreement but it seemed like communication was
breaking down all over the place. It was confusing, alarming,
and was consuming all our human attention and despite our
great human efforts we were not making any breakthrough.

I knew that gaining such an advance for the Kingdom
of God that would come with our building would not go
uncontested spiritually and I realised that we were missing
something about this situation. So somewhat belatedly,
I took myself off alone and asked God to show me what
was happening in the spirit realms. He revealed to me a
Stronghold of Darkness which was affecting the thinking
across the situation. It was a stronghold of pride whereby
people were not valuing other people's points of view but
sticking only to their own opinion. Once this was revealed to
me I took spiritual authority over the situation and banished
the power of darkness that was damaging the project. Within
two days conversations started to flow and agreements were

being made.

A week later negotiations came to a halt once more, this time I was quicker off the mark and went straight to God who showed that a Stronghold of Control was now trying to influence the communications resulting in various power struggles going on rather than collaboration. I took authority over this power of darkness, and within a day positive communication recommenced and within days and just within our deadline, agreements were reached which enabled contracts to be signed. The result is the Eastgate building which since opening has provided blessings to thousands and thousands of people from many different nations. For myself, I have learnt to be quicker to consider the influences outside of the human realm that influence our advance with the Kingdom of God, and have grown in confidence in the authority God has given to his people to influence that realm.

When dealing with delay, trust God that He has heard your prayers, and keep on praying until you have assurance.

Delay is sometimes caused by spiritual battles, be confident in the authority God has given you to play a part in that battle.

There are many other examples of people dealing with delay in the Bible, for example the Apostle Paul spent many years in development, interacting with God and other people before the moment in Antioch where we come to this point in his and Barnabas' story: Acts 13 *1 Now in the church at Antioch there were prophets and teachers: Barnabas, Simeon called Niger, Lucius of Cyrene, Manaen (who had been brought up with Herod the tetrarch) and Saul. 2 While they were worshiping the Lord and fasting, the Holy Spirit said, "Set apart for me Barnabas and Saul for the work to which I have called them." 3 So after they had fasted and prayed, they placed their hands on them and sent them off.*

Paul had been called many years previously, the ensuing

years were his development for the time when he would be released into the fullness of that calling.

Indeed delay, often more aptly called waiting, is a normal part of life. If I book a holiday I look forward to it and prepare for it in advance until the moment it arrives - we would probably not class this as a delay. At the age of 15 I decided I wanted to be a doctor, the reality of that did not come true until I was almost 24 and the continuing development of that calling happened throughout my life. Many delays are taken in our stride as we wait for things to happen and prepare appropriately, often this is a positive experience.

To my mind the challenging delays are the ones linked with disappointment, discouragement, frustration and other negative emotions. When our waiting time seems too long to us and our expectations are unmet. Also it is often linked to areas where we allow our hopes to rise the most. I have found a particular verse in the Bible extremely helpful when confronted by such times (as well as being useful all the time); it is Romans 8 v 28 *"And we know that God causes everything to work together for the good of those who love God and are called according to his purpose for them."*

I learned this verse early in my Christian life and I have applied it diligently to my thinking ever since. When things seem to be going wrong or not as I anticipated I call upon this promise that God will work everything for good and I trust Him with the outcome. Often there is an emotional conversation with God as part of the process, where I express my disappointments and confusion, but I always finish by stating that I trust Him with the outcome. That trust is not based upon my own understanding of the situation or even a potential solution or outcome, it is a trust in the nature of God.

I have learned that God is not disturbed by my emotions

and my honesty but understands them and values the truth being expressed in our relationship; ultimately I come out more strongly connected to Him and my faith grows.

One of the most challenging episodes in the life of our church involved a building project. Kim and I, along with David and Kerry, joined the church in New Ash Green in 1988. It was a small church and our Sunday meetings were in the Youth and Community Centre which we hired for the purpose. When we outgrew that we hired a local primary school and when there was not enough room there we moved on to hiring a local secondary school which gave us plenty of room for growth. We had to set up every Sunday for music, creche, children's activities, refreshments and so on.. By the year 2000 a common dream was developing amongst us all to have a building of our own for seven day a week use, so we started special offerings for this purpose, and started to explore possibilities. Eventually we settled upon a joint project with the Secondary School where we met on Sundays. A new school building was being planned and we joined forces with the school to provide extra resources for the school and a home for ourselves. Everyone was excited by this collaboration, with gains for all involved, especially in the rural setting where we were, which meant that community facilities would be enhanced, a new school and sports facilities would be built, with a spiritual presence involved in it, and there would be a home for our church.

We continued to save money, and by 2004 we had accumulated about £500,000 for the project. We developed a very good working relationship with the school and were involved in the governance system of the school, extracurricular activities, and delivering some of the teaching programme. The day arrived when the architectural drawings were to be unveiled for the new school, and I went along with members of the school staff for a preview. As I greeted the architect, with whom I had interacted during the planning process, to say I was excited would be a large understatement. I looked at the drawings and initially was puzzled, not understanding what I was looking at. That puzzlement turned to dismay when I could find no reference nor sight of the part of the buildings which included our church facility. So I went to talk with the architect explaining my confusion. His reply floored me. He said that it had been decided that the project with the church would not continue and there was nothing included for us in the plans for the new building. This was the first I had heard about this and I had no idea how to react especially as I was feeling extremely angry and betrayed.

I spoke with the head teacher who confirmed what had already been said, and I asked why I hadn't been involved in this decision, but there was no satisfactory answer to be had. I left and went home, all sorts of thoughts swirling around in my head. I explained to Kim what had happened, she was equally perplexed and upset, and after something to eat and drink I took myself off for a long walk and a conversation with God. The hopes for our church seemed to have been shattered, and I in particular felt responsible for leading the church along this path (although all of our leaders were in agreement and responsibility was shared). There was no solution that I could see, I believed God had led us along this path that had led us to a dead end, and I was angry with God. I also felt foolish.

I had a long rant at God and kept on walking. Eventually I stopped and sat in a field. It was a warm summer evening, with meadow flowers all around me, birds singing and insects buzzing. I only knew of one thing to do - I presented Romans 8 verse 28 to God and told Him that I trusted Him to work this all out for the good of the church. As I did this 'the peace that passes all understanding,' settled in my heart and mind and started to guard me. Next I chose to worship God as I started to walk home.

Explaining the course of events to the church was extremely difficult. Corporate disappointment was very evident, leaders' meetings came up with no new ideas, and we all agreed that we needed to keep trusting God through this trial and into the future. We made worship of God simply for who He is our main priority (as always) and called upon His faithfulness to His own nature.

In addition, we pulled on the verses in Ephesians chapter 3 which say, *"Now to him who is able to do immeasurably more than all we ask or imagine, according to his power that is at work within us, to him be glory in the church and in Christ Jesus throughout all generations, for ever and ever! Amen."*

There is an extremely important principle to be drawn from these verses. God wants to do more than we ask or imagine, and He has chosen to do that through his power at work within us. This is an amazing statement, and it is one that has helped me navigate the path of life. If I limit my expectation of God to working within the bounds of my imagination, I am very likely to miss the greater opportunities that God will present to me. I need to be continually ready to be surprised by God, and also expectant that He will do so. Sometimes this can be a confusing path, where we are convinced that God has heard our requests, our hearts cry and our dreams, and yet what He delivers to us looks completely different.

Imagine that I offer to give you a £5 note. You can picture it in your mind's eye, you know its colour and shape, you could recognise it anywhere. I reach into my pocket and bring something out and offer it to you. You instantly recognise that it is not a £5 note, it is the wrong colour and size. What has gone wrong? Have I lied to you, broken my promise, even deliberately set out to disappoint you? Your heart drops and you are tempted to walk away, your trust in me damaged by my action. But then you take another look, and you focus more closely on my hand still outstretched to you, containing something different. Your thoughts and emotions start to change. You begin to recognise that what is before you is actually a £20 note, more than you had asked or imagined. How easy it would have been to miss this if you only had eyes for what you had imagined. I believe that many people miss some of the greater opportunities that God offers them, because they have limited their eyes to only looking for what they have already asked or imagined, and even grow disappointed with God as a result.

As we navigated the weeks of disappointment after the news of the building project, we resolutely decided to keep our eyes and ears open to 'the more than' opportunities that God had in store for us, understanding that if we were faithful with small opportunities God would give us greater ones. Two weeks into this period, I went to preach at the church that Kim and I had been part of previously, where we still had many friends. At the end of the meeting a friend came up to me and said that he had a prophetic word for me. He went on to explain that the word from God made no sense to him because he knew of our context, that we lived in a village and that our church served villages in a specific area of North Kent and God had confirmed that calling to us very clearly. He told me that *"God says that He is going to place you at the East gate to the City."* My heart was stirred inside me as he spoke, God had spoken something that was far beyond our imagination. I drove back to New Ash Green, along narrow country roads, contemplating what had been said, confident that God had spoken. As soon as possible I shared this with other leaders in the church, and we weighed the prophecy. We concluded that God was directing us along a different path than we had previously known or imagined, and we started to pursue that opportunity.

We relocated the church to an urban setting, we were granted permission to design and construct a building in a new area of development in North Kent and in December 2013 we finally opened the building, a home for our church but also a community centre for the developing area. Three months later, in March 2014, the area was designated by the UK government as Ebbsfleet Garden City, the newest city in the UK which is now being constructed quite literally around Eastgate. And guess where in the city Eastgate stands? At the eastern end, which is the first part that has been developed, the rest of the city is being developed and Eastgate is involved in developing the community and influencing other sectors of life in the city.

Looking back, if the project with the school had gone ahead as we had hoped we would have been delighted and happily existed there. However, God had more than that in store for us and we are extremely glad that we listened to Him, didn't park on our disappointment, but instead pursued the new dream that He had in mind for us. More than we could ask or imagine!

Story by Dave Foggon:

Whilst on a mission trip, our team decided to go to downtown Mexico City to do some sightseeing on our day off. We split into smaller groups and I was in the group who decided to go to see an old cathedral. Outside the cathedral we saw a man who was mute and unable to walk, sitting on the street begging. Two of us gave him some money and prayed for him. He indicated he felt strength come into his legs and was able to say a word - "Jesus" - for the very first time. Without thinking it through, suddenly I stood up and shouted loudly, "God is doing miracles right now! If you need healing in your body, come here because God is here to heal!"

Crowds quickly gathered around us and we began praying for people. Healings started to happen frequently with ease. People with crutches were walking off with them under their arms. Broken bones, backs, and legs were healed. People with diseases in their bodies felt the pain completely disappear. One man had a disease in his colon. After his arm was healed, he revealed this problem and the pain instantly left for the first time in over a year. A retired medical doctor who was 90% deaf took her hearing aid out after I said to her, "Receive your hearing right now", and walked off with it in her hands, no longer needing it. Everyone on the team saw a continual outpouring of miracles for two hours. A few team members prayed for a man who was severely disabled and didn't believe he could be healed. He'd had very little movement in his body for years due to severe arthritis and other medical problems. After prayer he suddenly got up, stood up straight, and ran off! We didn't do any more sightseeing – God had other ideas! By the end of our time there, God had healed between 40 and 50 people right there on that street corner!

Chapter 16 Why is God not Answering my Prayers?

This is one of the most common questions that Christians ask:

- we ask ourselves
- we ask other people
- we ask God

It is a very good question indeed it is even a Biblical question and it can lead us to great answers. Biblical answers are the best source to turn to as other sources run a risk of introducing error into our thinking. The Bible does not shy away from this subject and contains within it plenty of places where this question is being asked. The Psalms are full of 'Why' questions, the book of Job likewise. The Gospels also contain such questions, for example: Matthew 17 v 18-19 *"Then Jesus rebuked the demon, and it came out of the boy, and he was healed from that moment. Afterward the disciples came to Jesus privately and asked, "Why couldn't we drive it out?""*

If the Bible does not shy away from the question, why do we sometimes shy away from the answers that the Bible provides?

I find that many treat the question of God not answering prayer as if it is a mystery with answers hard to come by, but I have not found that to be the case. If we are not careful about this 'mystery mindset' it can result in us not pursuing the very answers we need so that we can overcome the problem. Another problem that I observe is that people often don't like the answers that the Bible gives and find ways to discount them. For example, the question in Matthew 17 is immediately followed by an answer from Jesus.

> *v20 "Because you have so little faith," He answered.*

That seems very straightforward to me. Jesus supplies an answer to the question - insufficient faith.

I am hoping that having come this far in this book you know my heart on this subject. My heart is to encourage you, stimulate you, teach you, and challenge you to grow in faith. That applies to every one of us, and I definitely include myself. We can all grow in faith. So I have no intention of condemning you, blaming you, offending you or discouraging you.

Why am I saying this? Well my experience is that many people take offence when this Bible verse is talked about and believe that somehow they or others are being condemned for a lack of faith.

So let's ask another question - was Jesus trying to condemn his disciples or rather instruct them, encourage them and stimulate them to grow in faith? I believe we find the answer as we read further in the passage.

> *"For truly I tell you, if you have faith the size of a mustard seed, you can say to this mountain, 'Move from here to there,' and it will move. Nothing will be impossible for you."...*

Jesus is trying to encourage them, build them up, and make it attainable for them to "move mountains". A mustard seed is small - so Jesus was not creating a massive burden for them, rather he was encouraging them to have a very simple (childlike) trust in God. He leaves them with this thought "Nothing will be impossible for you."

It would be sensible for us to look at other answers from the Bible to this question so that we can *"throw off everything that hinders and the sin that so easily entangles, and run with perseverance the race marked out for us."* Hebrews 12 verse 1.

I have compiled a list of answers that I have found in the Bible that address this issue. It is not an exhaustive or exclusive list but it should be enough to help you throw off things that may be hindering you from expressing and enjoying the fullness of your Christian faith. As you study the Bible yourself, you may well find other answers supplied within its text.

Being double minded.

James chapter 1: "2 Consider it pure joy, my brothers and sisters, whenever you face trials of many kinds, 3 because you know that the testing of your faith produces perseverance. 4 Let perseverance finish its work so that you may be mature and complete, not lacking anything. 5 If any of you lacks wisdom, you should ask God, who gives generously to all without finding fault, and it will be given to you. 6 But when you ask, you must believe and not doubt, because the one who doubts is like a wave of the sea, blown and tossed by the wind. 7 That person should not expect to receive anything from the Lord."

Let's have a look at this passage in greater detail, and to my mind verse 5 is key to understanding it:

"If any of you lacks wisdom" recognising an area of lack in my life is very important because if I don't perceive it, refuse to recognise it, or even perversely take delight in it, then I won't pursue an answer. I believe true humility is rooted in great self-awareness, by which I mean being aware of areas in my life where there is a lack and at the same time rejoicing over the areas of strength.

"You should ask God": you should approach God with the issue. The Bible says that as we draw close to God he draws close to us and that if we ask we will receive.

"Who gives generously to all without finding fault": God is generous in his answers, his measure is pressed down and flowing over, his desire to do more than we could ask or imagine. This applies to 'all' in other words God deals with everyone in the same way. God deals with us on the basis of his grace towards us, it does not depend upon us having faultless behaviour. In other words, we cannot earn blessing and favour from God. We do not have to do things or perform in order to extract answers from God.

(Romans 8 verse 32 "He who did not spare his own Son, but gave him up for us all—how will he not also, along with him, graciously give us all things?")

Let's move on to verses 6 and 7 which as first glance look confusing:

> *"6 But when you ask, you must believe and not doubt, because the one who doubts is like a wave of the sea, blown and tossed by the wind. 7 That person should not expect to receive anything from the Lord."*

That doesn't seem to fit with 'ask and you will receive' because it actually says that in. this circumstance we should not expect to receive anything from the Lord. However, the question "why' is answered in the passage itself. When you ask, what you believe and doubt are both very important: if doubt is so spiritually powerful in a negative sense, it makes sense to ask 'what are we not meant to doubt?'

The context for verse 6 is verse 5. Doubting the truth contained in verse 5 will result in various unhelpful thoughts:

- I need to add works of my own in addition to resting on the grace of God in order to get answers to my prayers.
- Somehow I am not included in the "all" and I am less favoured in God's eyes.
- God treats me differently to other people.
- I am not worthy of God answering my prayers because of my faults.
- Such thinking within us will wage war with our understanding of the grace of God, our minds will be blown around, our thoughts tossed up and down, we will move away from the place of grace and peace, and miss the answers that are being provided.

Husbands disrespecting wives.

> *1 Peter 3:7 Husbands, in the same way be considerate as you live with your wives, and treat them with respect as the weaker partner and as heirs with you of the gracious gift of life, so that nothing will hinder your prayers.*

How we interact with other people is important (especially important for married couples). Being loving, respectful, considerate, kind, patient, forgiving, faithful, gentle, and thankful are aspects of godly (heavenly) behaviour that help to form a heavenly culture in which heaven's answers to our prayers are less likely to be hindered.

> *Matthew 22: 37 Jesus replied: "'Love the Lord your God with all your heart and with all your soul and with all your mind.'38 This is the first and greatest commandment. 39 And the second is like it: 'Love your neighbor as yourself.'40 All the Law and the Prophets hang on these two commandments."*

Love God and love other people - it has very important outcomes.

Sinful behaviour

> *Gal 5: 19 The acts of the flesh are obvious: sexual immorality, impurity and debauchery; 20 idolatry and witchcraft; hatred, discord, jealousy, fits of rage, selfish ambition, dissensions, factions 21 and envy; drunkenness, orgies, and the like. I warn you, as I did before, that those who live like this will not inherit the kingdom of God.*
>
> *22 But the fruit of the Spirit is love, joy, peace, forbearance, kindness, goodness, faithfulness, 23 gentleness and self-control. Against such things there is no law. 24 Those who belong to Christ Jesus have crucified the flesh with its passions and desires. 25 Since we live by the Spirit, let us keep in step with the Spirit. 26 Let us not become conceited, provoking and envying each other.*

In this passage we see the contrast in behaviour between the Kingdom of Darkness and the Kingdom of Light and the contrasting outcomes.

In verse 26 the passage urges us *"Let us not become conceited, provoking and envying each other"* which implies that we need to guard against becoming something which cuts across our life in the Spirit, instead we are urged to *"Keep in step with the Spirit"* or in other words "walk with the Spirit and follow his leading". When someone is born again they not only receive salvation, but they have an inheritance to pursue and uncover. In Ephesians chapter 1 we find an explanation of this.

> *v 3 : Praise be to the God and Father of our Lord Jesus Christ, who has blessed us in the heavenly realms with every spiritual blessing in Christ.*

v 17: I keep asking that the God of our Lord Jesus Christ, the glorious Father, may give you the Spirit of wisdom and revelation, so that you may know him better. 18 I pray that the eyes of your heart may be enlightened in order that you may know the hope to which he has called you, the riches of his glorious inheritance in his holy people, 19 and his incomparably great power for us who believe.

We have received every spiritual blessing in Christ, but our eyes need to be opened to see them and the power to accomplish them. Sinful behaviour distracts our eyes away to earthly realities rather than heavenly ones so that we are less likely to pursue our inheritance. Also note that much sinful behaviour is detrimental to human relationships eg hatred, discord, jealousy, fits of rage, selfish ambition, dissensions, factions and envy; and as we have already seen, damaged human relationships hinder our prayers.

The parable of the prodigal son also gives us insight into the squandering of inheritance, both sons had the same level of opportunity, both squandered their inheritance, the younger son by obvious sinful behaviour, the elder son by bad attitudes and poor relationships. But note that the Father reached out to both to restore them to their full inheritance - but the key lay in the willingness to repent and change behaviour, which the younger son did and was restored, unfortunately the older son did not and continued to miss out on his full inheritance.

1 Cor 6: underlines this for us:

Verses 9 and 10: Or do you not know that wrongdoers will not inherit the kingdom of God, nor thieves nor the greedy nor drunkards nor slanderers nor swindlers will inherit the kingdom of God.

No matter what your circumstances are, as a child of God your

Father in heaven is reaching out to you with your inheritance. Turning away from sinful behaviour and attitudes is one of the keys to seeing more of the Kingdom of Heaven.

Asking for selfish reasons.

> *James 4:3. When you ask, you do not receive, because you ask with wrong motives, that you may spend what you get on your pleasures.*

The motivation and reason for praying is very important. It is not wrong to pray blessing for ourselves, but if the motivation is without thought to the overflow of that blessing to other people there is a danger of selfishness.

The Bible instructs us to "love others as we love ourselves." Therefore, we can conclude that having a loving attitude towards yourself is important but without that love overflowing to others it is likely to become a spiritual dead end. I remember a man I knew, who had recently been born again. He was learning about the Biblical principle of tithing income. He decided to apply the principle in his life but did so in a very questionable manner. He decided how much income he wanted to earn each month from his self-employed business (a lot of money, much more than his previous income at that time!). He was planning for a rich lifestyle. He then started giving one tenth of his desired amount to the church as his tithe, with the expectation that God would supply the other ninety per cent for him to enjoy.

About three months into this plan he talked with me about it and complained that God hadn't kept his side of the arrangement! He explained that his finances were in jeopardy and he no longer trusted God. What went wrong? I would suggest he asked with selfishness without a thought about generosity. Generosity is an aspect of love, and I have found it a very useful indicator of my own motivations. James chapter 3 has some very strong things to say about selfish ambition and jealousy, and we would be very wise to take note.

> *James 3: 13 Who is wise and understanding among you? Let them show it by their good life, by deeds done in the humility that comes from wisdom. 14 But if you harbour bitter envy and selfish ambition in your hearts, do not boast about it or deny the truth. 15 Such "wisdom" does not come down from heaven but is earthly, unspiritual, demonic. 16 For where you have envy and selfish ambition, there you find disorder and every evil practice.*

Praying and giving in order to impress other people.

> *Matt 6: 1. Be careful not to practice your righteousness in front of others to be seen by them. If you do, you will have no reward from your Father in heaven.*
>
> *2 "So when you give to the needy, do not announce it with trumpets, as the hypocrites do in the synagogues and on the streets, to be honored by others. Truly I tell you, they have received their reward in full. 3 But when you give to the needy, do not let your left hand know what your right hand is doing, 4 so that your giving may be in secret. Then your Father, who sees what is done in secret, will reward you.*
>
> *5 "And when you pray, do not be like the hypocrites, for they love to pray standing in the synagogues and on the street corners to be seen by others. Truly I tell you, they have received their reward in full. 6 But when you pray, go into your room, close the door and pray to your Father, who is unseen. Then your Father, who sees what is done in secret, will reward you. 7 And when you pray, do not keep on babbling like pagans, for they think they will be heard because of their many words. 8 Do not be like them, for your Father knows what you need before you ask him.*

Generosity is a good thing, but when it is done for the selfish reason of impressing other people and gaining influence God is not impressed. Similarly with prayer. God does not reward such prayers with an answer from himself, indeed that is not the reward sought by such behaviour. However, when we genuinely seek God He will reward us. In addition, we do not have to use long prayers to impress God, a simple cry from our heart is what will move His heart to respond.

A lack of patience and perseverance

Hebrews 6:12 We do not want you to become lazy, but to imitate those who through faith and patience inherit what has been promised.

Inheriting the fullness of the promises and inheritance of God requires perseverance and patience. In the modern world where so much is obtained and expected instantly it is possible to become lazy in terms of waiting with expectation. This can be a challenge to our modern mindsets. I would suggest that a Bible study on the word perseverance could be very helpful in this regard.

Being moved by the wrong spirit.

Luke 9: 53 But they did not receive Him, because He was traveling toward Jerusalem. 54 When His disciples James and John saw this, they said, "Lord, do You want us to command fire to come down from heaven and consume them?" 55 But He turned and rebuked them, and said, "You do not know what kind of spirit you are of; 56 for the Son of Man did not come to destroy men's lives, but to save them.

Jesus fulfilled the Old Testament law and brought us into a

new covenant. We need to make sure that we do not lapse into ways of thinking that are not consistent with this new covenant.

When we use prayer rather than authority

> *Matthew 10 verse 1: Jesus called his twelve disciples to him and gave them authority to drive out impure spirits and to heal every disease and sickness.*

When we continue to pray for God's intervention in regard to something that we have already received spiritual authority over, we are effectively not believing what God has already given to us. Jesus gave his disciples authority to heal the sick (in his name), he did not instruct them to pray to God, but rather to move in power and authority just as he did. Confidence in the authority already given to us is extremely important. For instance, we see Peter full of confidence in Acts 3:

> *6 Then Peter said, "Silver or gold I do not have, but what I do have I give you. In the name of Jesus Christ of Nazareth, walk." 7 Taking him by the right hand, he helped him up, and instantly the man's feet and ankles became strong.*

Peter didn't pray for the man because he himself was already confident in what he had received from God, he simply used his authority over the sickness. As the book of Acts progresses we see a passage in chapter 5 which tells us *"15 As a result, people brought the sick into the streets and laid them on beds and mats so that at least Peter's shadow might fall on some of them as he passed by. 16 Crowds gathered also from the towns around Jerusalem, bringing their sick and those tormented by impure spirits, and all of them were healed."*

Peter had learned many lessons, grown strong in his faith and was confident in his spiritual authority.

Another example would be in releasing people from demonic oppression; we do not need to ask God to drive away the demons, instead we simply tell them to "Go" in the name of Jesus.

Confidence (faith) in our God given authority is extremely important in order to see the outcomes we desire and sometimes that faith can be expressed in prayer (James 5 verse 15: *And the prayer offered in faith will make the sick person well; the Lord will raise them up*) but most often faith is simply expressed by words and actions. We need to learn how to confidently use the gifts God gives to us by growing in our faith.

When we continue to pray for God to do something in respect to which He has already given us authority, it is possible for us to slip into unbelief and try to achieve our goal by our own efforts and this will not produce the results we want, but rather this route of action carries with it the danger of leading us into a spiral of disappointment and discouragement.

Galatians 3 verse 3: are you so foolish that having begun in the Spirit you are now trying to achieve your goal by your own efforts.

Thinking in an individual way rather than a corporate way
In much of Western society great value is placed upon individual thought, individual freedom and choice, individual expression, individual dreams and destinies. Indeed, I myself grew up with the encouragement from my parents to pursue my dreams, think for myself and not to live in the fear of other people's opinions: and in many ways this was healthy. However, on its own that form of thought would be

unhealthy. I also had to learn to value other people's opinions, listen to their thoughts, respect their choices and celebrate their successes. More than that I had to learn to celebrate 'corporate success' which did not depend upon the success of an individual but rather a whole body of people working together.

I love sport and during my youth I played many different sports, some individual and some as part of a team. I enjoyed many individual successes, but when my team won it was not 'my success' but rather 'our success' in which I played a part. Individual losses were processed and learned from in a certain way, but team losses needed to be processed together in order to learn together.

Similarly, in medicine, doctors without nurses, physiotherapists, receptionists, administrators, etc, would not provide a good medical service. We need each other.

Christianity is not an individual endeavour, we are part of a body, a family, an army and we share a culture. Successes are to be celebrated corporately, likewise failures and losses need to be processed corporately, our individual responsibilities taken seriously but not separately. Often when prayers are answered more than one person has been praying and moving in faith - it is a corporate success in which you play a part. Likewise when prayers are not answered, the responsibility seldom rests upon one individual, and our corporate culture and belief/unbelief systems need to be analysed together so that we can improve and move forward.

One Christmas Eve I was working in my medical practice as usual, alongside my colleagues. It wasn't very busy for us as most people don't choose that day for medical appointments if they can avoid it, however the shopping precinct outside was swarming with people. I called the next patient into my consulting room and started talking with her. She was very late for her appointment and very apologetic. She went on to explain that she had "just popped into the supermarket for a few things, but the problem was that there were hundreds of people there doing their last minute shopping and they had caused her to be late because of the long line of people in front of her at the checkouts."

I chuckled inwardly at the way this lady had divorced herself from the problem and blamed it upon everyone else. She failed to see that she was part of the problem and part of that long line at the checkout.

The danger of false humility and comparison when it interferes with the pursuit of your individual destiny.
Although Christianity is a corporate venture it is very important to recognise the individual part you have to play in it. Let's look at a Bible passage to help us with this train of thought:

> *Galatians 6: 2 Carry each other's burdens, and in this way you will fulfill the law of Christ. 3 If anyone thinks they are something when they are not, they deceive themselves. 4 Each one should test their own actions. Then they can take pride in themselves alone, without comparing themselves to someone else, 5 for each one should carry their own load.*

Carry each other's burdens: We are to help one another and look out for each other

If anyone thinks they are something when they are not, they deceive themselves:

The Bible talks a lot about unity and difference, for example in 1 Corinthians 12 it says referring to a body "don't try to be an eye if you are an ear."

In Ephesians 4: it talks about Jesus giving different

gifts to his church which have a complementary function in equipping the church, each equally important but with different emphases, priorities and skills. It is important to recognise which gift you carry and be faithful with it rather than try to be something you are not.

Each one should test their own actions.
    Everyone has the responsibility to examine the outcomes of their activity as that will be good evidence of specific gifts and callings. For example evangelists are good at evangelism and have a specific grace upon them in that function.
    Then they can take pride in themselves alone, without comparing themselves to someone else.
    The ability to take delight (pride) in your own work is a godly attribute. In the story of creation at the end of each day God assessed His work and found that it was good, and on the sixth day it was very good. I believe that within Christianity there can be a strong culture of what I call false humility which creates a virtue out of self-criticism, self-discouragement and lowering of expectations of oneself. There can also be an unhealthy culture of hierarchy and inequality leading to comparison with other people in an unhealthy way which can lead to dissatisfaction with one's own gifts and calling. For instance, if we believe that a prophet is more important than an evangelist we might seek to attain a gift which we don't have.

1 Corinthians 12: If the whole body were an eye, where would the sense of hearing be? If the whole body were an ear, where would the sense of smell be? 18 But in fact God has placed the parts in the body, every one of them, just as he wanted them to be. 19 If they were all one part, where would the body be? 20 As it is, there are many parts, but one body.

God has formed each one of us in a unique way as part of his body. If we don't value our unique destiny and place in the body, not only will we not fulfil that destiny, we will diminish the overall effectiveness of the entire body.

For each one should carry their own load.
If we try to pursue a path God has not given to us, our prayer life could be a very frustrating thing. Your search for significance will only be fruitful in searching for and being faithful to your unique calling and destiny (your own load), not in comparing yourself with others. Self-awareness and self-contentment are very important factors in a fruitful Christian life.

I recommend you look further into the subjects touched upon in this chapter as I am sure that there are more answers to be found than just the ones I have mentioned, and by finding answers we can enter into the solutions.

Story by Sasha Caridia

Randy Clark has an excellent teaching about Reiki and other practices, called, 'Healing energy - whose power is it'

One day an agency colleague said to me 'I am a Reiki healer,' my immediate response was 'Great, I am a Holy Spirit healer!' Over the course of that shift we had various conversations and she asked many questions, the answers to which simply pointed to Jesus as being the one true source of love and power. My colleague explained that she had degenerative discs in her lower back and as a result suffered from chronic pain. Having explained how much God loves her and wants her to be well she was very happy to receive prayer. I felt prompted by the Holy Spirit to ask afterwards how she felt, not in relation to pain levels but rather in regard to what she experienced whilst being prayed for. She replied, "I have Reiki healing and spiritual healing which feel the same but this felt completely different. I can't describe it, it feels like nothing I have ever experienced before". She then described how the pain was travelling up and out of her body and 'leaving'. For her 'healing' as such was not the issue, but rather the true source of love and power needed to be demonstrated. I reminded her that the spirit of the living God lives in me and He loves her and wants her to know Him. She encountered and experienced the love and power of Jesus today, the one who is in passionate pursuit of her. We have worked together since and the conversation has continued, each time pointing towards Jesus as the answer to all that she is looking for.

Chapter 17 Familiarity with God -
The Nazareth experience.

I remember vividly one day when I was reading my Bible and I reached Mark chapter 6. It was not an unfamiliar chapter to me but on that particular day the Holy Spirit spoke to me in a very powerful way about the fact that Jesus was unable to do miracles (except heal a few people) in his hometown of Nazareth. A very physical 'what?!' escaped from my lungs. Jesus unable to do miracles! My mind was reeling somewhat and in all honesty I had to adjust my thinking considerably in the light of the truth being revealed to me. So let's have a look at this passage.

> *Mark 6: 1. Jesus left there and went to his hometown, accompanied by his disciples. 2 When the Sabbath came, he began to teach in the synagogue, and many who heard him were amazed.*
>
> *"Where did this man get these things?" they asked. "What's this wisdom that has been given him? What are these remarkable miracles he is performing? 3. Isn't this the carpenter? Isn't this Mary's son and the brother of James, Joseph, Judas and Simon? Aren't his sisters here with us?" And they took offense at him.*
>
> *4 Jesus said to them, "A prophet is not without honour except in his own town, among his relatives and in his own home." 5 He could not do any miracles there, except lay his hands on a few sick people and heal them. 6 He was amazed at their lack of faith.*

It was difficult for me to comprehend that Jesus was unable to perform miracles in a certain place. And it had all seemed to start so well: the people of Nazareth were amazed at his teaching and they wondered where he had received such wisdom and the authority and power to perform miracles, after all he was a 'local' and obviously they were not used to such things in their synagogue and town.

Then they started to process what they were hearing and witnessing. The main tool they used was their previous knowledge of Jesus and their familiarity with him, after all he was 'one of theirs'. They subjected the current experience to scrutiny, not by the revelation contained within it but by the constraints of familiarity and historical understanding. What they said about Jesus was true, "Isn't this the carpenter? Isn't this Mary's son and the brother of James, Joseph, Judas and Simon? Aren't his sisters here with us? And they took offense at him."

What they said about Jesus was true but it wasn't the full truth being made available to them. An opportunity to grow in faith was presented to them but they failed to grasp it.

Limited truth can be a dangerous thing. For instance, if someone is on trial for an alleged offence and evidence is produced that is true but other true evidence is omitted, then the judgement could be wrong. Likewise, if I tell you all about myself as a teenager but not anything about my adult life you would not have a full picture of who I am and you may misjudge or misrepresent me.

The Nazarenes not only refused to put new knowledge into the equation of their thinking, but they took offence against Jesus for revealing himself in a way with which they were not familiar. When our current ways of thinking are challenged by new knowledge it is an opportunity that can progress in very different directions.

- The opportunity to grow.
- The opportunity to be offended.
- The opportunity to be indifferent.

In many ways this is the story of world history, for instance when Galileo in the early 17th century put forward the idea that the earth was not the centre of the Solar System but actually orbited the sun, he was vehemently resisted by the church on theological grounds.

Church history is unfortunately littered with the resistance to progressive ideas and revelations from God about himself. By this I don't mean ideas that are contrary to the Bible, but rather ideas resistant to the discovery of further Biblical truth. The Reformation would be a good example of something being resisted violently by the established church.

At Nazareth, Jesus revealed more about himself without denying that which was already known, and he made a fascinating statement-

> *Verse 4: Jesus said to them, "A prophet is not without honour except in his own town, among his relatives and in his own home."*

This warns of the danger of familiarity towards prophetic revelation, and explains much about the reasons that Christianity has faced such difficulties in transitioning from one generation to another with growing faith and endeavour. If we regard the truth that we currently have as the full extent of truth about God then we have limited our knowledge of God, effectively denying His infinite and eternal nature. The willingness to keep on learning and discovering more is to my mind the essence of true humility and is a vital key to growth. It is the opposite of the type of pride that seeks to stand above knowledge being offered by others and is destructive in its nature. The Bible refers to such humility and pride in a couple of places: *"God opposes the proud but gives grace to the humble."*

What does it look like when God opposes the proud? I would suggest verse 5 gives us a very good answer.

"He could not do any miracles there, except lay his hands on a few sick people and heal them."

I think the Bible is clear that Jesus did not set out for Nazareth with a desire to oppose them, but rather to bless them through his presence. However, their response to him governed the consequences of their attitudes and behaviour - they did not experience God in a way that had been offered to them. They missed out on the opportunity to know and experience God in greater measure.

They did not experience miracles.

And yet a few sick people were healed. Why were they healed when others weren't, and who were they?

When there is a prevailing culture of conservative belief and resistance to change it has a very powerful and restrictive effect upon the people who exist within that culture. It takes people of courage and fortitude to break through such cultural barriers and embrace new realities. I believe this was the reality in Nazareth - a powerful religious culture, resistant to change. And yet within that context there were a few people courageous enough or desperate enough to overcome such cultural strongholds and seek Jesus, in one sense to push through a hostile crowd and touch him with courageous faith. Their humility was rewarded as the Bible promises in Hebrews 11v6: *"And without faith it is impossible to please God, because anyone who comes to him must believe that he is, and that he rewards those who earnestly seek him."*

This is the opportunity that is open to everyone on Planet earth; to come to God, simply believing that He is the great "I am" with an infinite and eternal nature; to keep moving forward in humility and to continually discover more of Him. Hebrews 12 v 1-2 puts it this way:

Therefore, since we are surrounded by such a great cloud of witnesses, let us throw off everything that hinders and the sin that so easily entangles. And let us run with perseverance the race marked out for us, 2 fixing our eyes on Jesus, the pioneer and perfecter of faith.

In this section of the book we have focussed on throwing off everything that hinders us in our faith. Now it is time to focus on how to continually grow in faith, and how to run the full race marked out for us by fixing our eyes on Jesus, with confidence that He is the pioneer and perfecter of our faith.

Story by Dave Foggon:

A few years ago, one of my good friends got married. He and his new wife came to visit us as she'd not yet met all of the family. As they sat in the lounge, she began to explain how they'd been trying to conceive since they got married but hadn't been able to. She then started to tell us how, the night before they came to us she'd had a dream in which a little boy appeared to her. She described in detail what the boy looked like and his personality and temperament. We said it sounded a lot like our three year-old son, Joel. She told us that the boy in the dream came up to her and said, 'God is going to give you a baby', before praying for her. Right as she was telling us this, Joel woke up from an afternoon nap and walked into the lounge. She looked at him and said, 'That's the boy from my dream!' She had never met him before. A week later, they contacted us to say they were pregnant!

SECTION 3. HOW TO GROW IN FAITH

I find the concept of faith as a continuing journey rather than a series of events a very helpful way of thinking and that has helped in the format of this book.

In Section 1 we sought to understand what faith is.

In Section 2 we looked at things that will oppose us in our faith journey and seek to hinder our progress.

In Section 3 we are going to look at how to Grow in Faith.

It is a very exciting journey, an adventure where you will gain things that money cannot buy and experience things beyond your imagination and even your known desires. So let's start on the next stage of understanding about Faith.

Chapter 18 Where do I start?

When you are planning a journey there are two very important facts that you need to know:

Where am I starting from?
Where am I going?

Without these two facts the journey is likely to be much more complicated than necessary. Having said that, these two facts do not tell us about everything we will encounter upon that journey. For instance, if you are using Google maps or some other reactive GPS system you will be asked for your present location and your destination and a suggested route is given. That route may well be adjusted in response to real time circumstances but always with the aim of getting you to your destination. We are very used to this reality in modern life and I am amazed how often I refer to such technology and trust in its outcomes. I realise I put a lot of trust in Google! This is also a useful framework when it comes to our Christian journey of continually growing in faith. The above questions are important to our faith journey as well. Let's have a look at a Bible passage and study it in order to help us with this:

2 Peter chapter 1:

3 His divine power has given us everything we need for a godly life through our knowledge of him who called us by his own glory and goodness. 4 Through these he has given us his very great and precious promises, so that through them you may participate in the divine nature, having escaped the corruption in the world caused by evil desires.

God has given us everything we need to live a godly life - that is quite a statement. We lack for nothing.

This is true because of our knowledge of him; in other words, we find everything we need through our relationship with God. Our calling is rooted in the glory and goodness of God, so our mission is to make his glory and goodness known to other people. We have received great and precious promises from God and as we pursue them we in some way participate in the divine nature. What is natural for God becomes natural for us, and we become naturally supernatural in our earthly lives.

'We have escaped the corruption of the world' - what does this mean and how do we proceed with our journey? Let's read on:

> *5 For this very reason, make every effort to add to your faith goodness; and to goodness, knowledge; 6 and to knowledge, self-control; and to self-control, perseverance; and to perseverance, godliness; 7 and to godliness, mutual affection; and to mutual affection, love. 8 For if you possess these qualities in increasing measure, they will keep you from being ineffective and unproductive in your knowledge of our Lord Jesus Christ.*

The Christian journey starts when a person receives forgiveness from God for their sin and is born again of the spirit. Prior to that we are *"dead in our transgressions and sins"* (Ephesians 2:1), meaning that we are spiritually separated from God by our sin, and the Bible describes the consequence of that in Romans 3:23 *"All have sinned and fall short of the glory of God."* Our sin causes us to fall short of experiencing the

Glory of God and also to fall short of our glorious divine
calling.

Jesus paid the price for the forgiveness of all our sins
and if we ask God for forgiveness through repentance he will
purify us of all our sin (I John 1:7), restore us to relationship
with him and also restore us to our glorious calling. The word
'purify' means to remove all contamination and corruption.
This forgiveness and repentance is a gift of grace from God,
paid for by Jesus. The Bible also tells us that the faith we need
to respond to God's grace is a gift from himself to awaken
our spirit to the opportunity of eternal life. So our journey
starts with gifts given to us by the grace of God, not by our
own endeavours but by a simple choice to receive the grace
and love of God. We start purified, with a glorious calling and
with great and precious promises.

And then we start walking with the Holy Spirit and
put all our efforts into our calling and growing into his
likeness (partaking in his nature) with ever increasing glory
(2 Corinthians 3:18). What an adventure to embark upon,
and as we move forward we grow by increasing in our godly
characteristics, adding to our faith. This is the journey of
faith.

Are there any obstacles in our way? Let's read on:

9 But whoever does not have them is nearsighted and blind,
forgetting that they have been cleansed from their past sins.

There is a very interesting diagnosis within this verse: if you
are not growing something is wrong. Broadly speaking we can
expect that if something is healthy it will grow, lack of growth
indicates a problem. This verse states that a lack of spiritual
growth can have at its root the issue of forgetting that you
have been forgiven of past sins. If you don't believe you have

been completely forgiven you will keep seeking forgiveness rather than godliness and this will hinder your growth.

Christianity should not be centred around the avoidance of sin and an ongoing search for forgiveness but rather a glorious pursuit of our divine calling. We need to be very clear in our minds that we have already been forgiven. For certain we need to resist temptation that could lead us into committing sin, which by definition is destructive in nature and carries consequences. But please note that temptation is not sin, otherwise Jesus would not have been without sin. If we do sin we have a responsibility to 'clean up our mess' and deal with the consequences, but it does not take away from the fact that once born again you are a new creation with a God given destiny.

Over the years I have noticed that there is some confusion within Christianity about the difference between forgiveness and righteousness, which leads to problems understanding what it means to be clothed in the righteousness of Christ. The righteousness of God is spoken about across both Old and New Testaments, for example Psalm 65:5 says *"You answer us with awesome deeds of righteousness, O God our Saviour"*

An outcome of righteousness is awesome deeds. Forgiveness leads us to being clothed with the righteousness of Christ which means to be clothed in his nature and righteousness is an expression of that nature. Jesus never sinned, he carried our sin and paid the price for it, but Jesus is not a forgiven sinner. Therefore, our identity and our starting point in Christianity is not as a forgiven sinner focussing on what has already been removed from us, but as righteous sons and daughters of a Glorious King who have awesome deeds of righteousness prepared in advance for us to do, firmly rooted in the present and looking to a glorious future. When God looks at us this is how he sees us.

This thought leads us to the last verse we will look at in 2 Peter 1:

> *10 Therefore, my brothers and sisters, make every effort to confirm your calling and election. For if you do these things, you will never stumble, 11 and you will receive a rich welcome into the eternal kingdom of our Lord and Saviour Jesus Christ.*

Bearing in my mind what has been stated in the previous verses, we are urged to live our lives straining forward into our calling and election, expectant that we will be fruitful and play our part in God's unfolding plan for the earth. We are also urged to keep our eyes on our final destination into the eternal kingdom.

To summarise:

> Forgiveness wipes away our past sin.
> We start our born again lives as new creations, righteous and expectant.
> We grow in faith as we journey through our lives being transformed from one degree of glory to another.
> Ultimately we will enter into the full reality of God's eternal kingdom.

This is the mindset we need to start our journey with and build upon adding to our faith in a continual fashion.

Story by Janice Pleasants:
I went into a hardware store. As I walked in I heard 'clip-clop, clip clop', so I turned to look out of the front window for horses but there were none there. I then heard the sound again, but still no horses. I noticed the store was empty, there was just one shop assistant behind the counter and the Holy Spirit said, "It's for her." So I approached her and said, "This may seem strange but do horses have any particular significance for you?" "Yes," she said, "I ride every day and have a horse stabled. Why do you ask?" As she said that I saw a picture in my head of her walking badly. "I'm a Christian practising hearing from God, I also wondered if you had either back or hip pain?" "Yes," she replied, "I put my back out this morning! I'm covering for others who are on sick leave but I'm more sick than they are." I looked around, still no one was in the shop. So I asked if I could pray for her pain to go away. She agreed and I asked if I could hold her hand as she was behind the counter. I prayed and her eyes became like saucers and she rocked on her feet, holding my hand tightly. "Who are you?!" she asked, "I'm just a Christian practising hearing from God,' I replied. "I think it's gone a bit past practising!" she said, "Don't you feel that incredible peace around us? I do yoga and I have never experienced peace like this." "How's your back? I enquired. "Forget about my back that will get better, but this peace is priceless!' I said, "You can ask God for that peace any time, just ask him to make himself real to you today and give you more of His peace and He will." She was still holding tightly to my hand when she said, "I'll do that!" At that point three customers came into the shop and so I let go of her hand. I bought the item I had intended to purchase and left a peaceful lady.

Chapter 19 Continuing the Journey

Having considered our starting point we need to move on and consider our destination, and in order to do that we will look at some more Bible passages. Let's start with:

> *2 Corinthians chapter 10:13 We, however, will not boast beyond proper limits, but will confine our boasting to the sphere (metron) of service God himself has assigned to us, a sphere (metron) that also includes you. 14 We are not going too far in our boasting, as would be the case if we had not come to you, for we did get as far as you with the gospel of Christ. 15 Neither do we go beyond our limits by boasting of work done by others. Our hope is that, as your faith continues to grow, our sphere of activity among you will greatly expand,16 so that we can preach the gospel in the regions beyond you.*

These few verses lead us into a very interesting line of thought: As our faith continues to grow it increases the potential impact of the gospel beyond solely our own reach. To my mind this underlines the importance of "continuing to grow in faith" because the consequences of doing so will extend the kingdom of heaven on earth in ways that go beyond our limits (metrons) and beyond what we can imagine, even extending beyond the limits of this temporary earthly existence.

As we study these few verses it will be helpful if we can gain understanding of the Greek word 'metron' which appears twice in this passage and thirteen times in total in the New Testament. It is translated from Greek into a few different English words including 'sphere', 'measure' or 'portion. 'Also stemming from this is the Greek word 'ametros' which is translated 'without measure.'

Paul is talking about spheres of service that God has allocated to his people, in an individual and also a corporate (local church) sense. These spheres have limits or boundaries in order to help definition and clarity, and they also have a measure allocated to them so that faithful pursuit can have a measure of success resulting in encouragement, delight and joy being taken as we fulfil our calling. They can also give us a destination to aim for and arrive at with great celebration.

It is important to note that these 'limits' are not lifelong limitations but rather lifelong invitations. The Bible teaches a clear principle that if you are faithful with a small thing God will entrust you with greater things. As our faith grows spheres of activity expand around us.

This is a continual reality with an ever upward trajectory and has been my experience throughout my Christian life. When I have been faithful with a small thing with which God has entrusted me, He then opens up larger opportunities of service towards him. In turn as I am faithful with this and get comfortable with a 'measure,' effectively conquering the challenge it represents then it becomes a relatively small thing in terms of ongoing faith and effort. God will then give me an even larger portion of his kingdom advancement to be faithful with.

Our church is an example of this: we started the church in the village where we lived with about 25 adults and 10 children, it was called New Ash Green Community Church. New Ash Green is a large village of about 6,000 people and at that stage a very large proportion were children and teenagers. God put in our hearts a desire to bless our village and for the church to grow and become influential there. It was our 'sphere' and we decided to 'dream big' with the idea of a church numbering 200 people and having social influence. We had our Sunday meetings in the village youth and community centre. For Kim and I this mission started with our immediate neighbours and other friends; we found that indeed the harvest is plentiful.

We grew slowly and steadily, placing major emphasis upon our children (we had no teenagers in the church at that stage). Before long we were a church with 40 adults and 40 children. In response to a request from the village for help we took over the management of the Mother and Toddler group which we then ran for about 20 years helping to establish other such groups in our village and surrounding villages.

The church outgrew its Sunday premises and we started to meet in school premises within the village which enabled further growth until we had about 100 adults and 100 children as part of our church community. We also started to rent office space to give us a base to work from. We were asked by the Village Association to regenerate the whole social life of the village which we did successfully by building a new vision and organisational structure.

At this point people from surrounding villages started to be attracted to us and become part of the church, and they wanted an expression of the church in their own villages. Also we had outgrown our Sunday venue once again.

Had we reached 'our limit'? Had we fulfilled that part of our faith journey? Did God want to increase our sphere of influence?

We thought and prayed about it a lot and concluded that God was moving us on from the idea of reaching one village to the idea of reaching a whole rural area with expressions of the church in at least seven different villages. Quite a jump forward. Also we needed to move our Sunday meeting to a larger school which was situated in a village 3 miles away. This would give us room for further growth well into the future. However, it would break many of us out of our comfort zones - we were used to walking to church on a Sunday with little need for cars because we were all so close together. We were used to knowing each other extremely well, bumping into each other at the shops or on the school playground. We would also need to change the name of the church.

We became North Kent Community Church designating our new 'metron', no longer just influencing one village but rather affecting a larger area. Would we prove ourselves faithful once again?

The church grew and was expressed across our designated rural area, with activities going on in seven different villages. A youth group developed alongside our children's work, at its height our youth group numbered seventy 11-18 year olds, and we did a lot of work amongst teenagers across the area especially in New Ash Green. Our influence also spread beyond that as we were asked to teach and help other churches across the UK and other nations the 'secrets of our success.' However, we were not convinced that we had any secrets, rather simple Biblical principles that we lived by in the power of the Holy Spirit.

During this time, we arrived at the conclusion that a church building of our own would be not only desirable but also help us to fulfil our God given mission. So we started a building fund and the congregation gave approximately £100,000 each year towards this common dream, in addition to the usual regular church income. We looked at various options and eventually came up with an ambitious plan to build something as part of the redevelopment of the school premises where we met on a Sunday. I have already told this story in some detail in a previous chapter but I need to pull out a few other relevant points in the context of this chapter.

When we received the prophecy that God would place us at "The. Eastgate to the City" a question dawned in my mind, had we reached our limit once again? Had we fulfilled our metron?

We discussed this amongst the leadership team and with the congregation. We felt very strongly that God had spoken clearly to us and we needed to obey Him. God wanted to move us on from our rural calling into an urban one (we had previously resisted all attempts and encouragements by other people to send us in that direction because we were certain about our calling). It would be a massive change and the cost would be high.

About eight miles north of us just south of the River Thames was a large area of housing development and within that context was the requirement for the house builders to set aside land for community and worship use. We submitted an application and were asked to move forward in that process, needing to put forward a comprehensive business plan including ideas of the design and use of the building. We asked to put the worship and community facilities together as one building as that had always been the way we worked - a worshipping community amongst the community. Our bid was accepted by Land Securities and Countryside builders and the Director in charge of the project, Steve Atkins, told me afterwards that a couple of the reasons we were chosen was our track record of community development in different areas, and the fact that we had £500,000 in the bank demonstrating our commitment to the project.

So we moved forward taking our congregation into a completely new context - into our new metron. God had found us faithful with our previous calling and now he was expanding us once again and we had a lot to learn. It was a long journey towards the construction of our building amongst the new housing development which was part of the Thames Gateway Project, the largest building development in Northern Europe. We were pinching ourselves - we started with a few people in a village largely unknown to anybody and relatively inaccessible, now we were at the heart of this massive endeavour not far from the city of London with responsibility for helping to create community across the whole area.

Three months after we started to use our building the area of development that we were part of was re-designated by the central government - it became Ebbsfleet Garden City, the first new garden city to be created in the UK for about 100 years.

Where was our building situated in this city? At the eastern edge. God had quite literally placed us at the "Eastgate to the city" fulfilling the prophecy given to us many years previously when there were no plans for a new city except in the mind of God.

How did we get here? Faithfulness to your current calling and metron will lead to God enlarging your sphere of influence as your faith continues to grow through new challenges. In Acts 1:7 Jesus promised his disciples that *"you will receive power when the Holy Spirit comes on you; and you will be my witnesses in Jerusalem, and in all Judea and Samaria, and to the ends of the earth."*

What next for us? Quite literally 'God knows' and we trust and follow Him in the power of the Holy Spirit "to the ends of the earth". But is that the final destination?
Another Bible passage that is very helpful in this whole context is Ephesians chapter 4:

> *7 But to each one of us grace has been given as Christ apportioned it.*

Jesus apportions parts of his work on earth to each one of us:
in other words, each of us has a portion to contribute in the
completion of the whole picture.

> *8 This is why it says: "When he ascended on high, he took many
> captives and gave gifts to his people."*

Every one of us has been given gifts to help us fulfil our calling.

> *9 What does "he ascended" mean except that he also descended
> to the lower, earthly regions? 10 He who descended is the very one
> who ascended higher than all the heavens, in order to fill the whole
> universe.*

Jesus' metron is the whole universe which he intends to fill
with his glory and goodness. This is his divine purpose.

> *11 So Christ himself gave the apostles, the prophets, the evangelists,
> the pastors and teachers, 12 to equip his people for works of service,
> so that the body of Christ may be built up 13 until we all reach
> unity in the faith and in the knowledge of the Son of God and
> become mature, attaining to the whole measure of the fullness of
> Christ.*

In order to fulfil his calling Jesus has equipped his people with
different gifts which have the purpose of equipping people to
fulfil their metron/portion and in this way we can attain to
unity in the faith and attain the whole measure (metron) of
the fullness of Christ.

> *14 Then we will no longer be infants, tossed back and forth by the
> waves, and blown here and there by every wind of teaching and
> by the cunning and craftiness of people in their deceitful scheming.*

15 Instead, speaking the truth in love, we will grow to become in every respect the mature body of him who is the head, that is, Christ. 16 From him the whole body, joined and held together by every supporting ligament, grows and builds itself up in love, as each part does its work.

We will continue to grow in faith and love until the fully mature body of Christ is formed as each part does its work and is joined to the other parts of the body.

That is our ultimate destination - it extends beyond this worldly existence into the Universe and Eternity.

To quote a well-known character - "To infinity and beyond."

Story by Pete Carter:

A team from another church who wanted to advance in the realm of healing had asked us if they could come to the Eastgate Healing Centre to be trained by our people. One of their team was an elderly lady with hearing loss requiring hearing aids in both ears. She had travelled in the back seat of a car on busy roads to Eastgate and had trouble following any conversation in that noisy environment.

In order to understand the training we suggested that each member of their team go through the process of a normal visit to the Healing Centre with regard to healing for themselves or someone else who was on their mind. This lady wanted her hearing restored.

Along with the others she entered into the atmosphere of love, joy, peace, hope, faith and power that we deliberately create at the Healing Centre. She rested in that atmosphere for a while and then Helen and another member of our team approached her to release healing to her. Having identified the issue of hearing loss Helen suggested that the lady might like to remove her hearing aids so that she could sense if any improvement was happening. The lady did this and Helen instructed her to "keep the hearing aids in a safe place" (Helen recounted this to me later telling me that it hadn't been a great statement of faith!)

"OK" the lady replied. Then a look of surprise and realisation hit her; she had just heard Helen perfectly without her hearing aids. She put her hearing aids away in a bag not needing them in her ears.

A few days later I saw her at the Eastgate School of Spiritual Life and she was delighted to tell me that she didn't need her hearing aids, that she had heard every bit of conversation from the back seat during the car journey home, and that she had noticed her hearing continually improving.

Chapter 20 A Blind Lady in Brazil

This is a favourite story of mine and demonstrates part of my own personal story of continuing to grow in faith.

A shout of joy erupted from the back of the large room and attracted my attention. A lady had prayed for her friend and the result was great joy and wonder. It was October 2011. These two ladies had come to our annual Healing School very much in hope of a miracle and they didn't have to wait long. Towards the end of the first session everybody was encouraged to lay hands on people who wanted prayer for healing and to put into practice the teaching that all Christians can bring healing to other people.

One of these two ladies had a secondary malignant tumour behind one of her eyes causing that eye to be blind; her friend placed a hand gently on her and prayed in the name of Jesus. The sight in the affected eye was immediately restored and thus came the shouts of joy, which spread throughout the whole room as people became aware of what had just happened amongst them.

I was overjoyed, these ladies had reached out in faith to touch Jesus and had received a miracle. Many more miracles happened that day such as deafness disappearing, knees being healed and back pain being relieved. It was a great day.

I talked with the lady whose sight had been restored, and I was rejoicing with her. For many years I had been hoping and waiting for blindness to be affected by the power of Jesus in a place where I was present to witness it. And yet a part of me was provoked in a way that made me want to see it happen again, only this time as I prayed for the person.

I remembered the time in 2009 that I was in Wisconsin at another healing conference hosted by a church. It is the story I related fully in chapter 1 of this book: the lady, who had been profoundly deaf since birth. As I reflected on that memory, a memory money simply could not buy, I remembered the picture of this lady's joyful face now indelibly etched upon my mind, and I realised once again that faith can produce joy beyond comparison.

My mind turned back to the affliction of blindness and I asked God to give me the privilege of seeing the joy on someone's face as their sight was restored right in front of my own eyes. I came to the conclusion that this was definitely one of my life's dreams.

About that time that I was also grappling in my head with some Bible verses.

John chapter 14 verses 12-14.

12 I tell you the truth, anyone who has faith in me will do what I have been doing. He will do even greater things than these, because I am going to the Father. 13 And I will do whatever you ask in my name, so that the Son may bring glory to the Father. 14 You may ask me for anything in my name, and I will do it.

I had come to terms with verse 12, anyone who has faith in Jesus can do the works of Jesus and even greater things. Faith in Jesus is a powerful and remarkable thing. However, verses 13 and 14 were still stretching my thinking - " whatever you ask", "you may ask me for anything" are words that I was finding difficult to fully comprehend and believe. Don't get me wrong I believe the Bible is true, but was it a truthful reality in my own life? I came to the conclusion that I needed to continue growing in faith and to literally 'step out in faith.'

I had organised for myself to go on a mission trip to Brazil at the beginning of December that year as part of a team with Randy Clark, who is a man of great faith and compassion, and sees many miracles of healing on a regular basis. A friend had recommended that these trips were a great opportunity to grow in faith in the realm of healing. I was expectant and in my preparation I prayed in general terms that many people would receive healing and that God would use me and the rest of the team in the process. However, there was one thing that I really wanted more than anything else, and that was to see a blind person's sight restored as I prayed for them. I decided to ask God specifically for what I wanted.

The journey to Brazil from the UK was long and somewhat tiring, and I was glad that our first evening was scheduled for rest and relaxation in order to be ready for what was a full schedule of meetings for 6 days. We got to our hotel and it was announced that we had half an hour to get ready because an extra meeting had been arranged for that evening. We set off through the streets of Rio de Janeiro trying to take in the sights of the city through our coach windows. Eventually we got to the church building and Randy gave us some teaching about Healing and receiving 'Words of Knowledge' from God with regard to healing, (these are messages that God gives to people to help others understand that God knows about them personally; and also to increase faith in Him). Then he prayed for the whole team to receive more of the power of the Holy Spirit. Fortified by this, but still somewhat tired from the journey, I took myself into the meeting hall with the rest of the team. The place was packed with people of all ages, hundreds of them. The worship started and the congregation lifted their voices in praise to God. It was wonderful to join with people from a different nation in worship for a length of time. Then Randy Clark did some teaching about Healing, instructing people that Jesus loves to heal the sick, giving testimonies of actual healings, and then starting to give words of knowledge and seeing people instantly getting healed. Miracles were definitely happening and joy was breaking out. Then it was the turn of the team! There were about 40 of us, and we were invited to the front of the hall and asked to each give one word of knowledge as the microphone was placed in front of us.

Words of knowledge with regard to healing were not new to me, in fact I had been experiencing them for more than twenty years. I say experiencing, as the most prominent way that God speaks to me with regard to healing is by giving me a sensation (often painful) in a relevant part of my body indicating that I will encounter someone with such a problem within a short space of time. I first experienced these sensations during worship at the Sunday morning meetings of our church at that time. I did not recognise that God was speaking to me, instead I thought it was a distraction from worship either due to some physical affliction or to spiritual attack by a demon. So I ignored the distraction and rebuked the demon - the pains, however, continued to come each Sunday morning. I was a bit confused but determined to press through in worshipping God despite such distractions. The pains would disappear as soon as the worship times were finished, I was thankful for that. This continued to happen for about two years, and then a friend of mine went to a training conference with regard to healing and was taught that God sometimes speaks through sensations, sometimes painful, in people's bodies. Realisation occurred! And did I feel foolish! God had been speaking to me all that time, but I had not recognised his voice. Armed with this new information I started to share in our meetings the things that God showed me and more healings started to happen. I started to ask for more words of knowledge, even asking in advance and noting down what God had told me. This became a normal part of my Christian life.

Back in the meeting in Brazil, I was experiencing many different sensations in my body as God indicated different illnesses to me, but the one thing I wanted most of all He was not talking to me about. I wanted to see a blind person see. The microphone was moving along the line and approaching me; which word of knowledge would I choose? But I really wanted to pray for blind people, could I really ask God for this and expect him to do 'whatever I asked?' We had clear instructions to bring a word of knowledge, but in my mind I wondered if I could 'cheat' and say 'blindness' even though God hadn't spoken to me specifically about that. My brain was trying to process this as the microphone drew nearer. Suddenly it was in front of me and I heard the word 'blindness' exit from my mouth. 'Now you've done it!' I thought to myself. I guessed (and hoped in a strange way) that there would be some blind people in a crowd of such a size and I asked God to restore their sight. As I looked out into the mass of people I saw an elderly lady who clearly had one opaque eye - my heart went out to her and I asked God to heal her. She was seated about eight rows back and some way across to the left of my position. The microphone finished its course along the row of the team members and Randy Clark invited the congregation to come forward to receive prayer. It was pandemonium as people rushed forward. I dropped my head to pray and prepare myself, closing my eyes as I did so, asking God for his power and compassion. The elderly lady was in my mind and I hoped she would receive her miracle. I opened my eyes and lifted my head to see who was the first in line for me to pray with. To say I was astonished would be a severe understatement - standing right in front of me was the elderly lady with her opaque eye. 'How did you get to the front of the queue?' was a thought that immediately came to mind, surely that must be a miracle in itself in this mass of humanity. We looked at each other; hope seemed to come out of her one clear eye and I was encouraged. The other eye, however, was completely opaque. She was sightless in that eye. I have learned over the years that there is no formula for healing, no correct words, no correct process, no 'how to manual'. Healing happens because God loves people, and when we act in true faith in Jesus and reach out with compassion. As I stood before this dear lady, who must have been at least eighty years old, I was humbled that she was trusting me to enable her to connect with Jesus and that He would heal her. My heart went out to her. No words came to mind, so I started to pray softly in tongues, very little noise exiting from my lips. I placed a hand gently on her shoulder and simply asked Father God to touch her. I looked into her opaque eye and started to rejoice inwardly at the power and love of God. The opacity started to clear, the whiteness covering the entire front of her eye started to recede, and within two minutes her eye was completely restored to normal. She smiled. We hugged. Her daughters who were with her started to cry with joy and excitement. To say I was delighted would be an understatement - I will forever remember that moment when faith brought me something money cannot buy. I wanted to stay in the moment but the huge crowd expecting prayer became the priority. All too quickly for me this dear lady slipped into the crowd with her daughters and was lost to my sight. However, her sight was now restored. The meeting continued for a long time as we prayed for many people and saw God do amazing things. We made the journey back to our hotel and very, very tired I slipped into bed. As I was falling asleep a thought came into my mind - had I really experienced what I thought? Had I actually seen a blind eye healed before my own eyes?

The next morning the thought came back to me; knowing that the devil is a thief who would tempt me to disbelieve and thus rob me of joy and faith, I decided that I would reject the doubt and continue to believe in Jesus' love and power. Two evenings later, we were back in the same venue with crowds of people once again attending and the format was pretty much the same. Many people got healed and experienced the love and power of God. I was praying for many people and as the crowd started to thin out a lady who I did not recognise approached me with a broad smile on her face. She came close and engulfed me in an embrace as she burst into tears, saying words in Portuguese that I could not understand. She seemed ecstatic. As she let go of me another lady came through the crowd, an older lady, her eyes gleaming brightly, and I suddenly knew this was the lady who was previously blind and the younger lady was her daughter. Her face was radiant, she approached me, placed her hands on my face and kissed me on the cheek. She smiled at me and started to cry. My eyes began to moisten as well as I enjoyed the moment of celebration with this lady and her family who explained through translation that the miracle of restored sight had completely changed their lives and their experience and knowledge of God. I looked again into those two sparkling eyes and marvelled that God responded to my desires as well as to the cry of need from a family who called on the name of Jesus.

My faith continued to grow.

Story. By Dave Foggon:

I remember once being crammed into a small living room for a house church that I had been invited to speak at. After the meeting started, I felt prompted to share some testimonies and to call out some words of knowledge for healings. As I did this, a curious thing began to happen.

Multiple conditions and types of pain were revealed in that room but nobody was responding. We asked why no one needed prayer and the men and women began to reply. They said that no one had responded because they'd all been healed when we walked into the room. All kinds of pain had been either completely healed or partially healed by the presence of God at the moment we arrived for the meeting! It was astounding!

I noticed a man at the far end of the room who had been quietly enjoying the meeting without really saying a word. I asked if he needed healing of any kind to which he replied, "No." He then revealed that that very night he had been healed of the effects of a brain aneurysm as we walked past him at the beginning of the meeting. For years he'd been unable to sit upright in a chair for more than two minutes without falling onto the floor. As we arrived for the meeting, the presence of God healed him and he sat perfectly normally for the entire two-hour meeting! This suggested that God had done a creative miracle to restore parts of his brain that had previously died from the aneurysm. At the end of the meeting he had his photo taken with us to remember this momentous day in his life.

Chapter 21 The Faith Triangle: an Important Key

In 1997 something strange started to happen to me, it was disturbing and confusing. Generally speaking, I like to think of myself as easy going and not easily angered, enjoying peace of mind as a lifestyle and having an optimistic outlook. So it came as a surprise to me when I found myself unusually disturbed by a certain phrase whenever I heard it used. The phrase was "I haven't got faith for …" Somehow this phrase, used in any context, caused a reaction inside me that irritated me to such an extent that it bordered on anger. I wasn't sure what was going on inside me, but such negative feelings were not welcome. I talked with God about it, repented of any judgemental attitude and asked God to help me change. But it continued. I really was perplexed and kept on going to God for answers.

However, rather than improve, matters got worse: in addition to the one phrase annoying me another one started to do so, and this was even more confusing. When I heard the phrase "I have faith for..." I found myself equally irritated. I was put out that somehow I was negatively responding to a seemingly positive statement, something highly unusual for me as I choose to take great delight in other people's exploits of faith.

These two statements were seemingly opposite to each other and yet they invoked the same reaction inside me. I hadn't talked to anyone but God about this, uncertain of what to say as I was struggling for understanding.

This carried on for a couple of months and at the end of that time I set off for a two week working trip to India. The first week was to look at medical relief work in Mumbai and Nassik, the second week to spend teaching ethics at a Bible School. During this second week I found that I had quite a lot of spare time and there was a good library available so I decided to do a Bible study on the subject of faith with particular reference to the phrase "Faith for". I got out a large Bible concordance and then over the course of a few days looked up every verse in the Bible that contained the word "Faith" (there are a lot of them!)

As I worked my way through the Bible I noted that the phrase "faith for" could not be found, indeed the words only appeared next to each other once in the Bible and even then were separated by a comma.

Something was becoming clearer in my mind - "Faith for" is not a Biblical concept.

Instead my studying revealed a different concept; the Bible teaches the concept of "Faith in God".

Let me illustrate this from a few Bible verses amongst the many.

2 Chronicles 2 v 20: Have faith in the Lord your God and you will be upheld; have faith in his prophets and you will be successful.

Mark 11 v 22: "Have faith in God," Jesus answered.

Acts 3 v 16: By faith in the name of Jesus, this man whom you see and know was made strong. It is Jesus' name and the faith that comes through him that has completely healed him, as you can all see.

Acts 24 v 24: Several days later Felix came with his wife Drusilla, who was Jewish. He sent for Paul and listened to him as he spoke about faith in Christ Jesus.

Acts 27 v 25: So keep up your courage, men, for I have faith in God that it will happen just as he told me.

Romans 3 v 22: This righteousness is given through faith in Jesus Christ to all who believe. There is no difference between Jew and Gentile.

Galatians 2 v 20: I have been crucified with Christ and I no longer live, but Christ lives in me. The life I now live in the body, I live by faith in the Son of God, who loved me and gave himself for me.

Ephesians 1 v 15&16: For this reason, ever since I heard about your faith in the Lord Jesus and your love for all God's people, I have not stopped giving thanks for you, remembering you in my prayers.

1 Thessalonians 1 v 8: The Lord's message rang out from you not only in Macedonia and Achaia—your faith in God has become known everywhere. Therefore we do not need to say anything about it.

Hebrews 6 v 1&2: Therefore let us move beyond the elementary teachings about Christ and be taken forward to maturity, not laying again the foundation of repentance from acts that lead to death, [and of faith in God, instruction about cleansing rites, the laying on of hands, the resurrection of the dead, and eternal judgment.

- Having faith in God is the basic instruction of Christianity, indeed it is the essence of the Christian gospel.
- Faith in God leads to standing in the righteousness of God.
- Faith in God will lead to a supernatural lifestyle accessing the power of God.

- Faith in God gives us courage for the future.
- Faith in God defines a Christian lifestyle.
- Faith in God will ring out loud and clear, proclaiming Jesus to the nations.
- Faith in God is one of the foundation stones upon which the whole of Christianity is built.

Having gained this level of understanding, I came to realise that God had been speaking to me for months on this subject. He had got my attention through unusual means and I came to realise the source of my irritation was rooted in an incorrect concept very prevalent in Christianity. As this happened, my irritation ceased and instead a new determination started to grow in me to teach about faith in a more effective way than I had done before. Also came an acceptance that people's form of words do not always express precisely their thoughts or motivations. My job is not to judge people's language but help them to grow their Faith in God.

As I continued to speak to God about all this, he inserted another thought in my mind, a way to express what I had discovered. A tool that he gave to me. Wisdom given from heaven to someone who asked for it.

It is a tool that I have used at home and in many nations, it is very simple but profound and I continue to receive good feedback about it. I would like to share it with you, I call it the "Triangle of Faith."

Let me ask you to start using this tool by bringing to mind a circumstance that you would like to see change or develop, it can be any circumstance, a problem that you are facing, an illness to be countered, a dream to be pursued, a disappointment to be overcome, anything you like.

We are going to place this at the bottom right of the triangle:

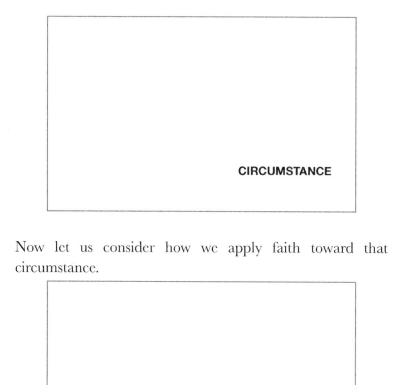

Now let us consider how we apply faith toward that circumstance.

How does your faith interact with this circumstance? Imagine drawing a line between the two words.

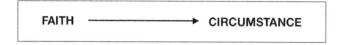

Then let's consider the concept of "not having faith for ...."

I don't have faith for this ——————> *circumstance*

The circumstance is bigger than the faith and nothing changes. Sometimes when this is happening we try to "stare down" the problem, making the circumstance in question the focus of our thoughts, efforts and beliefs. We can try harder to solve the problem, thinking that is a demonstration of faith, and question why God is not answering us.

Now let's consider the concept of "I do have faith for …."

I do have faith for this ——————> *circumstance*

This looks on the surface like a very positive statement, which is why I was so confused. But let me ask you a question; is anything missing in the diagram?

On its own this statement does not give any information about in whom or in what faith is placed in regard to this circumstance. It could be faith in our own ability or in another person's ability, it could be sheer optimism without any great basis or reason, it could be all manner of things.

Overall the statement lacks specificity, or in other words which specific thing or things lead to our confidence regarding the situation.

As we have discussed earlier, Christian faith is "faith in God", our confidence should stem from the very nature of God. So the answer in my mind is that the presence of God is absent in the diagram, and without God our own efforts cannot move spiritual mountains.

However, what happens when we put God in the picture?

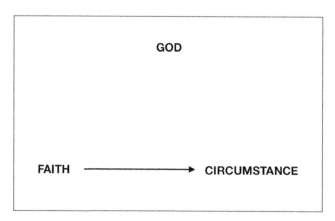

All of a sudden there is a different perspective that comes into play. How does God view this circumstance?

We can now start to think about how God would interact with the circumstance.

> Does He have sufficient resources?
> Is he disinterested or is He willing to intervene?
> What about his promises?
> What does the Bible say?

Suddenly our questions can be about God rather than the circumstance.

> What happens if we seek Him, will we find an answer?
> What happens if we ask, will we receive?

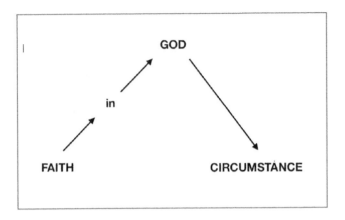

What happens if we knock, will the door be opened to us?

Now we are starting to exercise "Faith in God".

Broadly speaking Christians believe that "Nothing is impossible with God" so once we put God in the picture, the possibilities change. The resources of heaven can be poured out upon any circumstance so that the will of God can be done on earth as it is in heaven.

Faith in God releases the resources of Heaven

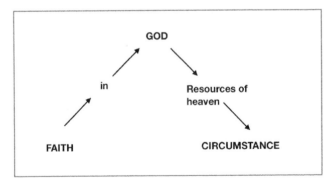

There is another important question to ask, "Why doesn't

God just do it?" He has all the resources available, why doesn't he intervene without involving us?

The Bible tells an overall story of God who has entrusted human beings with the responsibility of "ruling upon the earth" with Himself walking alongside in friendship and availability.

He is not a cosmic dictator simply enacting His will without any reference to mankind.

Also, His plan has never been for human beings to live on the earth without connection to Him, in fact if they try to do so the consequences will be ungodly.

God wants connection with us and for us to connect with Him, then his Godly rule can be exercised through us. That connection is called FAITH IN GOD.

So let's add that to the diagram.

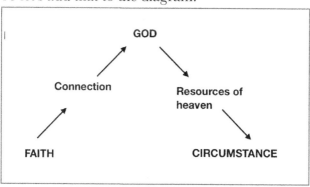

God has designed the world so that human beings can exist on the earth and rule over it, but always in connection with Him. There is no circumstance that will take him by surprise or for which he has no power or answer.

Faith in God is the connection between man and God that releases the resources of heaven upon any circumstance.

Let's look at a helpful Bible verse:

Hebrews 11 v 6: And without faith it is impossible to please God, because anyone who comes to him must believe that he is and that he rewards those who earnestly seek him.

- *"Without faith it is impossible to please God"*: God does not like to do anything without connection.
- *"because anyone who comes to him"*: God wants us to come to Him.
- *"must believe that He is"*: Belief about who God is, this is an essential key to faith.
- *"and that he rewards those who earnestly seek him."* God will reward those who connect with who He is.

This idea of "God is ...." requires explanation. Some Bible translations use the phrase "Must believe that He exists", but I don't find this very helpful as the logic in my brain tells me that I wouldn't come to Him if I didn't believe that He existed in the first place. So I looked up the Greek words and they are best translated as "God is"; in itself this is a very incomplete statement begging the question "What is He?"

However, the better question to ask is "Who is He?"

It reminds me of the story of Moses encountering God at the burning bush on Mount Horeb; during this encounter Moses asked God to let him know His name and God replied, "I Am who I Am"

This is a very strange answer.

Imagine if you met me for the first time, asked me about myself and I replied "I am" and went no further. You would know very little about me! However, if I were to say, "I am a doctor, I am married to Kim," you would start to build up a picture of me. If I add that "I am a father to two children and also a grandfather, I am a church leader and an author, I am keen on sports and I am a citizen of the United Kingdom" you would build up a fuller picture of me and interact with me accordingly. Yet you still wouldn't know me fully.

God is infinite and eternal and the fact that His name is "I am" is an invitation into an infinite and eternal discovery of the nature of God. No list of names can define God entirely. In fact, if God had defined Himself in any other way than "I am" He would have limited our expectations of Him.

He is whatever you need and all you need in order to meet any circumstance or opportunity you will ever face. Faith is the discovery of the very nature of God, and connecting to Him in such a way that more and more aspects of His nature are made real in and through our own lives.

- If there is a need for comfort - He is the Comforter
- If there is a need for healing - He is the Healer
- If there is a need for peace - He is the Prince of Peace
- If there is a need for provision - He is the Provider
- If I want to know the truth - He is the Truth
- If I want to know the way - He is the Way

We could carry on and on.

Christian faith looks like connecting to God and releasing the reality of his nature on the earth. There are no limits to the nature of God, therefore there are no limits on the growth potential of our faith.

This means that anyone can keep on growing in faith, and there is no problem admitting to a desire to grow in faith, in fact that is the very substance of Christianity.

I like the expression of the man in the Bible who said to Jesus, *"I do believe, help me overcome my unbelief."* (Mark 9 v 24). I think that is a very honest statement and brilliant request. All Christians have a mixture of belief and unbelief; some aspects of our faith are strong and it is good to recognise this; in some areas unbelief is a challenge to us, the solution is to connect with God so that He can help us overcome our unbelief by increasing our knowledge and experience of Him.

The Bible says that you only need faith as small as a mustard seed to move mountains, that is because a small amount of faith is sufficient to connect you to God who has all the power needed to move any mountain. Focussing on a mountain won't move it, indeed it might grow larger in your perspective and seem even more daunting. Focussing on God puts the mountain in its proper Christian perspective.

Faith focuses on God rather than the mountain.

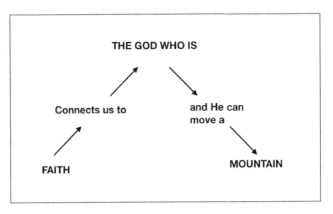

The outcome of this is not only that one mountain gets moved but also that our confidence/faith in God grows in a positive feedback mechanism so that any mountain comes within our grasp. Instead of the circumstance being a hindrance to our faith, it can become a conquered mountain that can help us look at other mountains with increased faith.

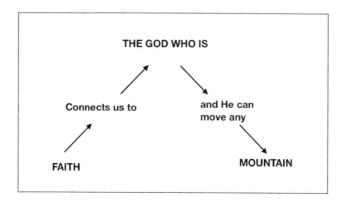

As our faith continues to grow through increased connection with God and increased confidence in Him, as we believe that God can do anything, and as we see the results of such faith then we will grow nearer to the Biblical truth:

> *Mark 9: 23 But Jesus said to him, "'If You can?' All things are possible for the one who believes."*

So let's press on in our journey and learn how to grow in faith.

Story by Janice Pleasants:

I felt the Holy Spirit highlight a homeless man to me and tell me to give him money for a hot meal. Before I could say what the money was for, he said, "Great! Now I can get a hot meal!" I felt prompted to ask if he had pain in his body as he was sitting on his case looking really miserable and supporting his shoulder with his other arm. He said that he'd been in a fight with two men in the night who had tried to steal his suitcase, in the ensuing struggle he had dislocated his shoulder. He was new to the area and didn't know what to do, he didn't know how to get to the hospital and didn't have any money to get a bus there. I said I was a Christian and could pray for him to be healed. I said, "Before we do anything else, why don't we see what Jesus does for you?" He agreed that would be okay and stood up with his eyes closed. Pete Carter at ESSL had taught us that week not to make assumptions before praying for healing but to pause and ask the Holy Spirit what to pray. So, I paused, became aware of God in me and simply stretched out my arm and said, "Jesus" (prior to speaking out what I thought would be a proclamation or prayer). I didn't touch the man. Before I could say anything else he jumped back and said, "What the **** did you just do?!" I said, "I didn't do anything" and he replied, "But no, I felt a hand manipulate my shoulder." In seconds his shoulder was back in place and the pain had completely gone! He laughed out loud, kissed my hand and did a jig around me, oblivious in his joy of what any passers-by thought of his celebration. He thanked God and went off pulling his case with his previously bad arm to go and get a hot meal, still laughing in amazement.

Chapter 22: Encountering God

Following on from the previous chapter I want to talk some more about encountering God. How can we meet him in his glory and majesty so that we get to know him more?

One of the ways I use in my pursuit of God is reading the Bible: I find it helps to stimulate me in various aspects of my life, and in particular there are certain Bible passages that I turn to more regularly than others to help me in my patterns of prayer: I literally pray my way through these passages as I read them, focussing on the different aspects of Christianity that are mentioned. Here are a couple of examples of such passages.

> *Colossians 1: 9 For this reason, since the day we heard about you, we have not stopped praying for you. We continually ask God to fill you with the knowledge of his will through all the wisdom and understanding that the Spirit gives, 10 so that you may live a life worthy of the Lord and please him in every way: bearing fruit in every good work, growing in the knowledge of God, 11 being strengthened with all power according to his glorious might so that you may have great endurance and patience, 12 and giving joyful thanks to the Father, who has qualified you to share in the inheritance of his holy people in the kingdom of light. 13 For he has rescued us from the dominion of darkness and brought us into the kingdom of the Son he loves, 14 in whom we have redemption, the forgiveness of sins.*

> *Ephesians 1: 15 For this reason, ever since I heard about your faith in the Lord Jesus and your love for all God's people, 16 I have not*

stopped giving thanks for you, remembering you in my prayers. 17 I keep asking that the God of our Lord Jesus Christ, the glorious Father, may give you the Spirit of wisdom and revelation, so that you may know him better. 18 I pray that the eyes of your heart may be enlightened in order that you may know the hope to which he has called you, the riches of his glorious inheritance in his holy people, 19 and his incomparably great power for us who believe. That power is the same as the mighty strength 20 he exerted when he raised Christ from the dead and seated him at his right hand in the heavenly realms, 21 far above all rule and authority, power and dominion, and every name that is invoked, not only in the present age but also in the one to come. 22 And God placed all things under his feet and appointed him to be head over everything for the church, 23 which is his body, the fullness of him who fills everything in every way.

In both passages the concept of continuing to pray so that we get to know God better is very clear. I personally encounter God as I pray this way and he reveals more of Himself to me. He gives me the Spirit of wisdom and revelation in increasing measure and his wisdom enables me to know how to apply such revelation in my life. As we continue in this book we will look into various different ways of encountering God in order to help us in our journey of faith.

Two key biblical principles appear at the top of my list

1) Faith in God rests on experiencing the love and power of God:

1 Corinthians 2: And so it was with me, brothers and sisters. When I came to you, I did not come with eloquence or human wisdom as I proclaimed to you the testimony about God. For I resolved to know nothing while I was with you except Jesus Christ and him crucified. I came to you in weakness with great fear and trembling. My message and my preaching were not with wise and persuasive words, but with a demonstration of the Spirit's power, so that your faith might not rest on human wisdom, but on God's power.

2) Faith rests on hearing the voice of God:

Romans 10:17 So faith comes by hearing, and hearing by the word of God.

Generally speaking, I have found that these two principles are keys to unlocking most of the other ways of increasing in faith. In this chapter we will look at experiencing the power and love of God. In the next chapter we will consider hearing from God and then we will build upon these two principles.

Faith in God rests on experiencing the power of God which will lead us further in our understanding of the love of God.

In 1 Corinthians 2 verse 4 - 5 Paul makes a very interesting statement about his thoughts in conveying the message of Jesus Christ and he chose this outcome as a priority *"so that your faith might not rest on human wisdom but on God's power."*

The historical context for this Bible passage is Acts chapters 17 & 18. Immediately before Paul visited Corinth for the first time he was in Athens and the Bible relates how he debated with the Epicurean and Stoic philosophers in the city even quoting their own poets. At the end of his time there the outcome was that a few people became "followers", which is a direct contrast to the "many who responded" in Thessalonica and Berea.

The account of Paul's visit to Corinth in Acts doesn't give great detail about Paul's methods and priorities in preaching there, however, the passage in 1 Corinthians suggests that he had reflected upon his experience in Athens' relying primarily upon "human wisdom" and resolved that preaching without a demonstration of God's power was comparatively unsuccessful.

I also find Acts 14: 3 very helpful in understanding this: *"So Paul and Barnabas spent considerable time there, speaking boldly for the Lord, who confirmed the message of his grace by enabling them to perform signs and wonders."*

If we take Jesus as our prime model of how to share the good news of the kingdom of heaven we can easily see that healing, the release of people from demonic oppression, words of knowledge and insight such as with the Samaritan woman in John chapter 4, miracles such as the feeding of the 5000, and power over storms were all part of the message. In the book of Acts, we read how the disciples followed this model as evidenced by the healings that accompanied Peter, bringing the dead back to life, angelic deliverance from prison, Philip in Samaria, Paul in Iconium, Lystra and other places.

God loves to confirm the glorious gospel of Jesus Christ by demonstrating his power through his people and it is fair to conclude that preaching and debate without a demonstration of God's power is less likely to be successful, indeed it is not following the most obvious Biblical model given to us. More than that, if we look at the story of the conversion of Cornelius and his household in Acts chapter 10, God is so keen to demonstrate his love and power to these Gentiles that He does not even wait for Peter to finish preaching before pouring out the Holy Spirit on them.

God loves all people and He wants them to know him in all his fullness, not just about him as a theory or intellectual process.

Jesus was a living experience of God on planet earth and

the Holy Spirit now invites people into that same experience.

When I was about 15 I became intrigued about the possibility of the existence of God, it wasn't an overwhelming thought in my mind but rather a small spark. I started to read a few books recommended to me by my sister, who had "somehow got God!" which was my explanation for the dramatic change in her life. I was intrigued on an intellectual level but with no intention of 'getting God' for myself. I read The Cross and the Switchblade, Run Baby Run and Chasing the Dragon all of which I enjoyed, but Christianity seemed to have little relevance or appeal to me even though I sometimes enjoyed the debate going on in my mind.

During this time, I would sometimes visit my sister at university for weekends and I was impressed by her group of Christian friends, the way they behaved and interacted with me was very kind and lots of fun. They 'had something' but never pressured me about it, and I wasn't particularly interested in getting it for myself, instead I enjoyed the benefits of it through them when I was around them but otherwise generally got on with pursuing my own way of life. Time moved on and I turned 16 years of age - I started to feel 'grown up.'

On one weekend visit my sister invited me to go with her and her friends to a church meeting: apparently it was going to be somewhat special because some of the friends were going to be 'baptised'. Surprisingly I accepted the invitation without any clear idea of what was going to happen. It was a large church building with a congregation of about 600 people packing the place out, and there seemed to be a buzz of excitement in the air. I was intrigued. An introduction to the meeting was given and some songs were sung (not by me) and then it was time for the baptisms! A line of people appeared from a side room and they were all dressed in flowing white gowns - what had I got myself into?! What was my sister doing here? It all seemed weird. Then one by one they got submerged in a pool of water and came out the other side very happy and this was accompanied by great shouts of joy and glee from the congregation.

My mind was trying to take this all in and I must admit I was not impressed.

Shortly after the baptisms it was time for the sermon and the atmosphere changed to respectful quiet and concentration on what was about to be said as the pastor (a title with which I was not familiar) made his way to the elevated pulpit. I remember it very clearly.

He began by asking a simple question: "What does it mean to say that 'I am a Christian'?"

My brain whirred into action and I concluded that I knew the answer to the question having investigated the subject to some degree. After all I was a good Boy Scout, I was British, and I had never stabbed someone, taken drugs or been part of the misdemeanours I had read about in the books mentioned. I was a good boy in my mind and that equated to being a Christian and more than that I had spent some time thinking about God.

The pastor went on to talk about the baptisms being a public demonstration of Christian faith - I wasn't impressed, and I had no intention of joining in! Then he painted a picture with his words taking us back to Rome in about 60 AD and the reign of Emperor Nero - this was familiar territory for me having studied Latin as a language and Roman history repeatedly at school.

He then made a statement using two Latin words "christianus sum" which translated into English means "I am a Christian".

Again familiar territory.

Then everything changed: the pastor said that by simply uttering these two words, "christianus sum" in Rome around 60 AD would carry a very high probability of being thrown to the lions to be devoured in the Coliseum. I changed my mind instantly - no way would I risk being thrown to the lions for some belief system or religious designation. I most certainly would not have said those two words.

And a sudden realisation/revelation burst upon my thinking - my sister and her friends had something worth dying for and I most certainly didn't. I had a very successful life, great family, good friends, dreams for the future, but nothing of such great importance that I would sacrifice my life for it. And a hunger was instantly birthed within me, a desire to know that "pearl of great price", a "treasure beyond measure." I realised what my sister and her friends had that I didn't - a relationship with God himself, not simply some thoughts about him, not a religion to be practiced, but an eternal life that went beyond the grave.

With this realisation came another one - I was not worthy of such a life, nor could I attain it through my own good works or efforts. I suddenly felt the weight of my own sin and separation from God. I was encountering the Holy Spirit and he was convicting me of my sin in order to lead me to Jesus the Saviour. I was experiencing the power of God.

The pastor continued to speak for a length of time, his eyes seemingly on me personally all the time. I had never felt so uncomfortable in my life, I even considered hiding under my seat! Somehow in the middle of all this my heart and spirit responded and my mind followed: I gladly chose to give up my life in exchange for the new, eternal life on offer, and as I responded to the Holy Spirit he brought me directly into a personal relationship with God.

I was born again, very much to my surprise and also the

surprise of everyone else.

I entered into the eternal and infinite adventure not through intellectual curiosity but through a demonstration of the Spirit's power.

I have seen this happen repeatedly over the course of the years. Julian was an artist and a musician, his wife had been born again and joined our church and our two families became close friends having children of the same age. Curious to find out more about what his wife had experienced, Julian started to come with the rest of his family to our Sunday meetings. During our worship it is not unusual for the congregation to 'sing in tongues' using that spiritual gift as part of our adoration of God, and one day as Julian and I were chatting he said to me that when this happened it felt to him like we were singing with angels. He was experiencing heaven on earth. Within a few weeks of such experiences and explanations from myself and others, Julian too was born again.

Tony came to church one Sunday morning for the first time: it was a powerful meeting with many different manifestations of God's power evident, some of them strange in various ways (the Bible recounts many strange experiences of God's activity). I was preaching that morning and I was aware of Tony observing what was going on and I wondered whether he might find it a bit 'too strange,' so at the end of the meeting I went straight away to chat with him. I asked him how he had experienced the morning with some of the odd things happening around him, his reply was instant, "There is an amazing atmosphere of love in this place." Tony was born again about two weeks later and became part of the church.

Kim and I had befriended one of our neighbours who had recently become a widow. She was a lovely lady who always dressed immaculately, was extremely polite and in some ways a little bit reserved. We invited her to join us one Sunday for church and she replied positively saying that she hadn't been to church for years. We arranged to collect her from her home and drive her with us to the meeting, carefully explaining what she could expect. She seemed very content and interested. We took our places at the back of the meeting hall and the worship started. Some people in the congregation had been at a John Wimber conference that week and shared about their experiences of miracles and God's power. Not only that, they started to pray for people and powerful things started to happen. I started to wonder how our neighbour would feel about this and I have to confess, I was a bit concerned that it might be off putting for her. This thought was multiplied when the man standing next to her was prayed for and fell to the ground under God's power. At the end of the meeting I asked her what she thought of the meeting, and she replied: "You won't need to collect me next Sunday" , my concerns seemingly being realised. She continued by saying "I have had a lovely time; I will make my own way here next Sunday." She became part of the church.

I have found over the years that my concerns that demonstrations of God's power may somehow be off putting for people seeking him are completely unfounded and in actual fact the opposite is true. I should not have been surprised because the Bible is very clear about this, in Ephesians chapter 3:

16 I pray that out of his glorious riches he may strengthen you with power through his Spirit in your inner being, 17 so that Christ may dwell in your hearts through faith. And I pray that you, being rooted and established in love, 18 may have power, together with all the Lord's holy people, to grasp how wide and long and high and deep is the love of Christ, 19 and to know this love that surpasses knowledge—that you may be filled to the measure of all the fullness of God.

God has designed it that demonstrations of his power enable people to grasp hold of his love and that this is a core foundation of 'faith in God." This is true not just for initial salvation but also for our continuing growth in faith. I encourage people to encounter God simply for the experience, trusting Him that he can use such experiences to reveal himself in increasing measure.

At Eastgate we have a Healing Centre which is open on Saturdays for anyone who wishes to encounter God and seek miraculous healing. We carefully create an atmosphere of joy, peace and hopeful expectation.

We expect people to encounter God and expect that He will do amazing things. Week by week we see extraordinary things happen, backs healed, knees healed, coeliac disease eradicated, a broken ankle miraculously restored instantly, a teenager called Luke who had a congenital abnormality of the oesophagus which had caused him long term misery was instantly transformed to normal (watch the beautiful, emotional video "Love Breaks Through" on the Eastgate Plus YouTube channel), and many, many more. As people experience God we generally find that they want to know him more and it is not unusual for people to be born again at the Healing Centre.

Another important thing I have learned on my journey is that a simple explanation is helpful to people and most people don't need an in depth explanation and understanding to benefit from their experience. The story of the outpouring of the Holy Spirit on the day of Pentecost is instructive in this matter:

Acts 2:

12 Amazed and perplexed, they asked one another, "What does this mean?"13 Some, however, made fun of them and said, "They have had too much wine."

A mixture of amazement and being perplexed is to be expected when God demonstrates his power. We can expect people to have questions.

We can also expect some people to mock us and not want to find genuine answers, such people are unlikely to respond to God at this moment in time. It is very important that we don't centre our thoughts and activities around this group of people by worrying about their response and being governed by it in such a way that we try to lessen the activity of the Holy Spirit and become apologetic for what God is doing. This is sometimes described as being 'seeker sensitive' and I have strayed there in the past (as I have related in this chapter). To my mind it is a fearful reaction that needs to be resisted and then we need to overcome such fear by trusting God that he knows what he is doing when He demonstrates his power.

I have learnt to always try to help people understand what they are experiencing through explanation, but I will never apologise for the activity of God. Let's continue to look at the story of Pentecost.

14 Then Peter stood up with the Eleven, raised his voice and addressed the crowd: "Fellow Jews and all of you who live in Jerusalem, let me explain this to you; listen carefully to what I say. 15 These people are not drunk, as you suppose. It's only nine in the morning!

Peter gives an explanation of the experience; he is not trying to persuade people into an experience. He explains that the 'drunken behaviour' has a different explanation to what they might be thinking

> *16 No, this is what was spoken by the prophet Joel:*

He uses Scripture to help his explanation.

> *22 "Fellow Israelites, listen to this: Jesus of Nazareth was a man accredited by God to you by miracles, wonders and signs, which God did among you through him, as you yourselves know.*

He connects the experience to Jesus and the fact that God accredited Him through signs, wonders and miracles.

> *36 "Therefore let all Israel be assured of this: God has made this Jesus, whom you crucified, both Lord and Messiah."*

He connects people to Jesus the Lord and Messiah.

> *37 When the people heard this, they were cut to the heart and said to Peter and the other apostles, "Brothers, what shall we do?"*

The Holy Spirit interacts with people by touching their hearts.

> *38 Peter replied, "Repent and be baptized, every one of you, in the name of Jesus Christ for the forgiveness of your sins.*

Peter leads them towards salvation.

And you will receive the gift of the Holy Spirit. 39 The promise is for you and your children and for all who are far off—for all whom the Lord our God will call."

Peter leads them towards the reality of the promise of the Holy Spirit's presence in their lives.

41 Those who accepted his message were baptized, and about three thousand were added to their number that day.

Three thousand people responded to Jesus, demonstrated their new found faith in God by being baptised, and became part of God's community, the church. The early church had been birthed according to the design of God.

God's church is designed to be full of love and power, and our faith in God rests on these two foundations.

Story by Janice Pleasants:

I was in a tearoom enjoying some tea and cake. A lady sitting at the adjoining table smiled at me, so I started to strike up a general social conversation. As I did, I saw a picture of barbed wire and prison bars, but the woman seemed a real genteel lady so I really couldn't understand why I was seeing that. So I explained that I sometimes received impressions or pictures about and for people and wondered if I could share something with her that I'd just seen. She agreed, when I shared the picture, she stared for a long time at her table and finally said, that she was a Jew, a holocaust survivor having been in a concentration camp as a child in the war. She was amazed, so I explained I was a Christian practising hearing from God and He had shared that information about her with me for a reason, as He wanted her to know He loved her and knew the details of her life. She had a bad back and was due for spinal injections that afternoon. I offered prayer but she said she would be happy to rely on the procedure. We went on chatting and I ended up telling her about healings I'd received from our loving Father God. She shared that she had been married twice, both times to committed Christians! As I got ready to go she said, "You've really made me think. I've always resisted Jesus but I'm not sure if I can resist Him anymore!"

Chapter 23 Hearing God

Most human beings have many different relationships, for instance I have friendships based on common interests such as sport, workplace friendships, and friendships within our church.

> *John 17: 3 "Now this is eternal life: that they know you, the only true God, and Jesus Christ, whom you have sent."*

Jesus defined eternal life as 'knowing God' thus Christianity is basically a relationship with God and in any relationship there is communication. Indeed, the nature of communication is defined by its relational context.

For example, when I go shopping for something my interaction with the staff is centred around my desire for a product and their desire to sell something to me. The level of trust involved depends upon the amount of money being spent and is unlikely to spread beyond the boundaries of the purchase.

My interaction with my wife is extremely different to that with a shop worker and far more complex because we are seeking to build a life together. My relationships with my children are different to that I have with my wife, and also different with each child. These relationships have developed over the course of time and adapted in accordance with their stages of life. My relationship with my grandchildren is also different to those with my children.

In all these relationships good and appropriate communication is very important to their healthy development. Good communication will help to create trust, whereas poor or inappropriate communication can damage trust.

What about our relationship with God?

A helpful verse to start our exploration is "Romans 10:17 *"Faith comes by hearing, and hearing by the word of God."*

This verse talks about how our relationship with God starts, how we become born again and enter into this new life offered to us. In some manner we hear about the message of Jesus Christ and God speaks to our hearts. Faith/trust is stirred within us by his voice and we respond to the message by trusting God for forgiveness and new life.

That is just the start of the adventure and interestingly in this Bible verse the tense of the Greek word translated 'hearing' is what is called a continuous present tense. This means that the verb has a continuous meaning, not just in the present but also the future. To give an example of this let's consider a few phrases:

"I am parenting my children" is not only a present but also a future reality.

"I am married" is a lifelong commitment.

"I have just qualified as a doctor" indicates a long process of training and also implies an ongoing reality. Past, Present and Future all in one phrase.

In the same way 'hearing the word of God' has a past reality, a present practicality and a future promise.

Our relationship with God has many different aspects to it and should be continually growing and developing. He communicates with us in many different ways and we need to develop our hearing so that we pick up all that he is saying to us at any one particular time.

Our relationship with God is described in many different ways such as:

- A child of God.
- A temple of the Holy Spirit.
- A worshipper.
- A friend of God.
- A part of the bride of Christ.
- A part of his body, the church.
- A servant of the King of Kings.
- A unique creation with a unique part to play in God's divine purposes and history.
- An heir of an extraordinary inheritance.

Different aspects of our relationship require different styles of communication and as we grow in our relationship we utilise these different aspects with some becoming more relevant at different times.

When I was born again, Christianity seemed to work very simply. God supplied my needs and guided me very clearly. I was aware of his voice and his response to my interaction with him. It was similar to that of a newborn human baby which has a very limited skill set of communication. Let's examine that for a moment.

When a baby is born everyone in attendance is waiting for a certain noise to announce a healthy arrival. Regarding the birth of my own children, at no other time in my life have I awaited a 'cry' with such eager expectation, nervousness, relief and then joy; for David it took over a minute, for Kerry just a few seconds. The cry announced 'I am here', a new life beginning.

The communication skill set for a baby is based around the ability to cry to gain attention and to smile to increase affection; both gain the attention of other people. In addition, the baby is carefully observing their new found world, trying to make sense of it all and discovering their key relationships

- who will meet my needs? How do I communicate? Laughter is another inherent ability that enhances communication, and don't we love to hear babies and young children laugh?

As a 'baby Christian' I found that communication with God was quite simple and in some ways basic. He fed me, protected me, cleaned me up when necessary and responded to my cries. However, that was the starting point of a relationship not the fullness; it was a fundamental and elementary stage of life, however, to stay in that place would have meant not becoming more mature in my Christianity.

Hebrews 6: 1-2 puts it like this: *"Therefore let us move beyond the elementary teachings about Christ and be taken forward to maturity."*

In addition Galatians 4: 1-2 says: 1 *"Think of it this way. If a father dies and leaves an inheritance for his young children, those children are not much better off than slaves until they grow up, even though they actually own everything their father had."*

The process of maturity is essential to enable us to access the full resources of heaven that God has provided us with through salvation in Christ and maturity requires moving beyond elementary communication: it moves us on to questions, choices, opinions, conversation etc.

Hearing God is not a static concept, and the ability to develop the skills of communication with God is essential to growing in faith. Also the reality that God says different things to us as we move forward on our journey is important to understand. When people are in moments of spiritual confusion I have often heard them say, "But God told me to do this, I don't understand what is happening."

I usually respond to this by asking a question: "What is God saying right now?"

What God has said in the past is relevant and helpful knowledge, but it does not necessarily dictate our present or our future reality. For instance, when our children asked us what was for dinner, they didn't think that today's answer would necessarily be tomorrow's answer. Also they had various household chores as they were growing up which they did regularly such as clearing the table after a meal: it was an ongoing instruction. They were also sometimes asked to do specific tasks on particular occasions but they were not expected to do them every day. As they grew older they were given chores that required more maturity and responsibility. The things I communicated with David and Kerry when they were 5 years old were not all relevant when they were 15 or 25 years old.

In the book of Genesis, we follow the story of Abraham and during that story God clearly communicates to him to sacrifice the life of his son Isaac, who is his heir and upon whom the family line is dependent and with that the promise of God to Abraham that 'he will become the father of nations'. It is a somewhat puzzling command. Nevertheless, Abraham responds in faith and sets off with Isaac up a mountain to sacrifice him.

> *Genesis 22: When they reached the place God had told him about, Abraham built an altar there and arranged the wood on it. He bound his son Isaac and laid him on the altar, on top of the wood. Then he reached out his hand and took the knife to slay his son. But the angel of the Lord called out to him from heaven, "Abraham! Abraham!" "Here I am," he replied. "Do not lay a hand on the boy," he said. "Do not do anything to him. Now I know that you fear God, because you have not withheld from me your son, your only son."*

God speaks to Abraham again but in a way that is directly contrary to the original command.

How important was it that Abraham kept on listening

to God?

How important was. It that he recognised the voice of God even though the words were seemingly contrary to what had been said before?

What would have happened if Abraham had stopped listening, or he obstinately held on to the first command? I would suggest that he would have killed the promise of God and cut across his line of inheritance, which is a shocking thought.

Are you still listening to God? Do you recognise his voice even when what he says seems confusing? These are relational realities and are key issues in regards to growing in faith.

Let me give you some reassurance, the Bible is quite clear that it is normal for Christians to hear and recognise the voice of God. John 10: 27 *My sheep listen to my voice; I know them, and they follow me.*

Knowing the voice of God is a Christian's birthright, it is not a spiritual gift to be sought after but an inherent right of being a child of God. The prime purpose of this is intimacy with God rather than service for God. As an intimate relationship with God develops towards maturity, following God's leadership is framed in this context of love and the acts of service that accompany this. I believe that I am a beloved son of God with whom he is well pleased and my response to that is joyful obedience and sacrificial service.

Luke 8:18 is a very helpful verse with regard to listening to God although at first sight it can seem confusing and for many years I failed to understand it.

> *"Therefore consider carefully how you listen. Whoever has will be given more; whoever does not have, even what they think they have will be taken from them."*

My experience was that I was so confused by the second part of this verse that I didn't pay attention to the first part. The second part seemed to me to be unfair and an example of inequality: the rich getting richer and the poor getting poorer. However, when my attention was drawn to the first part of the verse and I considered the verse as a whole suddenly it made sense. The instruction is to "consider carefully how you listen" and the rest of the verse explains the consequences of listening in different ways.

Listen positively or listen negatively.
Listen to gain understanding or listen to criticise.
Listen with trust or listen with suspicion.
Listen with love or listen with hatred.
Listen with grace or listen with judgement.
Listen with belief or listen with unbelief.

These are just a few contrasting ways of how it is possible to listen differently to the exact same words being said.

Let me give some examples to help:
When I am speaking to a group of people and share some testimonies of miraculous healing, I am giving everyone in the group the same chance to benefit from those stories. The opportunity to grow or shrink back. The benefit received is dependent on how an individual (or the group as a whole) listens. If a person listens with an attitude of trust and celebration they will effectively own the story for themselves ("whoever has") and they will position themselves to grow in that area. If a person listens with unbelief and chooses not to believe then they lose what they have just received. If a whole group listens with faith then the whole group will grow in faith, and if a whole group listens with unbelief then they

will shrink back in faith (Nazareth being an example). Also it is not uncommon for there to be a mixture of faith and unbelief amongst the same crowd of people.

Please understand I am not suggesting that questions shouldn't be asked to help understand the testimony further, but I do suggest that questions should be asked with a view to gaining information and growing in faith, rather than simply trying to confirm what you already believe or don't believe thereby extinguishing the opportunity to grow in belief. The crowd on the day of Pentecost are a good example of a mixture of attitudes, some asked "What does this mean?" and listened to gain understanding, these people entered into a new experience of faith; others mocked and dismissed the experience of God in front of them and missed the opportunity and lost what had been given to them.
Consider carefully how you listen, because the attitude with which you listen will determine the consequences of the opportunities given to you.

Let me give another simple example: if I were to give you some money, say a £20 note, when I was out with you one day, but you didn't put it somewhere safe, such as a purse or wallet, and by the time you got home you had lost the money or it had been stolen from you, it would not mean that I hadn't given you the money. It would mean you hadn't considered carefully how to steward that gift, the responsibility would be yours for that outcome. Similarly I often hear Christians talk about not receiving from God like other people, but there is a simple Biblical principle 'If you ask you will receive.'. The issue is not reception but wise stewardship. If you are faithful with a little you will be given more.

The attitude we have about stewarding the resources given to us helps to determine our spiritual future.

In an ongoing relationship, ongoing communication

is normal and it will have many different aspects. Let's examine briefly what that looks like and let's consider some of the different ways that we can listen; this is by no means an exhaustive list but hopefully a useful framework to help develop great ways of listening. I think the best place to start is whether we listen as sons and daughters or as slaves.

Listening as a slave is different to listening as a son or daughter: slaves don't listen for intimacy but for instructions; they often fear punishment; slaves don't dream much and have little hope for the future. Their purpose is to serve their master. Christians are called to serve God but service that doesn't flow from intimacy with God effectively causes us to function as spiritual slaves and the only part of God's voice we will regularly recognise are the instructions he gives to us about things to do. We will miss the intimate parts of communication about love, delight, pleasure etc.

Galatians 5:1 warns us not to allow ourselves to become slaves once again, and how we hear the voice of God and what we listen for are vital towards this.

If we only listen for instructions we tend towards being slaves in our mindsets and primarily respond to God as our master, whereas daughters and sons hear the voice of their loving Father as the context for other communication. In addition, children who understand about being heirs of a great inheritance need to learn lessons of responsibility and opportunity for stewarding the resources at their disposal.

Here are some other ways to develop your listening in a positive direction and take hold of the ongoing opportunities to grow in faith:

- I am a child of God therefore I am confident that I will hear words of love from my Father in heaven because that is my birthright.

- I am a temple of the Holy Spirit therefore I am confident of the presence of the Holy Spirit and his voice inside of me.
- I am a worshipper of the living God and I expect to encounter and experience him every time I worship.
- I am a friend of God therefore I am confident that I can have fun with God and share my everyday life with Him.
- I am a part of the bride of Christ therefore I am part of the greatest ever romance and I have a responsibility to get myself ready for the bridegroom (Jesus) which includes making plans together with other people and with God.
- I am a part of his body, the church, therefore I expect God to communicate to me in a corporate way not just an individual way.
- I am a servant of the King of Kings and I find it a great privilege and pleasure to listen for his words of guidance and instruction, confident that his plan for my life is good, pleasing and perfect.
- I am a unique creation with a specific part to play in God's divine purposes and history therefore I pay careful attention to listening to God in my specific areas of calling and gifting.
- I am an heir of an extraordinary inheritance therefore I have a privileged responsibility to listen to the wisdom of God so that I can be a good steward of what has been given to me, understanding that if I am faithful with little he will give me more, so I need to be ready to grow into that reality.
- I expect God to give me more than I could ask or imagine therefore I am prepared to be surprised by God.

As I continually communicate with God my connection and relationship with him will grow and so will my trust and faith in him.

Story by Janice Pleasants:

I was in an office when a PA came in to apologise that she wouldn't be able to help me today as her back pain was "killing her" and she could hardly move. I explained that I was a Christian and could pray for her but she said she "wasn't really into all that Jesus stuff." I said, "It's okay, it wouldn't be spooky or weird or anything, all I'd say is something like, 'I rebuke the pain in your back and I command it to go in Jesus name and I bless your back with life, health and flexibility." She paused and said, "Oh, okay." I asked her to let me know if she changed her mind and she said that she would and she left the room. About 15 minutes later she came back in and said, "Janice, it's the strangest thing but ever since we had our 'little chat' about my back, all the pain has gone and I can move again!" I said, "There's power in Jesus' name even when we chat about it." She said, "Yes, I guess so!"

Chapter 24 New Year's Eve

It was 31st December 2005, New Year's Eve, and we were preparing ourselves for a new era. There were only two of us in the room, facing a memorable but difficult moment.

As the clock drew close to midnight I offered my mother a drink and she gratefully said yes in the little voice she still had left. I cradled her frail body and lifted her head towards the straw through which she could suck a few drops of refreshing cool, iced water into her parched mouth, mumbling her gratitude towards me. As the clock struck midnight and 2006 arrived I said "Happy New Year" to my mum, celebrating that she would very soon be entering into a very new existence, but also mourning the forthcoming loss to our family of someone very precious to us all. She was dying of an unusual form of cancer which was overwhelming and destroying her body - it was incurable.

A few days previously she had fulfilled her last earthly wish, to spend Christmas with her family. My dad had somehow loaded her into his car, her emaciated body surrounded by blankets to protect her and keep her warm. Christmas presents filled most of the rest of the car, my mum loved Christmas and giving presents! When they arrived at our house I carried her from the car to a bed where she laid, too weak to do anything else. We would take it in turns to be with her, she loved her family, she was content.

Christmas Day passed and we knew she had done what she wanted to do and we realised the end was coming. We phoned the hospice in Margate who had a bed ready for her. Her grandchildren said goodbye to her for the last time and then I carried her to my father's car - she knew what was happening. I followed in my car and helped to settle her into the hospice room and I decided I also had a last wish in this regard - to celebrate the New Year with my mum.

So I returned on 31st December, mum was drifting in and out of consciousness, but she recognised I was there - her Pete. I sat down next to her and held her hand; from time to time she would squeeze my hand and I knew it was an expression of love. She had no strength left for words.

After we passed midnight and had our very personal and intimate celebration I laid her head back on the pillow of her bed in that small but pleasant room and I continued to hold her hand. I prayed out loud so that she could hear, thanking God for his love, faithfulness and power, for his kindness towards us and for a sure and certain hope of eternal life. Mum mumbled "Amen." That was the last word I remember her saying.

She no longer wanted me to pray for her healing as she had told me she was ready to "go home and be with Jesus" and would look forward to us joining her later. However, she had also been very clear in her encouragement to me when she had said to me, "Pete, never stop praying for the sick to be healed." She remembered being healed of lifelong sinus problems when she was in her sixties, never to suffer with that problem again; her hip had been healed of arthritis and she had walked freely following that. She knew the healing power of Jesus and we had prayed together many times during the course of her battle against cancer and experienced occasional breakthroughs, but we didn't see full healing of that condition. Our journey of faith needed to continue.

She fell back into a deep sleep shortly after midnight on 1st January 2006, I stayed by her side, holding her hand and occasionally stroking her hair. No more words passed between us, we had celebrated a new beginning together. Her spirit and soul were strong, her earthly body fading away.

She died a few days later, her earthly journey complete. I was sad about the loss of my mum on earth and disappointed that she hadn't been healed and in all honesty I wasn't interested in praying for people to be healed at that exact moment in time. I simply needed to be comforted and have my hope restored, so I focussed my faith on connection with God, my comforter and hope.

Six days after her death I was on a plane to Peru where I was due to be teaching and training Christians about healing. My mum had specifically encouraged me to continue with that planned trip despite circumstances but it was a strange feeling. Whilst there I saw God do remarkable things and I marvelled at his grace, love and power being used through me in such a time of weakness. I experienced a very strange mix of emotions, sadness and disappointment at the loss of my mum, joy and excitement from the miracles I was witnessing. Christianity is a challenging mixture at times, but the Biblical instruction to 'mourn with those who mourn, and rejoice with those who rejoice' was very meaningful and helpful.

Mourning is an important and appropriate response to significant loss and it is not an enemy to be fought, rather it is a journey to be navigated.

However, discouragement, disappointment and lack of hope are enemies to be overcome and in this instance they were 'giants' to me. I was aware more than ever that for me there was still more ground to gain on my earthly journey, and I vowed to myself to continue with even greater endeavour my "Journey of Faith, from Hope to Assurance."

Almost exactly nine years later on the 3rd January 2015 a lady came to visit the Healing Centre at Eastgate. During those nine years I had pursued the God of healing and miracles with increased fervour along with the rest of our church. One expression of that was that we had started and established a Healing Centre as an expression of Eastgate and it was designed to gain the confidence of the local health services so that Christian healing could be accepted as a complementary service alongside standard medical services. We had built a team of faith filled, joyful Christians who created a spiritual atmosphere where people could 'touch Jesus' and get healed. We experienced many wonderful miracles and made sure that everyone left with an experience of heavenly peace, joy, love and power.

The lady in question was suffering from cancer which had been diagnosed a few months previously, and to my astonishment I discovered that she had the same form of cancer that had killed my mother. She had already received chemotherapy (like my mum) and surgery was due on the 13th January to try to remove as much cancerous material as possible from her abdomen in order to make life more comfortable but without any expectation of a cure (like my mum). This touched me in a very personal way, especially as 13th January is my son's birthday and my mum was very close to her grandchildren. This was personal!

The lady experienced the presence of God in a powerful way at the Healing Centre and then headed home with her family. We awaited news.

The surgery took place on the allocated day, the surgeon opened up her abdomen and to everyone's surprise and amazement not a trace of cancer could be found. Celebrations abounded. The lady herself was so surprised that she found it hard to believe what had happened. She started to live life with a new expectation. She attended the hospital for regular checkups as we would expect and continued in good health. The following January , ten years after my mother's death

I received news that the lady had thoroughly enjoyed her Christmas and one of her highlights was dancing in worship with her granddaughter. My eyes filled with joy and I asked myself a question: 'Who had won that particular battle of faith?'

Many people came to mind - friends and family who supported and prayed, the medical staff who provided such excellent care, the Healing Centre Team, Eastgate church, and I included myself. One other person featured prominently in my thinking - my mum. She had pursued God and continued to grow in faith throughout her life after she was born again. She had also continually encouraged me throughout life, and even with her dying breaths had urged me to never give up but keep on moving forward. She had left a great legacy. We might not have won the battle for her cancer but nine years later we had defeated that exact same enemy through the power of Jesus and my mum had played her part in that victory.

Disappointment was defeated by hope.
Discouragement was defeated by encouragement.
Temporary defeat was defeated by perseverance in faith.
Mourning was turned into joy.

Story from a weekend working with another church:

A mother of six young children in her mid thirties had suffered a compression of the spinal cord 6 years previously, six intervertebral discs were removed and surgeons fused the lower back. She was left with no sensation to her left leg and had been unable to walk unaided due to weakness, numbness and 'foot drop' as a result of nerve damage and muscle wasting. Due to the constant pain she had been on high strength medication, including oral morphine.

She responded in faith by raising her hand for prayer after listening to the stories of healings and miracles that had been seen recently and as she did so she met with the love and power of Jesus. As sensation and strength was being restored to her leg the woman was tearful and lost for words. She then had the courage to stand up and take steps unaided by her crutch for the first time in 6 years.

Her older children, smiling and crying, watched their Mother gaining more and more confidence with each step. A short while later she was able to pick up and hold her two year old son in her arms for the first time without help, pain or fear of falling.

We celebrated and continued to encourage her and her children, recognising that we were seeing God do far more than heal a body. We were watching hope, destiny and the ability to dream for all of them being restored.

We later received a message from this lady, she has given permission for it to be shared.

'I really am doing amazing I came home and cut my garden for the first time in 6 years it might be a boring job for most but I have dreamed of being able to get back in my garden with the kids for years, words cannot describe how much this means to me, even more so to my children.

Chapter 25 Keep your Hope High.

Romans 15:13 May the God of hope fill you with all joy and peace as you trust in him, so that you may overflow with hope by the power of the Holy Spirit.

What a beautiful Bible verse, in it we see that God is our source of hope; that hope is connected to joy and peace; that we can have so much hope that it overflows; and that this all happens as we put our trust in him. The bible also states that 'faith is the assurance of things hoped for' (Hebrews 11:1). In my mind I think of hope as the soil in which faith grows, also as one of the nutrients in my spiritual river that nourishes faith.

Hope is absolutely vital to Christian life and to our continuing growth in faith, therefore it should be no surprise that this is an area of our lives where we will experience intense spiritual opposition. Many of our enemy's tactics are designed to reduce our level of hope and therefore we need to recognise such tactics and know how to overcome them; not only that but we need to positively develop hope within ourselves.

There are a couple of quotes from a friend of mine that I often refer to:

'You are allowed to be hopeless about any situation that God is hopeless about.'

'There are no hopeless situations, only hopeless people.'

If we put these quotes alongside the 'Triangle of Faith' it helps us to understand them. When we are feeling a lack of hope (or feel hopeless) about a situation, if we put God in the picture our thinking and our attitudes can change. However, if we also consider the River Thames story we can understand that it is important that we keep our hope unpolluted and as we do so life will develop wherever our river flows.

Over the years I have found that the subject of hope is one of the essential keys to a healthy and fruitful Christian life. Hope is so important that I want to give it a bit more space in this book so that I can share with you some of the things I have found helpful in 'keeping my hope high'.

Psalm 37:4 Take delight in the Lord, and he will give you the desires of your heart.

God is aware of the desires of our hearts, he made us to have such desires, dreams and hopes and it is very important that we understand this. However, he does not want us to pursue these things in a way that is separate to him, nor does he want these things to become precious idols in our lives surpassing and displacing our love and pursuit of God himself. Rather he wants us to love and value him above all other things because he is our greatest treasure. As we delight in him, our hearts will increasingly be aligned with his heart and the overflow into our lives will be that we see more and more of our heart's desires fulfilled. As I pursue him his life pours increasingly into mine.

I recall an example of this from years back: family holidays have always been an important part of our life, taking time away from the usual busyness of life to have quality time together, and we always try to capture some of those memories by taking photographs. On the particular year in question we had a holiday planned well in advance as we found that the anticipation over the months leading up to the holiday increased our joy and resilience in busy times. As we drew closer to the holiday, our camera stopped working and we did not have enough money to replace it before the holiday would start. We were a bit disappointed that we wouldn't be able to capture our memories in the same way as usual, but we didn't allow it to get us down or affect us badly. We didn't talk about it with other people, we didn't even make it a particular subject for prayer.

A few days later a friend, Mick, popped round to our house unexpectedly; he was a very keen photographer. In a very excited manner he explained to us that God had told him to buy us a new camera and that he would like to take us to a specialist camera shop to buy one. We were overwhelmed both by God and by Mick's generosity; Mick was also significantly touched that God had spoken to him in such a specific manner. The next day I was talking to God about it and telling him how amazing it was that I hadn't even prayed about the camera and yet he had provided for us.

His reply surprised me: 'You did pray about it.'

Assuredly I replied, 'No I didn't'

'Yes you did' he replied back.

'No I didn't'

'Yes you did'

'No I didn't'

It seemed very strange to be arguing with God; then God asked me a question 'do you pray in tongues all the time?' and a sudden realisation hit me.

I realised that up to that time I had an inadequate understanding about the gift of tongues, believing that it is a spiritual language that affects spiritual realities without any specific application in everyday life.

'You mean it counts in my earthly existence?' I asked God.

'Yes' he replied, 'it is a cry from your heart about all things and it is not limited to your understanding. It is also linked to your worship of me.'

By that time, I had already developed the twin spiritual disciplines of worshipping in the spirit and praying in the spirit twenty four hours per day. This is possible because our spirit does not sleep and is in constant communion with the Holy Spirit inside us. Praying and worshipping in the spirit is not an intellectual exercise and does not originate in our minds. As 1 Corinthians 14 instructs us 14 For if I pray in a tongue, my spirit prays, but my mind is unfruitful. 15 So what shall I do? I will pray with my spirit, but I will also pray with my understanding; I will sing with my spirit, but I will also sing with my understanding.

Now I realised that as I had delighted in God in such a manner, my heart desires were expressed to him and he answered them. This newfound confidence increased my levels of hope and expectation. It also increased the attention I pay to both these forms of prayer and worship: "in the spirit" and "in my understanding".

A few days later Mick took us to a specialist camera shop – he was like a child in a sweet store, discussing all sorts of camera details with the shop assistant and getting very excited. The blessing was definitely overflowing to Mick. After a while we left the shop with a far superior camera than we would ever have imagined for ourselves and a very excited friend, keen to show us the full potential of our new camera and help us enter into the greater delights of photography.

As I have written this, I can hear all sorts of questions forming in people's minds, as they do in mine:

Is that selfishness?

Can you ask for anything?

Is this not 'self-centred Christianity?'

Let's look at another couple of Bible passages to try to help us find some answers:

John 14:12-14 Jesus said: Very truly I tell you, whoever believes in me will do the works I have been doing, and they will do even greater things than these, because I am going to the Father.   And I will do whatever you ask in my name, so that the Father may be glorified in the Son.   You may ask me for anything in my name, and I will do it.

James 4:3 When you ask, you do not receive, because you ask with wrong motives, that you may spend what you get on your pleasures.

The passage in John 14 states that we can ask for anything in Jesus' name and he will do it. However, this is a promise set in a context of faith in Jesus and living a life like Jesus.

The passage in James teaches us that if we ask with wrong motives, in particular selfish motives, we will not receive an answer. Selfishness is not a godly attribute but not all our personal desires are selfish. Sometimes it is very difficult to discern our own motivation and at such times I find it helpful to ask God to help me understand myself, I am confident that God will talk to me and correct me if that is needed; I am also confident that God can close doors that he doesn't want me to go through.

In addition, I know that God does not want me to live in fear of getting it wrong; such fear can hinder people to such an extent that they are suspicious of all their desires and that has a very negative impact upon their lives.

So what does it mean to pray 'in the name of Jesus'? What a massive question? I have already written a chapter in this book that touches on this subject and maybe it even deserves a book of its own, so let me give you a brief summary of my thoughts and leave you to do some further study if you wish.

My understanding is that 'praying in the name of Jesus' means to pray in a way that is consistent with the nature of God as his nature is described by his names. The example of the life of Jesus in the gospels is very helpful.

For instance: Jesus provides more wine for a wedding celebration; Jesus helps Peter pay his taxes; Jesus heals people; while Jesus was on the cross he ensured that his mother would be comforted and provided for; Jesus resisted religious authorities; Jesus provided himself with a donkey to ride into Jerusalem on Palm Sunday.

Another verse that I have found helpful is:

> *Proverbs 13:12 Hope deferred makes the heart sick, but a longing fulfilled is a tree of life.*

This verse affirms the idea that desires (longings) are not wrong as long as our motivation is right, in fact having desires and seeing them fulfilled is life giving to us. The verse also talks about 'hope deferred' and its detrimental effect upon our emotional wellbeing.

But what does Hope Deferred mean?

I think there are two aspects to this:

1. When we hope for something and it does not arrive as we desire or expect, disappointment and discouragement can be the result. If that continues to be the reality the negative emotions can get stronger. In that case we need to go back to God for comfort, strength, encouragement, peace, joy and renewed hope. Once our hope is renewed we can wait with positive expectation once again.

2. The deferring of our willingness to hope. Sometimes disappointment and discouragement in relation to a desire can become so strong that we choose not to hope and not to trust God in that area because we want to avoid the possibility of further emotional trauma. It is very important that we can recognise if and when this is true for us, because the remedy is to choose to trust God once again and dare to let hope arise once more.

Another common thing I have found is that some people think that it is unkind to allow people to raise their hopes when there is no obvious solution in sight, or when they don't believe that God wants to intervene in a certain situation. These thoughts are often based around Proverbs 13:12 as outlined above.

My answer to this is that God never wants us to live without hope in any area of our lives, and also that our hope in God should go beyond our previous experience. We can always return to the 'God of hope' to have our hope renewed.

Here are some other quick thoughts about keeping your hopes high:

Optimism

I believe that God is a realistic optimist; his outlook is fully informed and he is always confident in himself to work things out for good.

Therefore, I have chosen to have a mindset and lifestyle that reflects this aspect of God's nature – I am a realistic optimist. I choose to have an optimistic attitude towards life. I do not deny the facts of a situation but I always look for the positive aspect of any situation and choose to trust God for a positive outcome even when I cannot see how it will happen. Many times in my life, people have said to me, 'Pete we need to be real about this'. Almost never has that been an invitation to be more optimistic but rather an invitation to reduce my hope and expectation about a certain situation. I have learnt to answer by saying, 'It depends on which version of reality you want me to align myself with, which viewpoint do you want me to look from, Heaven or Earth?'

Reality with God in the equation is different from that without him.

I develop confidence within me in regard to what I need to achieve in life. Such confidence increases my hope, and also the hope of others around me. I confront false humility because it reduces hope.

Dreams and Imagination
Keep dreaming and imagining; God gave you your imagination therefore you can trust that he will use it for his purposes.

Rejoicing, Praying and Gratitude

> *1 Thessalonians 5:16-18 16 Rejoice always, 17 pray continually, 18 give thanks in all circumstances; for this is God's will for you in Christ Jesus.*

Develop a 'gratitude attitude' and make the 'choice to rejoice' in all circumstances, also train yourself to pray continually as the Bible instructs us. As you do this you can be confident that you are living 'in the will of God' as a result hope and faith will grow.

Perseverance
We need to understand the link between perseverance and hope: *Romans 5:3-5 we also glory in our sufferings, because we*

know that suffering produces perseverance; 4 perseverance, character; and character, hope. 5 And hope does not disappoint us, because God's love has been poured out into our hearts through the Holy Spirit, who has been given to us.

There are processes in life that lead to growth and maturity; one of these processes is persevering through suffering. In other words, keep on going when circumstances are difficult. As we walk with God through such times and persevere in trusting him then godly character will be increasingly formed in our lives. As that process continues, hope will grow within us and become strong enough to overcome the disappointments that confront us. The foundation upon which this is all built is confidence in the love of God and in the presence of the Holy Spirit inside us.

Encouragement

Encouragement is listed as a 'gift of grace' in Romans 12 so we can be certain that it is a godly attribute. It is a gift that I have very deliberately sought to develop in my life, I try to encourage as many people as I can and that includes myself! In fact, I regard it as my responsibility to encourage myself, and also to encourage others, for example by taking delight in things well done, in challenges overcome, in relationships developing well. One particular habit that I have found to be very powerful is encouraging any signs of progress being made no matter how small, I choose to encourage during the process not just at the final desired outcome. I most certainly don't wait for perfection as I believe such a target is unhelpful; perfectionism is a huge barrier to encouragement and the growth of hope.

Love always trusts

We are called to love all people, even our enemies, and the Bible instructs us that love always trusts. This is a very challenging concept that needs a lot of heavenly wisdom in its outworking: we need to understand healthy boundaries and many other things alongside. I have talked about this already in this book, but to summarise my personal attitude is that I choose to start with an intention to trust people (put my faith in them) rather than start from a place of suspicion. In this way I start with hopeful expectation which I have found to be a very powerful spiritual force for good and soil in which faith can grow. Trust increases hope.

We are also called to 'love ourselves' this will involve trusting yourself.

Romans 8:28

And we know that in all things God works for the good of those who love him, who have been called according to his purpose.

This is a Bible verse that I keep in my mind constantly and when nothing else seems to be working for me I return to it as a source of hope.

Story by Janice Pleasants:

I was on the upper deck of a crowded bus reading a book, 'Dreaming with God' by Bill Johnson. The man next to me looked over and said, "Are you a Christian?" When I said I was, he said he was a Christian too but had given up dreaming with God a long time ago. He was burnt out in ministry. As we chatted I saw a picture of a waterfall and joy over him. So I then offered to pray for him. He said, "What, here on the bus?!" I said that I'd do it very discreetly and no one needed to know what we were doing. So I prayed, and as I did he let out a deep sigh and started saying, "His yoke is easy and His burden is light," over and over again. Then he began to giggle, then laugh, then he was screaming with laughter, collapsed in his seat. I felt such a heavy Presence of God, like I would slide off of my seat if I didn't grip the seat in front. People around us began laughing. A couple in the seats in front turned around and asked, "What's the joke?" I said, through tears of laughter, "It's no joke, it's a download of heavenly joy." "How do you get that?" they asked. I said I can pray and you'll just receive it. As I did, they started laughing too. Then the man suddenly realised that he had missed his stop a while back. He thanked me, saying all the heaviness had lifted and he felt completely renewed and then staggered down the stairs. I heard him laughing on the lower deck as he waited to get off the bus. I had to stagger off soon afterwards with people still laughing around me.

Chapter 26 Standing Upon Shoulders

A friend told me at a young age that 'a wise man learns from his own mistakes, an even wiser man learns from other people's mistakes,' and I have found this very helpful throughout life. I have discovered that the principle not only holds regarding mistakes but also successes and triumphs. We have much to learn from those who have gone before us and Christians not only have the benefit of journeying through life with other Christians of their own era, but also get to stand upon the shoulders of previous generations.

I like riding on roller coasters and have done so since as long as I can remember. To me there is something exciting not only about the ride itself but also the anticipation of the ride, and in particular when the extent of the 'thrill' from the ride is beyond what you have experienced before. I guess you could call me a thrill seeker, ready for new excitement and adventures. My son and daughter grew up embracing adventure in different forms, from climbing trees at a young age through to white water rafting on the Zambezi river just downstream from Victoria Falls when aged 18 and 16 respectively. What is life if it isn't an adventure!?

When David was 15 years old, one day in October he had a scheduled day off school because of a training day for the teachers. This was a day when most children would be in School and before many tourist attractions closed for winter. An opportunity was presenting itself! I arranged to take a day off work and about 6.00am in the morning David and I set off from Kent for Alton Towers further north in England. The journey took us just under 4 hours and we arrived early in the day, leaving us plenty of time to savour the attractions before the park closed around 6.00pm.

Alton Towers is one of the largest theme parks in England with many great rides including various types of roller coaster; on a regular basis a new faster, scarier, more exhilarating ride would be introduced to the menu on offer with an underlying invitation to those brave enough to try.

In 1998 the major new attraction was Oblivion, the world's first ever 'dive coaster.' What is a 'dive coaster?' we thought to ourselves, already confident with the idea of roller coasters but this was a new idea.

As we entered the park we worked our way through the rides in a sort of progressive order of travel, enjoying the fact that there was very little queuing necessary on this day compared to some long waits on busier days. In our minds our route was taking us toward 'Oblivion' which was in one of the farthest corners of the park away from the entrance. Finally, we arrived in X Sector and came face to face with Oblivion. David and I had ridden many roller coasters in the past and thoroughly enjoyed our adrenaline filled experiences, many steep and fast rides, turning you this way and that, even upside down. We had even ridden one of the world's first purpose built 'stand up roller coasters', the 'Shockwave' at Drayton Manor. However, as we stared up at Oblivion we were somewhat surprised even uncertain. We watched for a few minutes as people already on the ride shrieked, gasped and shouted as they were dropped 180 feet (55 metres) vertically (well 89 degrees) into a hole in the ground to disappear from sight.

This was new! Previously all our roller coaster experiences had been in reasonably plain sight, steep but nowhere near vertical. We had never been dropped into the ground before. As we studied the ride, looking at the carriages carrying the passengers, there were certain reassuring things to give us confidence -

There was a track that the carriages followed and were strongly attached to.

After disappearing into the hole in the ground, the carriages (and their passengers) reappeared above ground a few seconds later still following the track which guided them to their destination.

People were whooping with delight as they ended their ride, many eager for another go.

Reassurance from what we had witnessed, the fact that people had gone before us and survived, and the excitement that ensued all served to persuade us that we would 'have a go'. The queue was short and soon enough we were seated in one of the carriages, David and I side by side, glancing at each other with nervous expectation. Locking mechanisms came down upon us, securing us very tightly in our seats with almost no room to move and a supervisor came to check that we were safely locked in. We started to move forward on the track and immediately we were ascending a very steep climb at what seemed to be a very slow pace. We were moving towards 'the dive.' David and I had chosen to sit right at the front of the carriage in order to maximise our experience and as we reached the top, our carriage tipped slightly over the edge and stopped! It was like we were in suspended animation. From our side came a voice through a loudspeaker with an instruction "Don't look down.". So what did we do? We looked down at the full 55 metre drop into a black hole in the ground, and thought 'that is where we are going, what have we done?!' I glanced across as well to see the carriage which had gone before us emerging from the darkness and found this reassuring.

Suddenly we dropped and started to fall, hurtling towards

the blackness, experiencing forces of 4.5G. Screaming was involuntary and genuine! Within a couple of seconds we entered complete darkness, with literally no sight of where we were going, and then a couple of seconds later we came out into the light, slowing gently as the track took us slightly uphill. Now we started to 'whoop' with delight, not only had we survived but we had enjoyed the ride. Adrenaline flowed through our bodies and a buzz of excitement surrounded us. The carriage came to halt, the lock mechanisms released us from our captivity, and we walked away from the ride straight to the back of the queue to have another go. This time we didn't travel in hope but rather in assurance as seasoned veterans showing the way for others to follow! In total I think we did that ride at least eight times that day.

To this day Oblivion is one of the roller coaster rides that lives in my memory more vividly than most others. In addition to the excitement on the day I also learnt some great lessons about faith:

There is a track specifically designed to carry me on the journey through life.

My carriage is very firmly attached to the tracks of my destiny and will carry me all the way to heaven.
I sit side by side with Jesus on this ride, taking his 'yoke' upon me and tying myself to him.

I am securely anchored.

The ride will include slow uphill climbs which do not seem very exciting but gain the height needed to enable the momentum for the next phase of the journey.

Don't just look down at the challenge, look to those who have gone before.

There will be periods of life where you are not 'in control', trust in your maker is paramount at such times.

There is much joy ahead of us. As the bible states "For

the joy set before him, Jesus endured the cross."

Experience leads to assurance.

I can become an example of breakthrough for other people.

I am not the first one to travel with God and there is much to learn from the experience of others.

I wrote about Hebrews 11 earlier in this book. It is a chapter about endeavours of faith and some giants of the faith. Some of the inclusions are surprising:

- A woman called Rahab, known as the prostitute!
- Abraham who put his wife in Pharaoh's harem, and later on he put her in Abimelech's harem.
- Jacob the swindler and deceiver.
- Moses the murderer.
- King David the adulterer and murderer.
- Samson who lacked self-control and wisdom.

I find it fascinating that God's choice of recollection for us in the New Testament is to hold them up as examples of faith. Sometimes we look at our errors and mistakes and think they discount us from being people of great faith, but the Bible doesn't teach that. Rather it takes human stories and follows them through their ups and downs as the people in them have the opportunity to grow in faith and connection with God. Every one of us can look at such examples and be encouraged, not by sympathy with their failures but by inspiration in overcoming and moving forward in faith.

No matter where you are in your faith right now as long as you step forward in faith nothing can stop you from becoming a 'Giant in the Faith.'

God gives the same opportunity of life and destiny to

all his children, he may have laid different tracks for us to journey on but we are all heading for the same destination. We can all learn from the examples of those who have gone before us and also those who are presently around us.

As the Bible puts it:

Hebrews 6:12 We do not want you to become lazy, but to imitate those who through faith and patience inherit what has been promised.

Hebrews 13:7 Remember your leaders, who spoke the word of God to you. Consider the outcome of their way of life and imitate their faith.

I believe that not only do we get to stand on the shoulders of giants so that we can move beyond their finishing place in extending the kingdom of God, but also that as we move forward in faith we will ourselves be an example for following generations to learn from and move ever further forward.

You can become a giant of the faith upon whose shoulders others will stand.

Story by Janice Pleasants:

I was in a bank queuing up for the counter service, standing
behind a young woman. I suddenly saw a picture of several
butterflies flying, I looked to my right and a customer being
served at the counter had a T-shirt on with a large butterfly
on the back of it and some place name. I was just wondering
if my picture had something to do with him when I felt the
Holy Spirit say, "It's not him it's for her," the woman in the
queue in front of me. I then got the impression that I should
tell her that she had new life in her. She was sideways, so
I caught her attention by commenting, "That's an amazing
butterfly on that guy's T-shirt isn't it?" As she turned to me,
she agreed and I said, "I just get the sense that butterflies are
somehow significant to you." She said, "That's amazing!" and
dropped her cardigan off her shoulder. There up her shoulder
were flying butterflies in a tattoo just like I'd seen in my head.
She said, "You can't have seen them, so how could you know
that?" I said, "I'm a Christian practising hearing from God
and I also feel the phrase 'new life' means something to you."
She immediately teared up and asked if she could meet
outside when we had finished. She was 19 years old and said
she had found out the previous week that she was pregnant
and she'd encountered a lot of family pressure, as a single
mum, to have an abortion. I felt the Holy Spirit say, "Love
her from Me." So I asked if I could pray for her, and I simply
prayed for His wisdom and peace to come to her. She felt His
Presence and I gave her a hug. I explained that God knew all
about her as demonstrated today, and He loved her so much.
She went away profoundly touched by this encounter with a
loving Father.

Chapter 27 Confidence and Humility

Imagine a woman walking into my medical consultation room and before conversation begins, in order to demonstrate my humility, I start by saying "I think it is really important for you to know that I am not really a very good doctor." I think she would be puzzled, probably alarmed, and her confidence in me would be eroded with the likely outcome that she would be looking elsewhere for medical advice in the future. I would probably have been a hindrance to her access to the resources of the health service that I have at my disposal. Such false humility is a hindrance to genuine relationships and confidence and yet it is not uncommon to find it expressed in Christianity and sometimes held up as a Christian virtue.

Confidence and trust are vital ingredients of a medical consultation enabling successful interactions and outcomes. I remember many occasions when a patient would start to tell me their symptoms and very soon I was confident that I knew what their condition was and that there was a solution readily at hand, this confidence could then be transferred to the patient and a good outcome achieved.

One such occasion was with a lady in her early eighties who had been struggling with pain in many of her joints, lethargy of a severe nature and general malaise. She was accompanied by her daughter and their mood was very downbeat as they expected bad news; it looked like she was 'accepting her fate' with little optimism for the future.

Having listened carefully for a few minutes, I smiled at her and confidently told her that I was pretty certain I knew what was wrong and that there was a very straightforward remedy. She would need some blood tests to confirm my thinking and we could progress from there. The lady and the daughter noticeably changed in demeanour, my confidence bringing hope into their situation. A few days later they returned for the result of the blood tests. I smiled as they entered the room, a different ambience came to rest upon them as I was able to confirm the diagnosis of Polymyalgia Rheumatica and confidently predicted a swift return to health after we started the correct medication. I asked them to return the following week for a checkup.

Imagine my joy when the elderly lady turned up the following week, more upright in stance and sprightly in step, she walked into my room without her daughter, sat down, smiled at me and said "You have given me my life back". She continued to live a fulfilled existence for many years, coming back for regular reviews, always with a smile and gratitude.

Confidence is a very important thing in life and is not to be confused with arrogance. As a General Practitioner I was confident in my own practice and knowledge, but I was also very aware of the limitations of my knowledge, experience and facilities. Someone who required surgery needed to be referred to a surgeon, likewise with someone suffering a heart attack immediate referral to hospital is necessary. It is not a weakness as a doctor to need other doctors, also it is not arrogant to be confident in your own area of work.

Over the years I have been involved in employing many people and helping them settle into their new work. Initially people are somewhat unfamiliar and uncertain, but with experience their confidence grows and this helps the whole environment. Confident people are more productive and can help other people more effectively.

Arrogance is where someone believes themselves to

be superior in some way, this usually results in less effective teamwork and togetherness. I saw this quite often in the world of medicine, where an individual would treat others as inferior in some way, thereby reducing camaraderie, support and encouragement which are all vital ingredients of a healthy working environment.

When I first qualified as a doctor, I knew that despite my five years of training at Medical School I still had a lot to learn; nurses, physiotherapists, receptionists, cleaners, porters etc were all part of the structure that makes a hospital work and generally had more experience of the working environment than me. I asked questions of everyone: "How does this work?", "What normally happens?", "What next?" "Where do I go for lunch?"

Alongside these questions I brought my skills as a doctor, quickly growing in confidence and playing my part in the 'hospital team.' I enjoyed working alongside others in this way, as we all confidently played our part to save and enrich other people's lives.

I believe it is very important to be confident in what I am good at so that I can give my best. I also believe it is important to know that I still don't know everything and that I need to learn more. Strangely to some ways of thinking I also believe it is important to be confident about what I am not good at. For example, I do enjoy music but I have next to no musical talent and I am quite certain about that. When I became a Christian at the age of 16 it seemed to me that all Christians could play the guitar; therefore I thought that I should try to learn. For some reason I had bought a cheap guitar as a souvenir from a family holiday in Spain but I had never attempted to play it, it just hung on my bedroom wall as an ornament. Now it's time had arrived!

I bought a book to instruct me: the first lesson was to

'tune the guitar', so I began following the instructions in a methodical fashion which required the ability to recognise when different strings were playing the same note. I was hopeless at it. I simply can't recognise musical notes but I could recognise that the sound I was making was far from musical. I sought help from 'proper' guitarists of whom there were a good number in my church. They endeavoured to help me with kind assurances that it was really very simple - but in my mind the musical notes simply didn't register. After a while I came to the conclusion that my brain was not equipped in that particular skill, and with a degree of relief I stopped trying to become good at something I was not equipped for. I am very confident in my lack of musical ability.

Other people are less confident in my inability in that area, and over the years many kind souls have offered to help me to enter into the realms of pleasure that they get from playing music. I turn down their kind offers knowing that my time and theirs is too valuable to waste in trying to become something God has not designed me to be. I do enter into the pleasure of music most avidly by enjoying the music produced by those with the gift to do so. I enjoy both live and recorded music and I have become very good at playing the iPod!

Some gifts you can ask God for, others are inherently part of the unique creation of each human being. We are all different and not everyone carries the same gifts, a lack of gifting in an area is not the same as weakness. Weakness is relevant to areas that respond to strengthening and that is a Biblical instruction. To recognise an area where you lack gifting is not a recognition of weakness but rather wisdom that can save you wasting a lot of time and energy on fruitless endeavour. My advice to you is to excel in being your God given self and don't strive to be what you are not; be confident in your areas of calling and gifting and concentrate on growing in and strengthening those areas.

Let's look at a Bible passage that I think illustrates principles about this extremely well.

Acts 3:

> *One day Peter and John were going up to the temple at the time of prayer—at three in the afternoon. 2 Now a man who was lame from birth was being carried to the temple gate called Beautiful, where he was put every day to beg from those going into the temple courts. 3 When he saw Peter and John about to enter, he asked them for money. 4 Peter looked straight at him, as did John. Then Peter said, "Look at us!" 5 So the man gave them his attention, expecting to get something from them.*

What was the man expecting? Obviously he was hoping for some money to continue his meagre existence, much the same as every other day.

> *6 Then Peter said, "Silver or gold I do not have, but what I do have I give you. In the name of Jesus Christ of Nazareth, walk."*

Peter was confident about what he did not have, this is wise. What you do not have you cannot give away.

> *7 Taking him by the right hand, he helped him up, and instantly the man's feet and ankles became strong. 8 He jumped to his feet and began to walk. Then he went with them into the temple courts, walking and jumping, and praising God. 9 When all the people saw him walking and praising God, 10 they recognized him as the same man who used to sit begging at the temple gate called Beautiful, and they were filled with wonder and amazement at what had happened to him.*

I wonder what would have happened if Peter had not been confident in the name of Jesus? I suspect the man would not have been healed on that day and other people would not have had the opportunity to see the power of God at work. Lack of confidence can sometimes be a learnt mechanism designed to keep people in a place of low expectation because of a fear of appearing arrogant, however, I believe that such a situation is actually false humility and that is a huge enemy of faith in God.

> *11 While the man held on to Peter and John, all the people were astonished and came running to them in the place called Solomon's Colonnade. 12 When Peter saw this, he said to them: "Fellow Israelites, why does this surprise you?*

Peter was not surprised because he was confident in what God had developed within him. He was inviting people into a similar experience.

Why do you stare at us as if by our own power or godliness we had made this man walk?

This demonstrates confidence and true humility.

> *13 The God of Abraham, Isaac and Jacob, the God of our fathers, has glorified his servant Jesus. You handed him over to be killed, and you disowned him before Pilate, though he had decided to let him go. 14 You disowned the Holy and Righteous One and asked that a murderer be released to you. 15 You killed the author of life, but God raised him from the dead. We are witnesses of this.*

Peter is confident in what he has witnessed.

16 By faith in the name of Jesus, this man whom you see and know was made strong. It is Jesus' name and the faith that comes through him that has completely healed him, as you can all see.

Peter explains about faith in the name of Jesus and the power experienced through such faith. He presents to them the opportunity to enter into the adventure of "faith in the name of Jesus". Peter's confidence and faith enable other people to enter into the realities of God.

In contrast false humility is a barrier not just to personal growth but also to the expansion of God's kingdom.

Faith is confidence in the power of God at work through his people. Examples of such confidence are numerous in the Bible for example in the story of Joseph in Genesis:

Genesis 40:8 Interpreting dreams is God's Business, Joseph replied. Go ahead and tell me your dreams.

Joseph was confident in his part to play in God's business.

Gen 41: 16 it is beyond my power to do this, Joseph replied but God can tell you what it means. So Pharaoh told Joseph his dream.

Confidence in God's power needs to be associated with recognition of our lack of power when we are not connected to God. This is godly humility.

God is our source of power and without connection there is no power.

It is similar to an electrical appliance not being connected to a source of electricity, it is a tool with no power. I am confident that I am a tool in God's hands for the extension of his kingdom but I also know that without proper connection to him I will simply become an ornament.

Story by Sasha Caridia:

Around a year after leaving the Ambulance Service to start working in a Minor Injury Unit I had a catch up with a friend and former colleague.

One cold winter's evening two years earlier, whilst at work, he asked me to pray for his shoulder and then decided that he wanted to accept the life that Jesus had for him after his shoulder 'got better!'

Around the same time another colleague had made a recommitment to follow Jesus after he saw his mother healed in front of his eyes when we prayed for her in a hospital cubicle.

My heart was so happy as my friend talked about the relationship that he and his children have with Jesus. He then went on to explain that the other colleague, who made the recommitment after his mother's encounter with God, was now, in his words, 'training' to become a vicar!

This was such an encouraging conversation, sometimes we don't get to hear about what happens in people's lives until after we have left a place.

Be encouraged, you bring the Kingdom of Heaven wherever you go and it is impossible for nothing to happen, keep going, keep praying, keep loving.

Chapter 28 Stepping out in Faith

One of the most important lessons that I have learnt in expanding my faith is being willing to step out in faith. I remember very clearly being in Mexico with Otilio, a young man who had been paralysed in all four limbs for ten years, and as I was praying for his healing God spoke to me very clearly that he wanted me to "pick him up, put his feet on the ground and let him go". Many thoughts passed through my mind in the few seconds that followed but they ended up in one question- was I willing to "Step out in faith?"

This story is told in full as the first chapter of my book "Unwrapping Lazarus" so I won't spoil it here by giving the outcome.

The choice to respond to the promptings of God is one that faces Christians all the time and the choices made will determine whether we will grow in faith in that moment of time. I remember a time many years ago when God told me to send a gift of money to my sister who is also a Christian. He told me that he wanted me to do it that very day and that the sum of money should be precisely £53. It seemed like a strange amount of money, "why not £50?" went through my mind but I dismissed that thought and did as prompted by God and sent the money by first class post to arrive the next day.

The next day my sister phoned me up and was very excited. She told me that they needed to replace the stair carpet in their house because it was very worn and torn and had actually become a safety hazard in particular to their children. Their problem was that they had no spare money to buy the carpet. She and her husband, Grantley, had prayed and asked God about it and were prompted by God to go out that very morning and order the carpet from a shop. They were a bit reluctant because they did not have the money but stepped out in faith, trusting the voice of God. They ordered the carpet and returned home to find my gift to them which had arrived whilst they were out at the shop. They opened the envelope and gasped in admiration of God - the carpet that they had ordered cost precisely £53. Their faith and mine grew on that day as we both stepped out in faith. Jesus truly is the author and perfecter of our faith.

We have friends in our church who took a step of faith as they obeyed God and decided to leave France in order to come and be with our church and training school in England. They have three children and it looked like an impossible task that required numerous miraculous provisions for it to happen. Their church in France was praying for them and someone gave them a 'prophetic image' to encourage them: it said, "Stepping out in faith is like walking towards an automatic door, it only opens as you walk towards it and get close."
How true, and how many of us have discovered this truth?

I often teach on this subject using a very familiar story from the gospels.

We find it in Matthew 14:

22 Immediately Jesus made the disciples get into the boat and go on ahead of him to the other side, while he dismissed the crowd. 23 After he had dismissed them, he went up on a mountainside by himself to pray. Later that night, he was there alone, 24 and the boat was already a considerable distance from land, buffeted by the waves because the wind was against it.

Setting the scene, Jesus has sent the disciples out in a boat to cross the lake, the wind is strong and the waves are powerful.

25 Shortly before dawn Jesus went out to them, walking on the lake.

Jesus walks on the water to catch up with the disciples.

26 When the disciples saw him walking on the lake, they were terrified. "It's a ghost," they said, and cried out in fear.

Not surprisingly the disciples don't recognise that it is Jesus as they have never seen him do this before, probably in their minds only ghosts walked on water. They are afraid.

27 But Jesus immediately said to them: "Take courage! It is I. Don't be afraid."

Jesus reassured them that it was him and there was no need to be afraid.

28 "Lord, if it's you," Peter replied, "tell me to come to you on the water."

This statement always amuses me as a thought comes into my mind that a clever ghost might well try to trick Peter into believing that it is Jesus. Anyway, enough of such distraction. Peter as always is quick to respond. We are not informed in detail the reason behind Peter's response and request but he was certainly up for new experiences!

29 "Come," he said.

Jesus extends an invitation to Peter. Will he step out in faith?

Then Peter got down out of the boat, walked on the water and came toward Jesus.

I try to imagine what this moment would have looked like:
    How tentative was Peter?
    How long did he hold on to the boat for?
    Did he try out one foot first?
    What were the other disciples saying? Encouragement or Discouragement? Excited shouting or concerned silence?
    And then he walked on water towards Jesus. What an amazing step of faith. What exhilaration.
    What happened next?

30 But when he saw the wind, he was afraid and, beginning to sink, cried out, "Lord, save me!"

I have often heard it taught that the issue that caused Peter to start to sink was that he took his eyes off Jesus; whilst this may be true it is not the Biblical explanation. The Bible says "when he saw the wind": Peter was distracted by the adverse circumstances he was facing.
    However, I have a question to ask - is it easier to walk on water when the weather is calm or when it is windy?
    The answer is obvious once you think about it: Neither is possible without God. Distractions often present circumstances as though they are serious challenges to the work of God. Could the wind stop Peter walking on the water? Only if he believed it could.
    At the Eastgate Healing Centre we have a principle of asking people only the minimum details necessary about their problem in order for us to engage meaningfully with them in an empathetic and loving way. We don't need to know the size and extent of the problem in full detail because we know that

God is bigger than any problem. Another reason is that we want them to be more focussed on God than their problems. We invite them into our atmosphere of faith, joy, peace and love and leave the atmosphere of their circumstances. Some people find this challenging to do and keep trying to remind us how extensive their problem is, often letting us know in addition that 'prayer hasn't worked for them in the past.' They are good at seeing the storm and that can distract them from encountering Jesus.

However, Jesus' hand is always stretched out towards us and he is willing and able to overcome any storm of circumstance.

> *31 Immediately Jesus reached out his hand and caught him. "You of little faith," he said, "why did you doubt?" 32 And when they climbed into the boat, the wind died down.*

Jesus caught Peter and stopped him from sinking below the waves. He then challenges Peter's faith and asks him why he doubted. To my mind Jesus is helping us to understand what "little faith and doubt" look like. They look like being more impressed by our circumstances than by Jesus, and doubting his power to carry us through the circumstances.

Please note that the wind didn't die down until they got back into the boat. Why did Jesus do it that way? In order to demonstrate that adverse circumstances cannot stand in the way of miracles.

Once again I let my imagination run across this part of the story and this is how I see it in my mind:

Jesus catches Peter and pulls him up on top of the water, he doesn't drag him through the water. He then walks with Peter on the water so that Peter's faith and confidence can grow. What an experience. When the lesson is over they both climb into the boat and at that moment the wind dies down. Jesus in complete control of all the circumstances and helping Peter to grow in faith.

What about the other disciples?

33 Then those who were in the boat worshiped him, saying, "Truly you are the Son of God"

The other disciples had witnessed what had happened and were moved to worship Jesus, acknowledging him as the son of God. Their faith had also grown because Peter had stepped out in faith; however, they did not have the experience that Peter had. Once again my imagination makes me wonder whether any of the other disciples asked Jesus to take them for a walk on the water, thereby moving from witnesses to participants?

Stepping out in faith usually involves moving from being a witness to being a participant.

I wonder how that story would be retold if you or I had witnessed it? What part would Peter's failure play in the story? If the telling of the story was stopped at the moment Peter began to sink below the waves it would contain truth but it wouldn't be the true story.

How often do we make people's shortcomings and failures our main recollection when they step out in faith, rather than follow the story through to its conclusion.

How often do we stop at the moment of our own failures not realising Jesus' hand is stretched out towards us to help us complete the journey of faith already mapped out for us. This can lead to such a fear of failure that we stop stepping out in faith and cease to grow.

When we started the Eastgate School of Spiritual Life (https://eastgate.org.uk/essl/) we taught people the principles of 'Treasure Hunting' as part of the very practical ways of developing a naturally, supernatural lifestyle.

It is quite simple really: spend time listening to God and ask him to give you 'clues' that will lead you to specific people. Every person is precious to God and therefore they are his treasure waiting to be found.

Our students learned to listen to God and write down the clues they had been given on their 'treasure map. Then they would go into our local town in search of treasure and, led by the clues would approach people and introduce themselves by saying something like: 'Hello we are on a treasure hunt, and we have some clues that have led us to you and we believe you are our treasure.' Often conversations would follow and we could explain to people about God's love and power and offer to pray for them. And what amazing things we see happen when we do this.

However, it takes courage to do this and run the risk of rejection or 'getting it wrong, and failing.'

On one day our teams set out in pairs around the town to find their treasure armed with their treasure maps. One team spotted a man who met about five of their clues so they approached him with confidence and introduced themselves to him as being on a treasure hunt. "Not interested," came back his reply and he walked off. The team was disappointed. Around the corner was another team who spotted the same man and he also matched their (different) clues. They approached him and got the same response. Further down the hill in town another team was excited when they saw a man who matched their (different) clues, it was the same man but this team had no knowledge of what had already transpired. They approached him and struck up a conversation.

"Who are you people?" he exclaimed and entered into the conversation. He had a serious problem with one of his ankles (the clues had pointed to this) and somewhat reluctantly he allowed the team to pray for him, and then he limped away. It was just before Christmas.

After New Year when we reopened the church office there was a message awaiting us on the phone. The man explained that he had encountered our teams in town and received prayer for his ankle. He then told us that the MRI scan he had shortly after prayer revealed that his severely damaged ankle was now normal on the scan, his pain and limp were gone and he wanted to thank us. In addition, he wanted to meet someone in town for coffee and to talk about Jesus. We were all thrilled and the story was shared around all the staff and students of the School of Spiritual Life. The first two teams who might have felt some degree of failure previously realised that they were part of this great success story.

We always teach the students that courageously stepping out in faith is always a success and pleasing to God no matter the seeming outcome. It is a mistake to stop the story at any seeming failure. Courage to risk rejection, ridicule and even persecution in order to step out in faith is always a huge success in God's eyes, and a huge growth point for our faith. The fear of failure and rejection is not our friend; it needs to be overcome by faith.

John Wimber, an amazing man of God and the founder of the Vineyard Church movement, helped to stir up Christianity in the latter part of the 20th Century towards believing in the supernatural aspect of our daily Christian lives. He talked about "doing the stuff" we read about in the Bible, and he stirred people to grow in faith. One of his famous sayings is "Faith is spelled R I S K."

The Bible explains that Christianity is inherently risky from an earthly point of view:

2 Timothy 3:12 In fact, everyone who wants to live a godly life in Christ Jesus will be persecuted.

Matthew 5:10 Blessed are those who are persecuted because of righteousness, for theirs is the kingdom of heaven.

Romans 12:1 Therefore, I urge you, brothers and sisters, in view of God's mercy, to offer your bodies as a living sacrifice, holy and pleasing to God—this is your true and proper worship.

Jesus called his disciples to lay down their lives for other people, to love their enemies, to not pay back evil with evil, and to expect suffering and persecution. Jesus didn't promise us a life of comfort and ease, but he did promise us a comforter, the Holy Spirit, to be with us. Jesus didn't call us to a life of leisure, but did offer 'Rest for our soul' and 'Peace that passes understanding'

Jesus asked us to lay down our lives as living sacrifices and in return offered us Eternal Life with joy beyond measure.

The Bible tells us that without the assurance of eternity in front of us our earthly existence as Christians doesn't make sense. 1 Corinthians 15: 19 *If only for this life we have hope in Christ, we are of all people most to be pitied.*

Christianity on earth is inherently risky, but the rewards in heaven far outweigh any troubles here. 2 Corinthians 4: 17 *For our light and momentary troubles are achieving for us an eternal glory that far outweighs them all.*

So we need to understand what RISK looks like in our own context as it varies with context.

For example, the risk of starting an open fire for warmth and cooking whilst camping in woodland is very different in wet conditions than it is in dry conditions where it could cause a forest fire.

The risk of swimming depends on the context: swimming in a swimming pool is low risk, swimming in the ocean far from land with no support and strong currents is higher risk.

What sort of RISK does openly displaying your Christianity place upon your life?

In some countries you could be risking your life itself, maybe imprisonment, separation from your family possibly, even loss of all your earthly possessions. Why would you take such a high risk?

The answer is that the rewards outweigh the risk.

The way to assess risk is to ascertain if the Benefit exceeds the Cost, and we do this all the time in our daily lives, for example:

We learn to decide how much money we want to spend on a certain purchase. Is it worth it?

Is it worth my time and effort? is a common calculation in our brains.

Close relationships require a degree of sacrifice and this enters our decision making about them.

The word 'safe' is linked to the concept of risk and it is a word I have found to be used increasingly commonly in our modern world.

'Is it safe?' is a question posed in relation to many walks of life, for example vaccines, medicines, eating various foods, modes of travel.

It is also a component of relationships, do people 'feel safe' with one another.

It can be applied to certain geographical areas where hostility and violence are more common. It can also be applied to the issue of Climate Change and other Global challenges.

'I don't feel safe' is a statement that seems to be increasingly common but what does it mean?

This is a subject to which I have given a lot of thought in recent times, and one of my observations is that it is common for 'safe' to be viewed as an absolute reality rather than a relative reality. For instance, during the CoVid pandemic which caused understandable massive concerns about safety in all sorts of ways, I heard some parents saying, "I am not letting my children go back to school until I know it is absolutely safe." I understood the concerns and sentiments but going to school has never been absolutely safe from risks:

Risk of rejection and bullying.

Risk of injury through playing sport or falling over.

Risk of crossing the road when walking to school.

For Christians some other considerations may come into play in our daily lives, for instance is there any risk to you if you display your Christianity in your workplace?

In my cultural context living in England, I am very unlikely to be imprisoned for my faith, be separated from my family or lose my life through persecution. So what risks do I actually face? What does sacrifice look like in my life? What cost is there to me because of my Christianity?

I will list a few areas where I have found it necessary to be willing to pay the cost and sacrifice associated with following Jesus, and some of the attitudes I have adopted to help me.

My time - my most precious commodity, you cannot buy it back. Jesus is worthy of my time.

My money - trusting God with my finances and adopting an increasingly generous lifestyle.

My reputation - overcoming the fear of man, overcoming rejection, and not compromising the truth of the gospel.

My comfort - following Jesus will take me out of my comfort zones.

My leisure - overcoming the pressure within the world to build a lifestyle of increasing wealth and leisure.

One specific example of a sacrifice that happened in my life was early in my medical career: I had applied for a new job which would take me forward for the next three years in my medical training and provide security and stability for myself and my family. The job was in the same hospital where I was currently working, my reputation was very good, and the senior doctors (consultants) I worked for were extremely supportive and had given me glowing references which included reference to my Christianity stating that it enhanced my work as a doctor. Everyone including myself expected me to get the job, one of two on offer. I was selected on a short list for an interview and the day of the interview arrived.

During the interview by a panel of senior doctors, one of them started to ask me about my Christianity in a somewhat hostile manner. I was a bit surprised because questions about personal faith were not usually asked in medical interviews, so I was not prepared for this line of questioning. I answered in what I believe was a wise way, in line with medical regulations and guidelines in the UK, and without compromising my Christian faith.

The result of the interview was that I did not get the job. It was a total shock, not only to me but also throughout the hospital. My Consultants asked for an explanation from the interview panel and found that I had been turned down because of my Christianity; to say they were angry would be an understatement, and they explained to me that those questions about my faith should never have been asked of me as it was unethical to do so and discriminatory towards to me. In addition, it flew in the face of their references which stated that my Christian faith was beneficial to my work and to those around me.

I did not know as I went into that interview that I was at risk for being open about my faith: the result was that I was without a regular job for a number of months, we came under financial pressure and I had to rethink my career path. Would I have changed any of my behaviour? Absolutely not. My faith is an integral part of who I am and I do not hide it, but I am wise in the way I demonstrate it to other people. In all my medical career I have never had a complaint from patients or colleagues against me because of my Christian beliefs. However, on that one occasion I suffered from discrimination - it was a cost I was willing to pay on my journey of faith.

Jesus continually calls us to step out in faith, to continue to accept the earthly risks involved in following him, confident that he will use us on earth to spread the blessings and good news of his kingdom, and bring salvation to other people so that they too can know the assurance of eternal life.

From an earthly point of view Christianity can look risky, but from an eternal point of view the risks are far outweighed by the benefits.

Story by Sasha Caridia:

Recently whilst out and about on a 'Treasure Hunt' a couple
of us were heading to a location we felt we should go to. We
had listened to the Holy Spirit for some 'clues' and we were
looking for specific people who matched the descriptions we
had. As we were arriving at the location I saw a man in a
wheelchair that I had met once before, he has a progressive
degenerative neurological condition, he is a follower of Jesus.
As we chatted, God dropped something very specific into
my heart for him. It wasn't related to his health rather it was
about remote working and him having his own consultancy
business. His face lit up, due to his worsening health he
was unable to continue in a very specialised job where his
knowledge and skills are not easily found. The man has been
in the process of setting up a consultancy and had just been
speaking to a recruitment agency. We decided to show the
man the various clues we had written down some minutes
before. They included the location, his name, his daughter's
nickname with a very particular spelling, specifics about a job
and recruitment agency! It was a wonderful moment as he
read through them and realised that Father God was in the
details of his life and had orchestrated his whole morning
to that point so that he would be in that place at that time
to hear the heart of God for him and his immediate family.
The wheelchair would have been the most obvious sign of
need, however, sitting in the wheelchair was a son, someone
of great value, who was sharing dreams about his business
venture and also his concerns for his daughter. He had given
her the nickname and was so touched that His Heavenly
Father would use this and the other clues to demonstrate that
what matters to him matters to Him. I asked what he would
like prayer for, he asked us to pray for his daughter, his wife
and his new business. Asking if we could also pray for healing

he emphatically replied "absolutely, yes" so we prayed and he prayed for us, it was a truly wonderful, joyful moment. We were somewhat awestruck at the love of God that once again had the power to break into a person's life at just the right time to build them up, cheer them up and draw them closer to their loving Heavenly Father. Our expectation is that when the love and power of God is released it is impossible for nothing to happen, the wheelchair is not part of God's dream for him.

Chapter 29 Never Walk Alone

The journey and adventure of following God is not to be walked alone. God has put us amongst a group of companions, fellow travellers, friends.

God desires that we should be part of communities of faith in committed relationships to one another with a common passion for God, the Father, Son and Holy Spirit. Learning together, supporting one another and creating something beautiful together. Such communities are called the church.

The church is a universal entity with an eternal reality, and also a local expression in a contemporary setting. The Bible tells us a lot about what churches should be like, with plenty of room for different expressions, but one of the most important common realities is that they should be environments of increasing faith and love.

Galatians 5:6 puts it this way *"the only thing that counts is "faith expressing itself through love"*

Faith expressing itself through love is given as a summary of the Christian life and of what churches should be like. This thought has been a governing principle in my personal life, my family life, my work and the church of which I am a part. In 1988, Kim and I with our two children, David and Kerry, moved house to live in a village called New Ash Green. This was a result of God speaking to both of us separately on the same day about that very same thing. I was a full time doctor in general practice, Kim a very busy young mother, great homemaker and woman of faith with a gift for hospitality amongst other things. We became part of a small church and added our faith to theirs. It was a church with quite a lot of struggles and which had seen little or no growth for a number of years but at that moment God seemed to be drawing people towards it.

Six months after our house move the church went through a very serious crisis and the leader at that time decided to leave and move on, a few other people decided to move on as well. The Sunday after this transpired, about 25 adults and children gathered at our Sunday meeting in a rather sad, perplexed and sombre mood. It was more like a funeral than a time of worship. Spontaneously Kim offered that anyone who wanted lunch together could come to our house straight after the meeting. We had planned lunch for the four of us!

Twenty-six people arrived!

And what we found was extraordinary - a bewildered group of people who loved God and believed that He could pull us through together somehow. Hope was still alive and faith began to grow in that soil.

Shortly afterwards this small group of people asked if I would lead them forward in faith and together we would build a great church, a faith filled community reaching other people with the love and power of Jesus. Kim and I were excited as we knew that God was suddenly bringing into being more of the reality of his calling upon our lives, to lead millions of people into the freedom that Jesus has purchased for them.

However, it was also daunting: I was a full time doctor who worked very long hours, we had a young family and we had a house that needed a lot of work doing on it. I remember when I told the church that I would gladly accept their invitation to lead them forward, but I made very clear some things about the way forward:

- The Presence of God was our paramount priority.
- If God told us to do something we would agree immediately and then work out how to do it afterwards, relying on him to provide the resources.
- Everyone would play their part in building this church.
- I was in no way superior or separate from them, we were all equal in value.
- I would play my part but that I would not do everything.
- I would lead them with love and faith.
- We would build an Oasis of Faith in the desert of unbelief.

That last image continues to guide our church to this day and it is extremely important to understand it. I live in the UK and in my opinion there is a cultural value of 'unbelief' in this nation, it is a 'stronghold' mindset in our culture. How can we recognise this stronghold, how does it manifest itself? Here are some thoughts:

- Valuing negative responses above positive ones
- Valuing cynicism
- Valuing suspicion above trust
- Valuing caution rather than careful evaluation of risk
- An unwillingness to acknowledge "unseen realms"
- Questions to dismiss the supernatural rather than to learn.

It is not only a secular stronghold but is a great enemy to the church, an enemy which has unfortunately infiltrated behind the defensive walls of many churches. It is a great enemy of individual and corporate faith, and environments with corporate unbelief do not provide a healthy environment for faith to grow, in fact they do the opposite.

Nazareth would be an example of corporate unbelief - Jesus could not perform miracles there, except for a few individuals who dared to break off the shackles of unbelief and to approach Jesus with faith. Unbelief is strongly linked to a suspicious mindset, a mind that asks questions to find faults rather than progressive answers based on trust.

So we set out as a church with a determination to create a culture of faith. As it emerged out of its crisis, still carrying some sadness at the loss of friends who had been journeying with us, our small church recommenced its journey with renewed faith and enthusiasm. The meetings became vibrant experiences of God, where the presence of God and his words to us were more important than our planned programme. We wanted to encounter Him. Miracles started to happen not only in our meetings but also through our everyday lives, people were born again and added to the church. God spoke to us and we said "Yes Lord." We served our village to enrich its community life. We engaged with other churches in the UK and other nations working with them to grow in faith together and do great exploits for God, one example of which is Farming God's Way which helps to overcome hunger, famine and poverty in developing nations. We resisted unbelief and any other stronghold we identified that would come against our mission of faith and love. We used our shields of faith to extinguish the enemy's arrows launched against us in the form of lies, accusations, temptations, fear, isolation, independence, guilt, shame. We learned how to 'speak the truth in love' knowing that this was essential in building a community of love and faith.

We were determined to grow in faith and become an oasis where anyone could drink of the glory, goodness, love and power of God. Over thirty years later we marvel at what God has done amongst us, he has been so faithful to us. As you know, the church is now called Eastgate in response to a prophecy from God about our destiny, and there are so many stories we could tell, however, I think I will need another book for that.

We have learnt many things en route, principles and values that have helped to guide us. Many have already been mentioned in this book but here are a few more to help you understand how to grow in faith. At the end of the book I will write a check list covering the key issues covered in the whole book; you might like to refer to it as a guide on your own journey.

Opening your eyes to the unseen realms:
In 2 Kings chapter 6 we find a story that illustrates this so well. The king of Aram is at war with Israel and the prophet Elisha sees in the spirit all the king's plans in advance, thereby helping Israel to avoid Aram's attacks. In response the king orders that Elisha be found and captured; they get news that he is in a city called Dothan so a large number of troops are sent overnight to surround the city. Next morning things are not looking good for Elisha and his servant - or are they? Let's take it up from there:

> *15 When the servant of the man of God got up and went out early the next morning, an army with horses and chariots had surrounded the city. "Oh no, my lord! What shall we do?" the servant asked.*

> *16 "Don't be afraid," the prophet answered. "Those who are with us are more than those who are with them."*

Elisha's servant sees the troops and is understandably alarmed and afraid. There seems to be no way out of this situation. Elisha himself is calm and at peace because he can see something his servant can't as yet. He replies to his servant that the enemy is outnumbered and there is no need to fear. On the face of it with only human reckoning and human insight Elisha is wrong. So we can imagine some of the thoughts going through the servant's mind. We can understand him being afraid.

> *17 And Elisha prayed, "Open his eyes, Lord, so that he may see." Then the Lord opened the servant's eyes, and he looked and saw the hills full of horses and chariots of fire all around.*

I love this prayer. It is one of the clearest examples in the Bible of a prayer of faith:

Elisha does not cry out to God in desperation for help because he knows that help has already been given. He can see the army of heaven. He asks with confidence for God to open his servant's spiritual eyes. The servant sees the resources of heaven that have already been given. Fear turns to Faith in an instant.

The Bible teaches us that we have already received every *"spiritual blessing in Christ"* (Ephesians 1:3). We need to continually have our spiritual eyes open to see the resources that God has already made available to us. Faith doesn't ask for what has already been received, but rather for "revelation and wisdom" to perceive what has been given and the wisdom to know how to put it into practice.

> *Ephesians 1: 17 I keep asking that the God of our Lord Jesus Christ, the glorious Father, may give you the Spirit of wisdom and revelation, so that you may know him better. 18 I pray that the eyes of your heart may be enlightened in order that you may know the hope to which he has called you, the riches of his glorious inheritance in his holy people*

I find that Christians often have questions about receiving things from God, or not receiving: in my mind the issue is often perception rather than reception. Let's ask God to "open the eyes of our hearts and be enlightened".

Generosity
God is generous beyond measure:

- Salvation and new life is given freely to us because Jesus paid the price.
- We receive the Holy Spirit freely because of Jesus' victory.
- The Holy Spirit gives us gifts when we ask.
- We have a divine destiny assigned to each one of us by grace.
- We have been blessed with every spiritual blessing.

The Bible teaches us that all these things become ours through faith. However, the journey of faith is not only about receiving but also about giving; it is also a journey into the likeness of God with ever increasing glory. One of the ways we become like God is through being increasingly generous - with our time, our energy, and our money.

Kim and I have been on a continual journey of generosity; we have both given 10% of our income to our local church since we were teenagers and this is the starting point for us in our financial management, all things follow from that. We believe that what we do with the other 90% of our income is where our generosity is fully expressed. We have endeavoured to make generosity a daily lifestyle rather than a special event, and we believe it is foundational for growing in faith. *Luke 16:11 So if you have not been trustworthy in handling worldly wealth, who will trust you with true riches?*

This principle is taught to people in our church so that we not only have generous individuals but we have sought to build a corporate culture of generosity. Our church corporately exercises generosity.

Placing your trust in God with regard to money and to provide for you to be increasingly generous is one of the key ways to grow in faith. The Bible summarises it well in this way:

> *2 Corinthians 9: 6 Remember this: Whoever sows sparingly will also reap sparingly, and whoever sows generously will also reap generously. 7 Each of you should give what you have decided in your heart to give, not reluctantly or under compulsion, for God loves a cheerful giver. 8 And God is able to bless you abundantly, so that in all things at all times, having all that you need, you will abound in every good work. 9 As it is written: "They have freely scattered their gifts to the poor; their righteousness endures .also supply and increase your store of seed and will enlarge the harvest of your righteousness. 11 You will be enriched in every way so that you can be generous on every occasion, and through us your generosity will result in thanksgiving to God.*

Service:

Service to God is part of our worship. It is putting him first in all things and recognising him as Lord and not only as Father. This is also a daily lifestyle, an attitude rather than an event; Jesus washed his disciples' feet as an example for us to follow. In a personal sense we serve in our own daily lives the people around us in our workplaces, communities and families. Additionally, there is a corporate expression of service together as a church community both serving the needs of the church itself but also serving the world around us.

The church provides a context for individual gifts to be expressed in a corporate manner so that we can all grow together: Ephesians 4:16 From him the whole body, joined and held together by every supporting ligament, grows and builds itself up in love, as each part does its work.

The church is a place that stimulates our faith, where we share encouragements, challenges and testimonies. It gives opportunities for individual gifts and faith to be expressed in a corporate dimension. One analogy I use is that of a jigsaw puzzle: every member of a church is like a piece of the puzzle, each finding their place as they find their connections, and each part of the big picture. Without every individual piece finding its place the picture cannot be whole.

Compassion:
This is almost a case of leaving the first to last! Compassion is the setting in which the jewel of faith is set. Indeed, compassion is the driver behind the mission of God on earth: God so loved the world that he sent Jesus.

The Bible tells us that Jesus was moved with compassion, his heart was touched by people's circumstances. and Jesus said that we are sent into the world in the same manner. Compassion should move our hearts to such a degree that we have an urgent desire to help people and reveal the love of God to them.

For me, feeling compassion for the world is like God taking a part of his heart and sharing it with me. It is such a strong force that it overwhelms me emotionally.

Compassion needs to be at the heart of Christian activity both individually and corporately and it gives the correct soil in which faith can grow. The Bible tells us that faith without love is not a good thing, however, faith stirred by love is necessary in order to respond to the calling that compassion places upon our lives.

In our school of spiritual life, I teach a lot about making the expression of our faith relevant to the world in which we live, looking at real life issues and challenges, facing the raw emotion of the circumstances of people's existence. In that context I pray for an anointing of compassion to come upon our students - it is a profound experience and many people weep as they feel a portion of the weight of God's compassion for the world. That experience often helps people to define their 'metron" or the calling of God upon their lives at that moment in time.

The fruit that emerges from such encounters with God have been phenomenal as people pursue their calling with faith and endeavour.

Such encounters with the compassion of God can also happen on an individual level. For me this has happened on a few occasions in my life which have elevated me to new levels of understanding of the love of God. One such experience was outlined earlier in this book in Mexico, the outcome of which was the experience of extraordinary miracles.

Some people I know have been led into their life's main calling as compassion for the world has stirred their hearts.

On another occasion it led to a surprising understanding of the pleasure of God in his children's dreams: the occasion was a "Heaven in Healthcare" conference at Eastgate with about 70 Christians who work in Healthcare. Most people who enter into the work of healthcare do so with compassion and the hope of making a difference in people's lives. Many of the people at this conference had expressed how dreams of their Christianity positively impacting their workplace had been crushed out of them and they felt deflated. Through the day we reestablished hope, started to increase faith, stirred compassion, and dared people to reignite their dreams. Towards the end of the day we split people into small groups of about six people and asked them to share their dreams regarding healthcare with each other; a buzz of conversation filled the room. We stuck some very large pieces of paper to the windows at the front of the auditorium and then asked everyone to come and write their dreams on them. People started to come forward and confidence, hope and joy increased in the room. We collected over 150 dreams and people took their time reading them - these were individual dreams becoming part of a common dream to see Heaven expressed in Healthcare. We had a ministry team prepared to lay hands on the delegates and as they were getting themselves ready they experienced the fire of God in the tangible way of every one of them suddenly becoming increasingly hot and needing to shed layers of clothing (decently I must add!). Then every delegate was prayed for and I witnessed them all encountering God in a profound way that left them lying on the floor in the presence of God for up to 30 minutes, myself and the ministry team included. During this encounter we experienced the compassion of God and the profound pleasure of God upon his children who dared to dream about heaven being expressed through their lives to the world around them. For me and others it was a life changing moment.

Once again the Bible has a great way of putting it when it says "the only thing that counts is faith expressing itself through love".

Please allow me to conclude this chapter with a prayer for us all drawn directly from the Bible, it is a prayer that I use regularly and is worthy of study and meditation. Indeed, I would recommend to you that you pray and study its reality into your own life.

Ephesians 3:

14 For this reason I kneel before the Father, 15 from whom every family in heaven and on earth derives its name. 16 I pray that out of his glorious riches he may strengthen you with power through his Spirit in your inner being, 17 so that Christ may dwell in your hearts through faith. And I pray that you, being rooted and established in love, 18 may have power, together with all the Lord's holy people, to grasp how wide and long and high and deep is the love of Christ, 19 and to know this love that surpasses knowledge – that you may be filled to the measure of all the fullness of God.

20 Now to him who is able to do immeasurably more than all we ask or imagine, according to his power that is at work within us, 21 to him be glory in the church and in Christ Jesus throughout all generations, for ever and ever! Amen.

Story by Sasha Caridia:
A while ago I was out and about, stopping off in a cafe before going to the hairdressers and then on to the supermarket. I was doing everyday stuff but have been learning over time that with an ear to Heaven and an intentional awareness of the activity of Holy Spirit in the day to day, our everyday stuff often leads to people encountering God through us as we are at rest in who and whose we are and the authority in which we walk.

At the cafe I felt the delight and pleasure of God for the person serving me, I took a risk and shared what I felt God was saying. The person has a relationship with Jesus but had been feeling that she was 'not good enough'. She was so encouraged by the specifics of what God had said to her that she kept coming back to the table between serving other customers to continue the conversation.

At the hairdressers, my hairdresser asked me what I had been doing since we last met. I told him stories about miracles and healings, about the love of God, about friends who are doing fantastic things in education, politics, media, arts and healthcare because they have a vision to see 'Heaven' influence those areas. I used words that were relevant to him, he is not a Christian. As a result of the conversation he is looking forward to hearing more when we next meet.

Then off I went to the supermarket. I saw a lady with crutches, pushing her trolley. Feeling the compassion of God and a tangible increase in His presence I took a risk and spoke to her. She knew Jesus and was happy to be prayed for. She said she had been feeling very low and had recently been housebound due to her limited mobility. The atmosphere around us felt like a thick blanket of 'love' as her pain diminished. She said she felt so energised and well within herself that she knew 'something had happened'. We celebrated, thanked God, chatted some more, hugged and then went on our way.

The 'everyday stuff' of our lives is about His presence, the Kingdom of Heaven, and all that comes with it, expressed in the here and now so that transformation happens wherever we are, whether in the immediate or over a period of time. As a result of these 'everyday stuff' encounters, some will come to know Jesus for themselves, others who already know Him will get to encounter Him in greater measure, perhaps in ways they have never done before as they experience the goodness, love and compassion of God in ways that are uniquely and divinely orchestrated for them in those moments. Presence, risk, love …

Chapter 30 Checklist

How to grow in faith/increase your connection with God

1. Encounter God. My message and my preaching were not with wise and persuasive words, but with a demonstration of the Spirit's power, so that your faith might not rest on human wisdom, but on God's power: 1 Corinthians 2:4-5.

2. Hearing God. Romans 10:17 17 Consequently, faith comes from hearing the message, and the message is heard through the word of Christ. What is God saying?

3. Receive a gift. Faith is a spiritual gift. Ask for it.

4. Keep your hope high.

5. Listen carefully. Luke 8:18. How do you interact with what God is doing or saying? In terms of manifestations, testimonies, prophecies and teaching.

6. Never lose your wonder at God's interaction with you.

7. Understand authority. Matthew 8, the Roman centurion.

8. Keep moving – it is a journey

9. Overcome disappointment. Constantly find the God of comfort and hope.

10. Coping with pressure. Example of drink cans when full they withstand pressure, when empty they are easily crushed. More faith will lead to more expectation on you, and often that means more spiritual battles.

11. Dealing with delay.

12. Hope involves waiting.

13. Overcoming fear of failure.

14. Communities of Faith. Be part of building great churches who are overcoming unbelief and growing in faith.

15. Unseen realms. 2 Kings 6, Elisha's servant. Open our eyes

16. Serving God, his church and other people.

17. Faith will be tested. 1 Peter 1. Example of New Zafira tyre pressure down to 23 from 29, (Nail in tyre). Faith is worth more than gold.

18. Grow your compassion. Faith needs the context of love. Love always hopes, Galatians 5:6. The only thing that counts is faith expressing itself through love.

19. Generosity: giving money, time and other resources demonstrates where your trust is placed.

20. Know your Metron: your faith will be expressed throughout all of your life and will be particularly effective in your metron, that is your area of calling.

21. Be faithful with what God has already given you and God will give you more. Expect growth in all areas. God is willing to continually entrust you with more responsibility in his kingdom.

Epilogue: The Never Ending Book!

This book has taken me a long time to write and I must offer apologies to my friends who have been urging me along for quite some time now. They are eager to read it and I have been eager to write it.

The problem lies within a fundamental Christian truth - God is infinite and eternal. Not that God is the problem in any way, simply that He is without beginning or end. So if we define faith as 'the discovery of who God is' then we can understand that growing in faith is an eternal adventure in no way limited to our current human existence. Furthermore, if we ask God to reveal more of himself to us, he graciously does and particularly so as we step out into new realms of faith filled endeavour.

As I have been writing this book I have experienced just that - new thoughts and revelations, new power encounters, increasing spiritual insight and understanding. Each one deserves to be included in this book and therein you can see the problem. How do I finish this book? In the end I had to face the self-discipline of writing a book to a conclusion knowing that within a few months I will be wishing that I had included something else that I have just learned.

So in many ways this book cannot ever be finished to a final conclusion, and this is paralleled in the Christian life. When we are born again we are given the gift of eternal life, a life that will never end, spent in the presence of God who has no end to his being. Christianity is beautiful and amazing. What an exciting, amazing future we have ahead of us, not just in this life but more so in the life beyond the grave.

I hope that this book has inspired, encouraged and instructed you to continually grow in faith and in your connection to God, The Father, Son and Holy Spirit.

I pray that you will understand, experience and share the love, power, beauty, majesty, grace and glory of God in ever increasing measure.

Amen.

Pete Carter